ADB Institute Series on Development Economics

Series editor
Naoyuki Yoshino, Tokyo, Japan

Asia and the Pacific has been advancing in many aspects of its development, but the potential for growth is vast. The Asian Development Bank Institute Series on Development Economics aims to identify and propose solutions using a multidisciplinary approach to important development issues facing economies in the Asia and Pacific region. Through edited volumes and monographs, the series showcases the research output of the Asian Development Bank Institute as well as its collaboration with other leading think tanks and institutions worldwide.

The current focus of the series is infrastructure development; financial inclusion, regulation, and education; housing policy; central and local government relations; macroeconomic policy; and governance. The series also examines the major bottlenecks to greater stability and integration in Asia and the Pacific, while addressing timely issues including trends in microfinance, fiscal policy stability, and ways of tackling income inequality. The publications in the series are relevant for scholars, policymakers, and students of economics, and provide recommendations for economic policy enhancement and a greater understanding of the implications of further capacity building and development reform in Asia and the Pacific.

More information about this series at http://www.springer.com/series/13512

Naoyuki Yoshino • Farhad Taghizadeh-Hesary
Editors

Japan's Lost Decade

Lessons for Asian Economies

ADBInstitute

Springer

Editors
Naoyuki Yoshino
Asian Development Bank Institute (ADBI)
Tokyo, Japan

Keio University
Tokyo, Japan

Farhad Taghizadeh-Hesary
Keio University
Tokyo, Japan

Asian Development Bank Institute
Kasumigaseki Building 8F
3-2-5, Kasumigaseki, Chiyoda-ku
Tokyo 100-6008, Japan
www.adbi.org

ADB recognizes "China" as the People's Republic of China.
Note: In this publication, "$" refers to US dollars.

ISSN 2363-9032 ISSN 2363-9040 (electronic)
ADB Institute Series on Development Economics
ISBN 978-981-10-5019-0 ISBN 978-981-10-5021-3 (eBook)
DOI 10.1007/978-981-10-5021-3

Library of Congress Control Number: 2017954305

Printed on acid-free paper

This Springer imprint is published by Springer Nature
The registered company is Springer Nature Singapore Pte Ltd.
The registered company address is: 152 Beach Road, #21-01/04 Gateway East, Singapore 189721, Singapore

This work is dedicated to the gentle soul of Sir Alan Arthur Walters (17 June 1926-3 January 2009), who was my PhD thesis supervisor at Johns Hopkins University, USA (1979).

Naoyuki Yoshino

This work is dedicated to Professor Naoyuki Yoshino, my PhD thesis supervisor at Keio University, Tokyo, Japan (2015) who taught me Japanese economic policy and to my parents, my wife Farnaz, and my brother Farzad, for their support and important roles in my life.

Farhad Taghizadeh-Hesary

Summary

This book analyzes the causes of Japan's long-term economic recession which started following the real estate and stock market bubble burst of the 1990s and provides remedies for this recession that could be useful for other Asian economies.

Japan has suffered from sluggish economic growth and recession since the 1990s, a period dubbed Japan's "Lost Decade." The People's Republic of China, the Republic of Korea, Thailand, and many other Asian countries may face similar problems in the future and are concerned by Japan's long-term recession.

This book addresses why Japan's economy has stagnated since the bursting of its economic bubble. The empirical analysis of this book challenges the beliefs of some economists, such as Paul Krugman (Nobel Prize laureate in economic sciences), that the Japanese economy is in a liquidity trap.

This book argues that Japan's economic stagnation stems from a vertical investment–saving curve rather than a liquidity trap and that monetary policy is ineffective for escalating its economic growth. The impact of fiscal policy has declined drastically, and the Japanese economy faces structural problems rather than a temporary downturn.

These structural problems have many causes: an aging demographic (a frequently overlooked problem), local governments' overreliance on transfers from the central government, high costs of energy due to a nondiversified energy basket as a result of the Fukushima nuclear disaster and nuclear plant shutdowns, and Basel capital requirements that have made Japanese banks reluctant to lend money to start-up businesses and small and medium-sized enterprises. This latter issue has discouraged Japanese innovation and technological progress. This book addresses all these issues empirically and theoretically and provides several remedies for Japan's long-lasting recession, which can also provide useful lessons for other Asian economies.

Preface and Introductory Remarks

In the early 1990s, Japan's real estate and stock market bubble burst and the economy went into a tailspin. Since then, Japan has suffered from sluggish economic growth. During this period, referred to as Japan's "Lost Decade," the country's economic growth rate has been the lowest among the world 's major developed countries. From 1995 to 2002, for example, Japan's annual average real gross domestic product (GDP) growth rate was only 1.2%, lower than that of all the other G7 countries (i.e., Canada at 3.4%, the United States at 3.2%, the United Kingdom at 2.7%, France at 2.3%, Italy at 1.8%, and Germany at 1.4%), lower than the eurozone average (2.2%), less than half that of all of the other larger Organisation for Economic Co-operation and Development (OECD) countries (the Republic of Korea at 5.3%, Australia at 3.8%, Spain at 3.3%, the Netherlands at 2.9%, and Mexico at 2.6%), and lower than the OECD-wide average (2.7%).[1]

Studying the causes of and remedies for Japan's long-lasting recession and low growth is crucial for other Asian countries, to prevent similar situations from occurring. Nobel laureate Paul Krugman has argued that the reason for Japan's recession is that the country is currently in a liquidity trap, a situation in which monetary policy is ineffective in lowering interest rates. However, our empirical results in Chaps. 1 and 8 of this book indicate that the problems in the Japanese economy stem from other sources. Theoretical and empirical results in this book will show that stagnation of the Japanese economy comes from a vertical investment–saving curve rather than a liquidity trap. This means problems are arising from structural challenges rather than from a temporary downturn.

There are several reasons for this long-term stagnation since the 1990s, which will be discussed in this book. One of these is Japanese companies' increased investment overseas and reduced investment in Japan. Because the aging population creates diminished future demand, companies have become wary of increasing investment, despite very low interest rates. In addition, the aging population has

[1]Horioka CY (2006), The causes of Japan's "Lost Decade": The role of household consumption. NBER Working Paper Series No 12142. National Bureau of Economic Research, Cambridge, MA

increased social welfare expenses. Japan has the highest life expectancy in the world, but the retirement age is still around 60 years old, resulting in a diminishing working population as the number of elderly and retired people rises and the population of the younger generation shrinks. Typically, elderly people consume less than younger generations, so this has added to the problem of reduced domestic consumption. Other factors include the high level of transfers from the central government to local governments, which reduced the productivity of local governments because of their reliance on central government money, and the Basel capital requirements, which made Japanese banks reluctant to lend money to start-up businesses and small and medium-sized enterprises and discouraged Japanese innovation and technological progress.

Many of these issues are also predictable for the future of other Asian countries. Hence, it is crucial for countries like the People's Republic of China (PRC), Indonesia, Thailand, and others to look at the causes of Japan's long-lasting economic recession and the possible remedies mentioned in this book.

Chapter 1 acts as a summary of this book. This chapter addresses, both theoretically and empirically, why Japan's economy has stagnated since the bursting of its economic bubble. It argues that Japan's economic stagnation stems from a vertical investment–saving curve rather than a liquidity trap. The impact of fiscal policy has declined drastically, and the Japanese economy faces structural problems, not a temporary downturn. The chapter provides both causes and remedies for Japan's long-lasting recession, which are expanded upon in the subsequent chapters.

Chapter 2 talks about the changes in economic effect of infrastructure and financing methods in Japan. The marginal productivity of public capital was high during the high-growth period (1955–1969) of Japan but declined from 1970 onward. It is likely that the misallocation of public capital also contributed to a lower rate of return from private capital, since public investments did not remove the "infrastructure bottlenecks" that lower the rate of return from private investment. This chapter analyzes the economic effect of infrastructure, focusing on the productivity effect of public investment, and discusses how to promote private sector investment in infrastructure through enhancing the rate of return to investors by utilizing part of spillover effects from the infrastructure. Private investors have found it difficult to obtain adequate rates of return. This chapter proposes one remedy: that the incremental tax revenues along the highway or railway should contribute a certain fraction of tax revenues (say 30%) to investors in infrastructure. To do so, the incremental tax revenues along the infrastructure investment must be computed. This chapter empirically estimates spillover effects by the use of both macroeconomic and microeconomic data.

Chapter 3 discusses Japan's high level of government debt and the optimal fiscal policy rule for achieving fiscal sustainability. Japan's debt to GDP ratio is the highest among OECD countries. This chapter firstly answers the question of whether the Japanese government debt is sustainable. Next, while the Domar condition and Bohn's condition are often used in the literature to check whether a government's debt situation is in a dangerous zone, this chapter shows that the Domar condition is obtained only from the government budget constraint (namely, the supply of government bonds) and does not take into account the demand for government bonds. A simple comparison of the interest rate and the growth rate of an economy using the Domar condition is not adequate to check the stability of a government's budget deficit. Both the interest rate and the growth rate of the economy are determined endogenously in the model. Thirdly, this chapter shows that Bohn's condition satisfies the stability of the government budget in the long run by imposing constraints on the primary balance. However, Bohn's condition does not achieve economic stability—even if the condition is satisfied, the recovery of the economy may not be achieved. This chapter proposes a new condition that satisfies both the stability of the government budget and the recovery of the economy. The chapter will shed light on these issues both theoretically and empirically.

Chapter 4 talks about macroeconomic volatility under the high accumulation of government debt in Japan. This chapter applies Bayesian estimation to an open-economy dynamic stochastic general equilibrium (DSGE) model of Japan to assess the effects of expanding government debt on interest rates, real exchange-rate dynamics, and real sector performance. The authors find that the emergence of even a small risk premium on government debt will trigger considerable instability in the real and nominal variables. The chapter shows that a switch to an exchange-rate rule for monetary policy would considerably moderate the instability induced by a rising risk premium.

Chapter 5 sheds light on Japan's postwar monetary policies and discusses whether they were developed according to Taylor rules or something else. This chapter investigates postwar Japanese monetary policies through the lens of the Taylor equation and the associated Taylor rule. Authors break from previous studies in extending the investigation back to the early postwar period and by examining the stability of the Taylor specification in various subperiods. In general, they find little support for the Taylor equation in the Japan case. A possible exception is the period from 1980 to 1997, but this was during the "bubble economy" and subsequent "Lost Decade."

Chapter 6 discusses the energy sector, especially Japan's oil consumption, by an empirical analysis. After the earthquake and tsunami that hit Japan's eastern coast in March 2011 (often referred to as the Great East Japan Earthquake) caused a nuclear disaster and shutdown of all the country's nuclear power plants, energy, especially oil and gas, became a more interesting topic as Japan substituted fossil fuels for nuclear power. This chapter sheds light on the impact of crude oil price volatility on the residential, transport, industrial, commercial, and nonenergy sectors in Japan, the world's third-largest crude oil consumer. The chapter's empirical results indicate that some economic sectors, such as the residential sector, did not have significant sensitivity to sharp oil price fluctuations, while others, like the commercial, industrial, and transport sectors, were strongly sensitive to such fluctuations. Moreover, the findings show that most sectors' sensitivity to oil price volatility declined after the Fukushima disaster in 2011, which led to the shutdown of nuclear power plants in Japan and increased reliance on oil imports.

Chapter 7 analyzes the three arrows of "Abenomics." Abenomics refers to the economic policies advocated by Prime Minister Shinzo Abe, who became prime minister of Japan for a second time when his party, the Liberal Democratic Party, won an overwhelming majority at the general election in December 2012. Abenomics is distinguished by sets of policies that comprise "three arrows": (i) an aggressive monetary policy, (ii) fiscal consolidation, and (iii) a growth strategy. This chapter explains these three aspects of Abenomics and the current state of the Japanese economy and examines what further remedies may be required if Japan is to recover from its long-term deflation. The authors look at such proposals as hometown investment trust funds, postponement of the retirement age by introducing a flexible wage rate system, and changing the pension system to 401(k)-style instruments.

Chapter 8 examines the effectiveness of Japan's negative interest rate policy. In April 2013, the Bank of Japan (BOJ) introduced an inflation target of 2% with the aim of overcoming deflation and achieving sustainable economic growth. But due to lower international oil prices, it was unable to achieve this target and was forced to take further measures. Hence, in February 2016, the BOJ adopted a negative interest rate policy by massively increasing the money supply by purchasing long-term Japanese government bonds (JGB). The BOJ had previously only purchased short-term government bonds, a policy that flattened the yield curve of JGBs. On the one hand, banks reduced the numbers of government bonds because short-term bond yields had become negative and even the interest rates of long-term government bonds up to 15 years became negative. On the other hand, bank loans to the corporate sector did not increase, due to the Japanese economy's vertical investment–saving curve. This chapter firstly explains why the BOJ has to reduce its 2% inflation target in the present era of low oil prices. Secondly, it argues that Japan cannot make a sustainable recovery from its long-lasting recession and tackle its long-standing deflation problem by means of its current monetary policy, particularly its negative interest rate policy. It is essential to make the investment–saving curve downward sloping rather than vertical. That means the rate of return on investment must be positive and companies must be willing to invest if interest rates are set too low. Japan's long-term recession is due to structural problems that cannot be solved by its current monetary policy. The last section reports the results of our simulation of introducing a productivity-based wage rate and postponement of the retirement age, which could help the recovery of the Japanese economy in light of its aging population.

Last but not least we are grateful to all contributors to this book. Without their valuable contributions we would have not been able to finalize this book. Special thanks go to Professor Paul D. McNelis, Professor Hiroaki Miyamoto, Professor Tetsuro Mizoguchi, Professor Masaki Nakahigashi, Professor James R. Rhodes, and Dr. Ehsan Rasoulinezhad. While editing this book we received support from many colleagues, policy makers, and scholars as well as from our families. We would like to mention some of them in particular. Our colleagues and friends, Professor Sahoko Kaji and Professor Masao Ogaki at the Faculty of Economics, Keio University, and Dr. Shinichi Nakabayashi and Dr. Peter Morgan of the Asian Development Bank Institute (ADBI). In addition, we are thankful to Muriel S. Ordoñez and Dr. Grant Stillman from ADBI, who helped us in the publishing process of the book and for finalizing the agreements with the publisher. We thank Ainslie Smith who supported us in the linguistic editing. Finally, we are grateful to Springer Nature for publishing this work. Of course, any mistakes left are ours.

Chiyoda-ku Naoyuki Yoshino
Minato-ku Farhad Taghizadeh-Hesary

Contents

Contents

About the Editors and Contributors

Editors

Naoyuki Yoshino is the dean of the Asian Development Bank Institute; professor emeritus of Keio University, Tokyo, Japan; and senior adviser at the Japan Financial Services Agency's (FSA) Financial Research Center (FSA Institute). He obtained his PhD from Johns Hopkins University in 1979, where his thesis supervisor was Sir Alan Walters (who was Margaret Thatcher's economic adviser). He was a visiting scholar at the Massachusetts Institute of Technology (United States) and has been a visiting professor at universities including the University of New South Wales (Australia), Fondation Nationale des Sciences Politiques (France), and the University of Gothenburg (Sweden). He was an assistant professor at the State University of New York at Buffalo before he joined Keio University in 1991 as a professor of economics. He was professor of economics at Keio University during 1991–2014. He was appointed chairperson of the Financial Planning Standards Board in 2007 and also served as chairperson of the Japanese Ministry of Finance's Council on Foreign Exchange and its Fiscal System Council. He was also a board member of the Deposit Insurance Corporation of Japan, chairperson of the Meeting of Japanese Government Bond Investors (Ministry of Finance), and president of the Financial System Council of the Government of Japan. He was conferred honorary doctorates by the University of Gothenburg (Sweden) in 2004 and by the Martin Luther University of Halle–Wittenberg (Germany) in 2013. He also received the Fukuzawa Award for his contribution to academic research in 2013.

Farhad Taghizadeh-Hesary is a faculty member and assistant professor of economics at the Faculty of Economics, Keio University, Tokyo, Japan, and a visiting professor at the Graduate School of Economics, University of Tokyo. Moreover, he is senior assistant to the dean of the Asian Development Bank Institute, where he conducts research on various topics. At the same time, he is advisor to the Ministry of Economic Affairs and Finance of the Islamic Republic of Iran. He obtained his PhD in economics from Keio University and master's in energy economics from Tehran University, Iran. He was a visiting scholar at several institutions and universities such as the Institute of Energy Economics of Japan from 2013 to 2015 and Credit Risk Database Association of Japan from 2014 to 2015. He has published three books, more than 40 academic papers in international journals, and book chapters on a wide range of topics, including energy economics, SME financing, the Japanese economy, monetary policy, and banking and finance.

Contributors

Paul D. McNelis Professor, Department of Finance, Graduate School of Business Administration, Fordham University, New York, USA

Hiroaki Miyamoto Project associate professor, Graduate School of Public Policy, University of Tokyo and visiting professor, College of Business, Rikkyo University, Tokyo, Japan

Tetsuro Mizoguchi Associate professor of economics, Faculty of Economics, Takasaki City University of Economics, Gunma, Japan

Masaki Nakahigashi Associate professor, Faculty of Economics, Niigata University; senior research fellow, Policy Research Institute, Ministry of Finance, Japan

Ehsan Rasoulinezhad Post-Doctoral scholar, Tehran University, Tehran, Iran

James R. Rhodes Vice President, Senior Professor and Emeritus Professor, National Graduate Institute for Policy Studies (GRIPS), Tokyo, Japan

Abbreviations

AD	Aggregate demand
AS	Aggregate supply
BOJ	Bank of Japan
CES	Constant elasticity of substitution
DSGE	Dynamic stochastic general equilibrium
GDP	Gross domestic product
HIT	Hometown investment trust (fund)
IRF	Impulse response function
IS	Investment–saving (curve)
JGB	Japanese government bonds
LM	Liquidity preference money supply (curve)
OECD	Organisation for Economic Co-operation and Development
PRC	People's Republic of China
QQE	Quantitative and qualitative monetary easing
SMEs	Small and medium-sized enterprises
US	United States
VAR	Vector autoregressive

Chapter 1
Japan's Lost Decade: Causes and Remedies

Naoyuki Yoshino and Farhad Taghizadeh-Hesary

Abstract Japan has suffered from sluggish economic growth and recession since the 1990s, a period dubbed "Japan's Lost Decade." The People's Republic of China, many countries in the eurozone, and the United States may face similar problems in the future, and they have been concerned by Japan's long-term recession. This chapter will address why Japan's economy has stagnated since the bursting of its economic bubble. Our empirical analysis challenges the beliefs of some western economists, such as Paul Krugman, that the Japanese economy is in a liquidity trap. We argue that Japan's economic stagnation stems from a vertical investment–saving curve rather than a liquidity trap. The impact of fiscal policy has declined drastically, and the Japanese economy is facing structural problems rather than a temporary downturn. These structural problems have many causes: an aging demographic (a problem that is frequently overlooked), local governments' overreliance on transfers from the central government, and Basel capital requirements that have made Japanese banks reluctant to lend money to startup businesses and small and medium-sized enterprises. This latter issue has discouraged Japanese innovation and technological progress. The chapter will address all these issues empirically and theoretically and will provide some remedies for Japan's long-lasting recession.

Another version of this chapter is available as Yoshino and Taghizadeh-Hesary (2016) Causes and remedies of the Japan's long-lasting recession: lessons for China. *China & World Economy* 24(2):23–47.

N. Yoshino
Asian Development Bank Institute (ADBI), Tokyo, Japan

Keio University, Tokyo, Japan
e-mail: nyoshino@adbi.org

F. Taghizadeh-Hesary
Faculty of Economics, Keio University, Tokyo, Japan

Graduate School of Economics, The University of Tokyo, Tokyo, Japan
e-mail: farhadth@gmail.com; farhadth@keio.jp

N. Yoshino, F. Taghizadeh-Hesary (eds.), *Japan's Lost Decade*, ADB Institute Series on Development Economics, DOI 10.1007/978-981-10-5021-3_1

Keywords Japan's Lost Decade • Aging population • Japanese economy • Vertical IS curve

JEL Classification E12, E62

1.1 Introduction

In the early 1990s, Japan's real estate and stock market bubble burst and the economy went into a tailspin. Since then, Japan has suffered sluggish economic growth and recessions (known as "Japan's Lost Decade"). Japan's growth rate during this period has been among the lowest of the major developed countries of the world. During 1995–2002, for example, the annualized growth rate of Japan's real gross domestic product (GDP) averaged only 1.2%. This was lower than the eurozone average of 2.7% and less than the other Group of 7 (G7) countries: Canada (3.4%), France (2.3%), Germany (1.4%), Italy (1.8%), the United Kingdom (2.7%), and the United States (US) (3.2%). Japan's performance was also poor compared with the 2.7% average of the Organisation for Economic Co-operation and Development (OECD) members, and was significantly less than the growth rates of the larger OECD countries: Australia (3.8%), the Republic of Korea (5.3%), Mexico (2.6%), the Netherlands (2.9%), and Spain (3.3%) (Horioka 2006).

Figure 1.1 shows the trend of Japan's real GDP and the real GDP growth rate during 1990–2015. After Japan's economic bubble burst in the early 1990s Japanese real GDP started to decline sharply. This long-term recession lasted almost 25 years.

It is crucial for the People's Republic of China (PRC), countries in Europe, and the US to study the causes of, and remedies for, Japan's long-term recession and low growth rates to prevent it happening to them. Economists such as Paul Krugman have argued that Japan's recession has happened because the country is in a liquidity trap, where monetary policy is ineffective in lowering interest rates. However, analysis in this chapter indicates that the problems of the Japanese economy stem from other sources. Theoretical and empirical results show that stagnation of the Japanese economy comes from a vertical investment–saving curve rather than a liquidity trap. This means problems stem from structural issues rather than a temporary downturn.

There are several reasons for this long-term stagnation. The main, greatly underestimated, reason is Japan's aging population. Japan has the highest life expectancy in the world, but the mandatory retirement age is still 65 years old.[1] The number of elderly and retired people in Japan is rising, while the population of younger people is shrinking. This results in a diminishing working population. Since elderly people tend to consume less than younger people this also shrinks the domestic consumer market, creating additional problems. Further issues stem from

[1]E Warnock (2012) Japan bill to raise retirement age passes lower house. The Wall Street Journal, 2 Aug. http://www.wsj.com/articles/SB10000872396390443687504577564800240852924

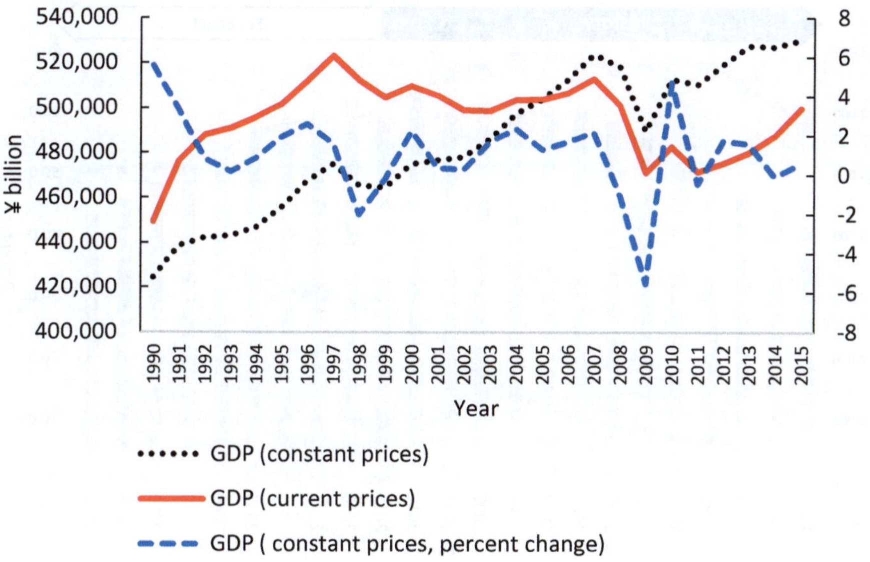

Fig. 1.1 Japanese GDP trends (1990–2015). *GDP* gross domestic product, ¥ yen (*Source*: World Economic Outlook Database, October 2015, International Monetary Fund (IMF). Data for 2015 are IMF staff estimates)

how the Government of Japan allocates transfers to local governments, and from Basel capital requirements that have made Japanese banks more reluctant to lend money to startup businesses and small and medium-sized enterprises (SMEs). This has discouraged Japanese innovation and technological progress.

In Sect. 1.2 we discuss the causes of Japan's long-term recession and provide a comparative study of Greece's economic collapse in Sect. 1.3. Section 1.4 is an empirical analysis of the Japanese economic crisis, and the ineffectiveness of the fiscal policies in stimulating the GDP growth after the bubble burst. It provides proof of our hypothesis that Japan's problems have been caused by the vertical investment–saving curve and not by a liquidity crisis. Section 1.5 provides remedies for pulling the Japanese economy out of recession and boosting its economic growth. Section 1.6 presents the concluding remarks.

1.2 Causes of the Long-Term Recession in Japan

Aging Population

Japan has achieved the highest life expectancy in the world, but its retirement age is still 65 years of age. Figure 1.2 shows that the working population (i.e., those aged 15–64) is diminishing drastically while the elderly population (those aged 65 and

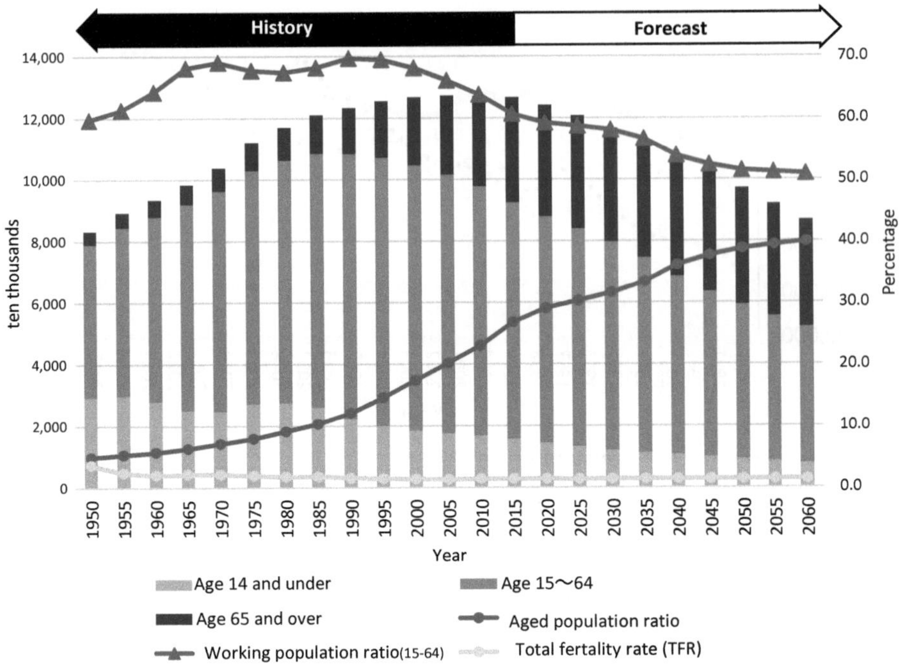

Fig. 1.2 Demographics of Japan (*Source*: Government of Japan, Ministry of Internal Affairs and Communications 2012)

older) is growing rapidly. The aging population and the shrinking workforce is one of the biggest causes of long-term recession in Japan.

On the other hand, Japan's method for calculating wages is based on seniority. Seniority-based wage systems make it difficult for companies to hire elderly people. They are often forced to retire, even though many of them would like to continue working. Because of the aging population, social welfare costs have started to increase and currently one-third of government spending is allocated to this, while the government budget deficit is rising every year.

Monetary Transfers from Central to Local Governments

Figure 1.3 shows expenditure from the general account budget of the Government of Japan in 2015. About 16% of total government spending is allocated to local governments, making it the second-largest government expense after social security. Local governments rely too heavily on central government transfers and do not make efforts to revitalize regional economies. In addition, a rigid distribution system within agriculture cooperatives has put farmers in a weak position, and they are unable to make innovations in agricultural production.

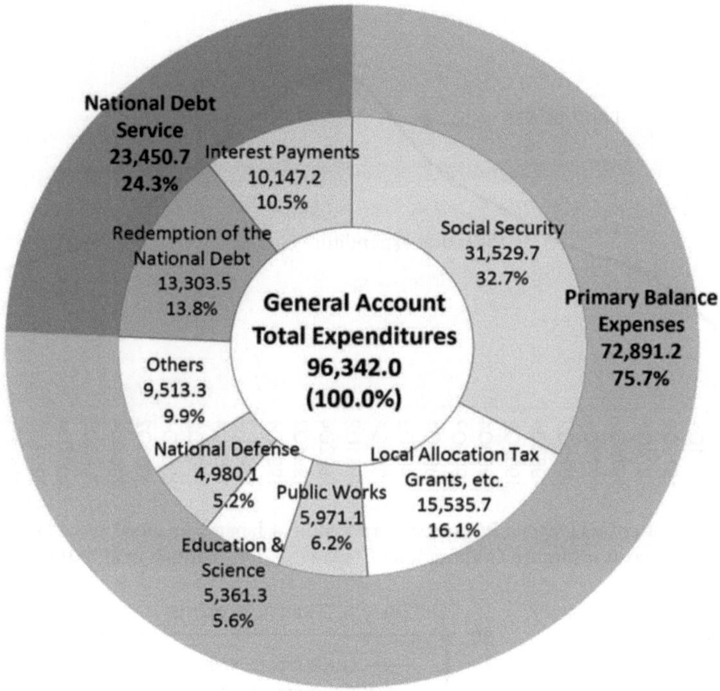

Fig. 1.3 General account expenditure budget, 2015 (¥ billions). *FY* fiscal year (*Source*: Government of Japan, Ministry of Finance 2015)

Banking Behavior

In the 1980s, Japanese banks issued loans based on collateral. From 1991 onward, land prices started to decline and banks began to accumulate bad loan assets. The number of banking failures started to increase immediately after the financial bubble burst, reaching a peak almost one decade later.

Figure 1.4 shows that before the bubble burst, there was no banking failure and assistance from the Deposit Insurance Corporation of Japan (DICJ), the financial system's insuring organization, was almost at zero. When banks began to fail after the bubble burst, the DICJ began to increase its financial assistance to help the failed banks. This assistance also peaked a decade after the bursting of the bubble.

Another obstacle in the banking system is the Basel capital requirements. Basel I regulations forced banks to hold 8% of its risk-weighted assets as capital, regardless of economic conditions. Japanese banks started to reduce their loans to avoid a shortage of capital, which created a credit crunch, and it became difficult for SMEs and startup businesses to borrow money from banks.

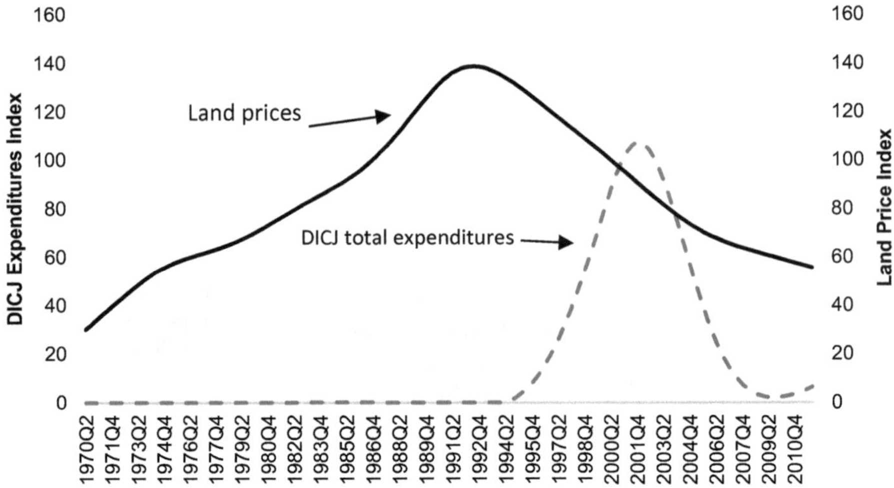

Fig. 1.4 Land price and Deposit Insurance Corporation of Japan's financial assistance for banking failure. *DICJ* Deposit Insurance Corporation of Japan (*Source*: Yoshino et al. 2013)

Fig. 1.5 Access to finance by large and small enterprises in Japan (percentage points). *CY* commercial year, *DI* diffusion index (*Source*: Bank of Japan (Tankan))

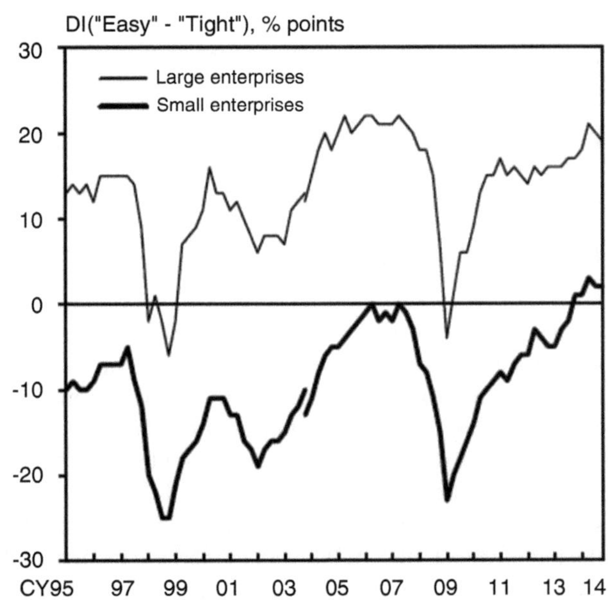

Figure 1.5 shows the results of a survey conducted by the Bank of Japan investigating the difficulty for large firms and small and medium-sized enterprises to raise money from banks or from the capital markets. Data points below zero signify difficulty for companies in raising money. The figure shows that smaller enterprises find it harder to raise money than larger firms.

Table 1.1 Estimated loan supply function

Dependent variable (bank loan)	Period I (1982–1989)	Period II (1990–1995)
Bank deposit	0.658 (19.69)	
Market share	0.426 (1.48)	
Loan rate- call rate	16.298 (2.611)	21.351 (3.028)
Call rate	8.564 (2.568)	6.755 (2.904)
BIS-ratio	8.658 (2.353)	
Rival Bank's previous period loan	0.066 (3.675)	0.038 (2.333)
Land price	0.123 (2.564)	−1.760 (−1.449)
Constant	−36.302 (−0.874)	

Adjusted-R^2 0.892, Hausman Statistic, CHI-SQUARE = 0.923, *P*-Value = 0.820
Source: Revankar and Yoshino (2008)
Note: Figures in parentheses are t-values. *BIS* Bank for International Settlements

Excessive Contractionary Monetary Policy

Japanese monetary policy in the late 1980s was too easy and contributed to the development of an economic bubble. After the bubble burst, Japan's monetary policy was overtightened, drastically reducing the lending capacity of Japanese banks. Revankar and Yoshino (2008) estimate Japan's loan supply function for the periods 1982–1989 and 1990–1995. The results are summarized in Table 1.1.

Findings from Revankar and Yoshino (2008) show the following:

(i) The interest rate policy was less effective from 1990 to 1995 than it had been from 1982 to 1989.
(ii) The capital requirement rule of the Bank for International Settlements discouraged Japanese banks from lending money to SMEs, startup businesses, and risky sectors.
(iii) During the period of economic boom, the increasing land prices pushed bank lending upward. Japanese banks were using land as collateral and the high land prices pushed up the value of the collateral, making the banks more willing to lend large quantities of money.
(iv) Japanese banks decided how to allocate their loans by looking at the behavior of other banks. Sumitomo Bank, for example, started to increase its loans during the economic bubble and many other banks followed suit. This is reflected in "Rival bank's previous period loans" in Table 1.1.

Reduced Effectiveness of Fiscal Policy

Kiichi Miyazawa, Prime Minister of Japan from 1991 to 1993, implemented fiscal policy when the Japanese economy was slow to recover in the 1990s. He followed a Keynesian policy, hoping for a high-growth period in which public investment

Table 1.2 Marginal productivity of private capital and public capital

Time period	Private capital	Public capital
1955–1959	0.8346	0.2468
1960–1964	0.8685	0.3216
1965–1969	0.8204	0.3610
1970–1974	0.4740	0.1802
1975–1979	0.3144	0.0944
1980–1984	0.2813	0.0722
1985–1989	0.2416	0.0621
1990–1993	0.2410	0.0592

Source: Yoshino and Nakahigashi (2000)

would help boost the Japanese economy. However, major highways and bridges had already been completed and investment in new infrastructure did not help the economy due to a decline in the multiplier for public investment. Public investment in Japan has tended to produce low stimulative effects on gross national product because of ineffective distribution. The bulk of public investment has been concentrated in the countryside, and research shows that such investment has a much smaller impact on rural areas than on urban areas and that public investment in the agriculture sector has been much less effective than public investment in the industrial and service sectors (Yoshino and Sakakibara 2002). The result of this increasing rural and agricultural bias in the allocation of public investment is that the multiplier of public investment declined sharply from about 2.5 to as low as 1.0 (Yoshino et al. 1998). This shows that such public investment only increases budget deficits; it cannot bring about a recovery of the Japanese economy.

The results of this misallocation are seen in declining returns from public and private investment, as reported by Yoshino and Nakahigashi (2000) in Table 1.2. The marginal productivity of public capital was high during the high-growth period (1955–1969) but declined from 1970 onward. It is likely that the misallocation of public capital also contributed to a lower rate of return from private capital, since public investments did not remove the "infrastructure bottlenecks" that lower the rate of return from private investment.

High Appreciation of the Yen in the Mid-1990s

Figure 1.6 shows fluctuations in the dollar–yen exchange rate during 1990–2014. Appreciation of the yen in the mid-1990s caused Japanese manufacturing companies to relocate from Japan to other Asian countries. Wage increases also pushed Japanese companies abroad. As a result, domestic production started to diminish. Figure 1.7 shows Japanese outward foreign direct investment to other Asian economies including the PRC; Hong Kong, China; India; and Indonesia from 1989 to 2004.

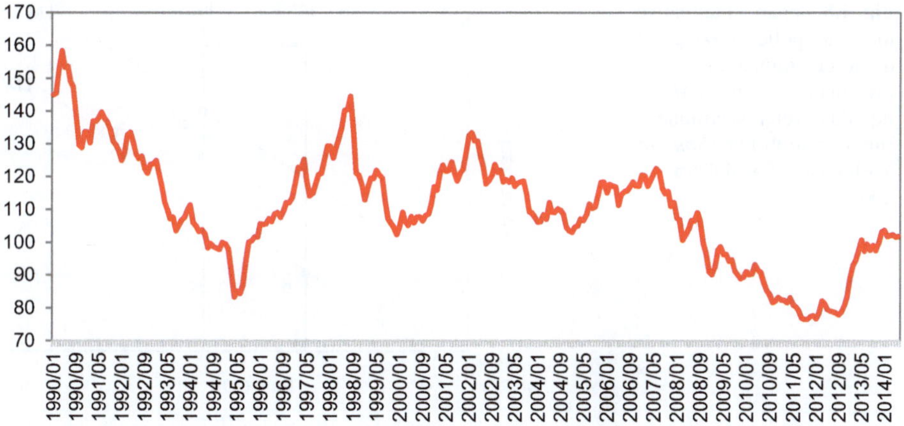

Fig. 1.6 Exchange rate, 1990–2014 (dollar–yen rate). *Note*: Dollar–yen spot rate at 5 p.m. Japan Standard Time, monthly average, Tokyo market (*Source*: Bank of Japan foreign exchange rate, time series database)

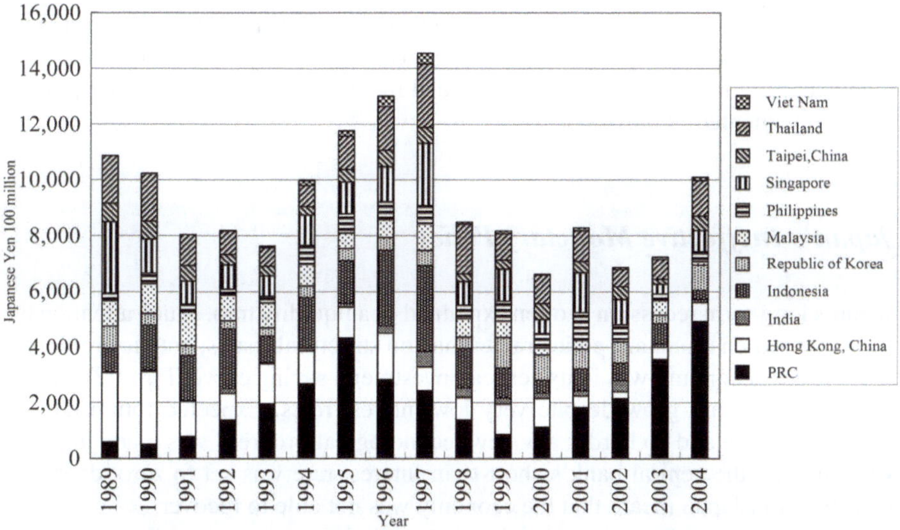

Fig. 1.7 Japanese outward foreign direct investment to Asia (¥100 million). *PRC* People's Republic of China (*Source*: Alvstam et al. 2009)

Banking Crisis of 1998

Japanese banks were in turmoil in the late 1990s. In total, 181 banks went bankrupt. Most banks that failed were small, or were credit cooperatives. The main reasons for failure were

(i) too much concentration on lending to specific sectors (such as construction and real estate),

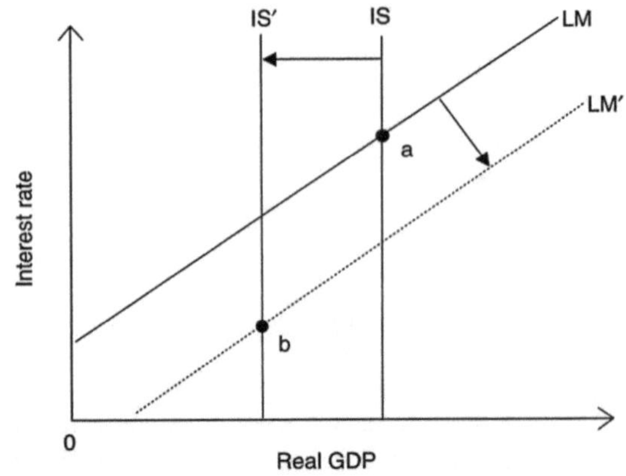

Fig. 1.8 Japan's ineffective monetary policy. *GDP* gross domestic product, *IS* investment–savings, *LM* liquidity preference/money supply equilibrium (*Source*: Yoshino and Sakakibara 2002)

(ii) increased focus on the lending of regional banks due to regional recessions,
(iii) mismanagement and fraudulent lending, and
(iv) failure in securities investment and a lack of investment knowledge.

The injection of capital into problem banks was regarded as a moral hazard in the 1990s. Many manufacturing companies opposed capital injections for banks since manufacturing industries were never rescued by the government. Capital injections were implemented in the 2000s.

Japan's Ineffective Monetary Policy

Japan's long-term recession is often explained as a liquidity trap. Much attention has been focused on monetary policy rather than on structural issues, but the problem of the Japanese economy was in its vertical investment–saving curve (Fig. 1.8). Private investment did not grow despite very low interest rates. Expected future rates of return were low and so hardly any new technological progress was made in Japan. Even though the central bank's short-term interest rate was set to zero, depressed investment in Japan meant that the economy was not able to recover.

Because so much effort was aimed at utilizing monetary policy instead of accelerating corporate restructuring, attempts to reduce idle capacity and start new investment through such restructuring were not pursued.

1.3 Comparison of the Economic Collapse in Japan and Greece

Although both Greece and Japan have high levels of net debt, it is helpful to understand why Japanese debt is still sustainable while Greece was declared bankrupt.

Japan's government debt is much higher than that of Greece, but it is sustainable because almost 95% of the Government of Japan's debt is held by domestic investors in banks, postal savings, life insurance, and pension funds. The Japanese government issues various kinds of bonds based on demand by differing sectors, and the government bond market has been quite stable in Japan. Japanese investors continue to hold government bonds since Basel capital requirements set the risk of government bonds at zero. On the other hand, more than 70% of investors in Greece's bond market are foreigners and they have been quick to move out of the market at times of risk.

Figure 1.9 depicts the supply of government bonds and the demand for government debt in Japan and Greece. The vertical line shows the supply of government bonds in the primary market since no matter what the rate of interest is, the government has to finance its budget deficits. The demand for government bonds increases when the interest rate rises. Thus the demand curve for government bonds is denoted by an upward slope in the figure.

Both Japan and Greece have increased their sales of government bonds, meaning that the supply curve of government bonds has shifted to the right in the primary market. Demand for Japanese government bonds by banks, insurance companies, and pension funds is increasing as the sluggish economy has reduced demand for corporate loans (Fig. 1.9). Monetary easing has increased bank deposits and these funds have often been invested in government bonds. Japanese interest rates, therefore, remain low.

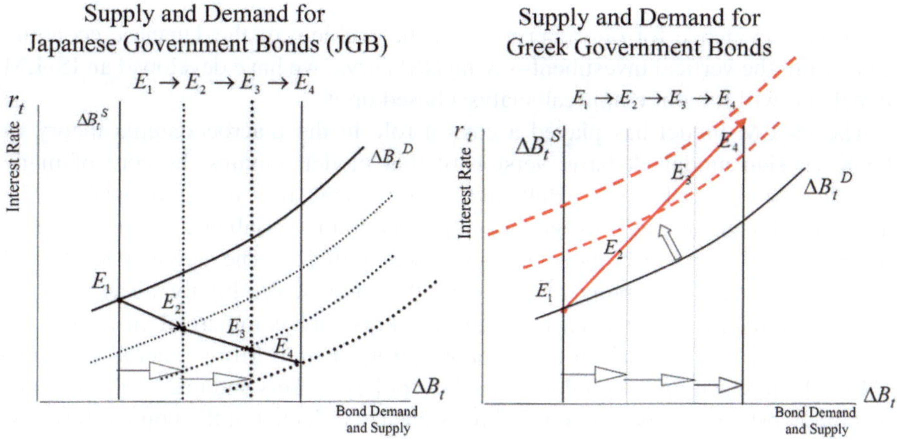

Fig. 1.9 Government bond markets of Japan and Greece (*Source*: Yoshino and Taghizadeh-Hesary 2014a)

Table 1.3 Holders of Japanese and Greek government bonds, 2011

Holders of Japanese government bonds	% of total	Holders of Greek government bonds	% of total
Bank and postal savings	45	Overseas investors	33
Life and non-life insurance	20	Domestic investors	21
Public pension funds	10	European Central Bank	18
Private pension funds	4	Bilateral loans	14
Bank of Japan	8	Social pension funds	6
Overseas investors	5	International Monetary Fund	5
Households	5	Greek domestic funds	3
Others	3		

Source: Yoshino and Taghizadeh-Hesary (2014b)
Note: In Greece, 70% of debt is held by overseas investors, compared with 5% for Japan

The behavior of holders of Japanese and Greek debt is distinctive (Table 1.3). Overseas investors, who hold 70% of government bonds in Greece, are very quick to sell them if they feel that risk is increasing. As demand for Greek bonds has diminished, the demand curve of the bonds has shifted to the left (Fig. 1.9, right-hand graph), which has progressively raised the interest rate on Greek bonds. The Greek interest rate increased to more than 20%, while the Japanese interest rate has remained at about 1% or less (Yoshino and Mizoguchi 2013). Since only 5% of the total bonds issued by the Japanese government are held by overseas investors, there is much less likelihood of capital flight, since domestic holders tend to retain their investments.

1.4 Empirical Analysis

Empirical Model

To provide evidence for our assertion that the problem of the Japanese economy stems from the vertical investment–saving (IS) curve, we have developed an IS–LM model and will run our empirical analysis based on it.

The IS–LM model has played a central role in the macroeconomic theory of the Keynesian model. A basic version of that model remains the core of many introductory textbooks (e.g., Hall and Taylor 1988) that use it to analyze the effects of changes in some exogenous macroeconomic variables and, in particular, the impact of alternative monetary and fiscal policies. The augmented IS–LM model is also the backbone of many of the large-scale, highly disaggregated, macroeconometric models used by governments and commercial firms for the purposes of policy evaluation and economic forecasting. More generally, the IS–LM model has a significant influence on how policy makers and market participants view the workings of the economy. This is clearly reflected in the popular business press (Galí 1992).

Below are two equations that constitute the simplest version of our IS–LM model. (Yoshino and Taghizadeh-Hesary 2016) They will be used simultaneously to run our empirical analysis. The first equation is the IS equation. It represents the equilibrium where total private investment equals total saving. Each point on the curve represents the balance between savings and investments. The second part of the simultaneous equation model is the LM equation. It shows the combination of interest rates and levels of real income for which the money market is in equilibrium. The LM function is the set of equilibrium points between the liquidity preference (or demand for money) function and the money supply function. The right money demand consists of the transactional demand, which is a function of real GDP, and the speculative demand, which is a function of the interest rate.

IS Equation

$$y = \alpha - \sigma (i - p) + u_{is} \tag{1.1}$$

LM Equation

$$m - p = \beta + \phi y - \lambda i + u_{lm} \tag{1.2}$$

In these equations, y denotes the log of real GDP, i is the nominal long-term interest rate, and p and m are the logs of the price level and the money supply, respectively. u_{is} and u_{lm} are the stochastic processes describing money supply and money demand (LM) and spending (IS) driving forces. To run our empirical analysis for GDP we used the Japanese real GDP, deflated by the GDP deflator (2009 = 100), seasonally adjusted using the X-12 quarterly seasonal adjustment method. For the interest rate, we used a 10-year government bond yield, which is a long-term, safe asset interest rate. For the price level we used the general consumer price index of Japan. For the money supply we used Japanese M1, adjusted using the X-12 quarterly seasonal adjustment method.

We used data from 1990Q2 to 2013Q4. All variables except the interest rate were used in logarithmic form. The data is sourced from Nikkei NEEDS and the Bank of Japan database.

Unit Root Test

To evaluate the stationarity of all series, we performed the unit root test on all variables at levels and first differences initially with the intercept, and then also with the intercept and trend. The test used was the augmented Dickey-Fuller test and the results are summarized in Table 1.4.

The results imply that almost all variables are non-stationary in levels. The variables include real interest rate, nominal interest rate, real GDP (in logarithmic

Table 1.4 Unit root test

		Intercept				Trend and intercept			
Variable	Definition	Levels (t-statistic)	AIC	First differences (t-statistic)	AIC	Levels (t-statistic)	AIC	First differences (t-statistic)	AIC
$(i-p)_t$	Real interest rate	−2.40	1.77	−9.64**	1.817	−2.19	1.78	−9.80**	1.816
i_t	Nominal interest rate	−2.06	0.33	−9.59**	0.37	−1.73	0.34	−7.65**	0.29
y_t	Real GDP	1.24	17.42	−8.20**	17.32	−4.77**	17.18	−8.36**	17.33
$(m-p)_t$	Real money supply	−0.58	62.21	−2.85*	62.20	−2.13	62.19	−2.82	62.18

Source: Authors' calculations

Note: * indicates rejection of the null hypothesis for the presence of unit root at 5%. ** indicates rejection of the null hypothesis for the presence of unit root at 1%. The optimal lag lengths for the augmented Dickey-Fuller test were found using the Akaike information criterion. *AIC* Akaike information criterion, *GDP* gross domestic product form), and real money supply (in logarithmic form).[2] However, the first differences of all variables show stationary results. These results suggest that the real interest rate, nominal interest rate, real GDP (in logarithmic form) and real money supply (in logarithmic form) each contains a unit root. Once the unit root test was performed and it was discovered that the variables are non-stationary in level and stationary in first differences, they were integrated of order 1 or I(1). Hence, they will appear in our empirical model in first differences.

Empirical Results

Both the IS and the LM equations are simultaneously estimated by the iterative seemingly unrelated regression. This method uses information about contemporaneous correlation among error terms across equations in an attempt to improve the efficiency of parameter estimates. The results of the regression are summarized in Table 1.5.

The upper part of Table 1.5, with the results for the IS equation, shows the relationship between the real GDP and the real long-term interest rate. Economic theory suggests that when the real interest rate goes down, investment should go up, so the sign of the interest rate in the empirical findings should be negative. Indeed,

Table 1.5 Empirical results (sample: 1990Q2–2013Q4)

Equation	Dependent variable	Explanatory variable	Coefficient	Std. error	t-Statistic	Prob.
IS	y_t	α	−0.16	0.08	−1.98*	0.049
		$(i-p)_t$	−0.0002	0.0004	−0.53	0.60
		y_{t-1}	1.01	0.007	147.63**	0.00
R-squared = 0.99, adjusted R-squared = 0.99, Durbin-Watson stat. = 1.70, std. error of regression = 0.01						
LM	$(m-p)_t$	β	0.02	0.19	0.11	0.91
		y_t	0.70	0.26	2.67**	0.008
		i_t	−0.025	0.009	−2.72**	0.007
		$(m-p)_{t-1}$	0.99	0.006	171.06**	0.00
R-squared = 0.99, adjusted R-squared = 0.99, Durbin-Watson stat. = 1.93, std. error of regression = 0.03						

Source: Authors' calculations

Note: Estimation method: iterative seemingly unrelated regression. *Std. error* standard error, *Prob.* probability

[2]Real GDP was stationary with "intercept and trend," but because the value of the Akaike information criterion with "intercept" was higher compared to "intercept and trend," we consider the "intercept" result. Hence, this means the variable was also non-stationary in level and stationary in first difference, i.e., I(1).

the sign of the real interest rate in Japan's IS equation from 1990Q2 to 2013Q4 was negative, but not significant. This means that when the interest rates were lower, investment did not accelerate. This is evidence of the vertical IS curve that can be seen in Fig. 1.8 and is in accordance with Yoshino and Taghizadeh-Hesary (2015), who did not find significant association between the long-term real interest rate and the real GDP of Japan during 2002Q2–2014Q2. The lagged GDP gap had a significant impact on the current value of GDP.

The lower part of Table 1.5, with the empirical results for the LM equation, shows the combination of interest rates i_t and levels of real income y_t for which the money market is in equilibrium. The LM function is the set of equilibrium points between the liquidity preference (or demand for money) function and the money supply $(m - p)_t$. The Y axis of the LM curve is the interest rate and the X axis is the real GDP (y_t). Usually, the LM curve is upward sloping and our empirical results for 1990Q2–2013Q4 of Japan are in accordance with an upward-sloping LM curve. Money demand consist of two parts; transactional demand (which is a function of the real income) and speculative demand (which is a function of the interest rate). Our results are in accordance with economic theory that suggests that transactional demand is a positive function of the real income, and that speculative demand is a negative function of the interest rate. Moreover, both coefficients show statistically significant values. These findings contradict Paul Krugman's assertions about the Japanese economy. He has argued that Japan is currently in a liquidity trap, which would equate to a horizontal LM curve (Krugman 1998a, b). However, our empirical analysis indicates that the Japanese LM curve has an upward slope, so the problems of the Japanese economy must stem from other sources.

Since we argue that the problem of the Japanese economy in the "Lost Decade" did not arise from monetary policy, and because the results show the Japanese economy is not in a liquidity trap, we suggest that the problems arise from other issues such as banking behavior, diminished effectiveness of fiscal policy, high appreciation of the yen in the mid-1990s, an aging population, and transfers from central to local governments.

1.5 Remedies for Stimulating Growth in Japan

We suggest 11 remedies for stimulating Japanese economic growth that could also help prevent other Asian economies from falling into long-term recession.

Remedy 1: Required Reforms Regarding the Aging Population

An aging population and early retirement age are key contributing factors to Japan's slow economic activity. Wage rates should be based on productivity rather than seniority. It is much easier for companies to hire elderly people if their wage rates are set according to productivity. Healthy elderly people should be able to find jobs based on their experience. The retirement age should be increased to boost the diminishing working population. Moreover, the government needs to encourage greater female participation in the labor force through measures such as improving child care facilities.

Remedy 2: Increasing Female Participation in the Economy

In Japan, female participation in the economy is far lower than in many other advanced and emerging economies. This may be due to several social factors, but there are ways to increase female participation in the economy.

In Japan, as in other countries, women usually join the workforce after graduation. However, in many cases, after having children they leave their jobs to dedicate time to child care. Figure 1.10 shows the percentage of female employees by size of enterprise. This shows that the smaller the enterprise, the higher the percentage of female employees. This is because many microenterprises are family run and wives work together with their husbands, so even after having children they can look after their children while working in the business on a part-time basis. As is clear from the figure, in large enterprises, female participation is lower. This is because large enterprises generally have higher discipline (stricter attendance and leave requirements) so it is more difficult for mothers to manage child care and work at the same time.

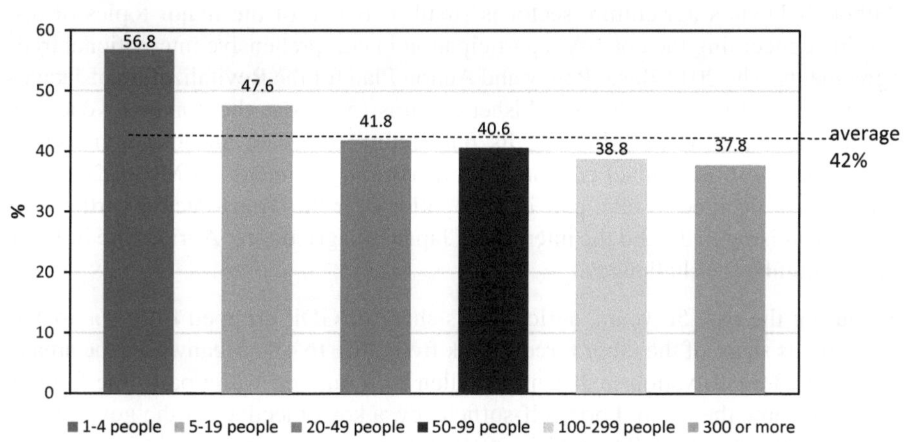

Fig. 1.10 Percentage of female employees by size of enterprise in Japan (percentage of employees). *Notes*: "Employees" refers to people who are company members, work in a private shop, or are otherwise employed at a company, by an individual, or in a private shop; the term excludes persons employed at public agencies and other groups and corporations, and furthermore excludes executive officers of companies, etc. The dotted line in the figure represents the average for all enterprises (42.0%) (*Source*: Government of Japan, Ministry of Internal Affairs and Communications 2012)

Due to the aging population and shrinking labor force, the government needs to encourage greater female participation in the workforce, in part by improving child care facilities. A good child care system could be a crucial tool for helping mothers return to work after having children. It could also have a positive effect on the birth rate, as a poor child care system may deter women from having children.

Remedy 3: Reduction of Transfers from Central to Local Governments

Government spending between central and local governments must be clearly defined. An incentives mechanism should be created to encourage local governments to reduce transfers from the central government. At present, local governments are more eager to receive transfers from the central government than to raise private funds. The central government should provide only limited transfers to motivate local governments to raise most of the funding from the private sector. Public–private partnerships and hometown investment trust (HIT) funds must also be promoted. The allocation of taxes and expenditure between the central government and local governments must also be determined.

Remedy 4: Reform of the Agriculture Sector

Although Japan's agriculture sector is small, it is one of the major topics of discussion concerning the country's participation in comprehensive international trade agreements. The 2011 Basic Policy and Action Plan for the Revitalization of Japan's Food, Agriculture, Forestry and Fisheries aims to bolster the competitiveness of farmers in the 5 years following its publication to create an agriculture sector compatible with high-level economic partnership agreements. In March 2013, the government decided to take part in negotiations for the Trans-Pacific Partnership, while promising to defend the interests of Japanese agriculture. Agriculture in Japan faces a number of challenges:

- During the past 50 years, agriculture's share of GDP dropped from 9% to 1%, while its share of the labor force shrank from 28% to 4%. Meanwhile, the area of land under cultivation in Japan has fallen by a quarter, while part-time farming has become the norm. Food self-sufficiency, a key objective for the government, fell from 79% in 1960 to 39% in 2010, in terms of numbers of calories.
- Productivity in land-intensive agriculture is low, reflecting the small size of Japanese farms, which average only 2 hectares, compared with farms in the European Union (14 hectares) and the US (170 hectares) (Government of Japan, Ministry of Agriculture, Forestry and Fisheries 2012). Farms tend to be small in Japan because of land reforms following World War II, Japan's mountainous terrain, the production adjustment program that allocates output of rice to specific farmers, and subsidies that make small-scale farming profitable.

- High levels of support for certain commodities impose heavy burdens on consumers and taxpayers. The overall level of assistance in Japan, as measured by the Producer Support Estimate, was 51% in 2009–2011, about double the average of the OECD. Higher prices boosted consumer spending on agriculture products to 1.8 times more than it would have been without government policies.
- Border measures, including a 2012 tariff of ¥341 per kilogram of rice, which amounted to a 780% rate, isolated farmers from international competition and complicated Japan's participation in comprehensive regional and bilateral trade agreements. Still, some parts of the agriculture sector are thriving. In particular, vegetable production increased its share of agriculture output from 9% in 1960 to 28% in 2010, exceeding the share of rice. Vegetable production is a labor-intensive sector with business-oriented farms that receive relatively little government support and are not necessarily large scale. A more open and competitive environment is essential to secure the growth and competitiveness of agriculture and promote Japan's integration in the world economy. Demographic factors create an opportunity for farm consolidation and other reforms to boost productivity. Indeed, in 2010, the average age of farmers was 66, and 56% of rice farmers were over 70, while a further 36% were aged 50–70 (Fig. 1.11). Only 8% were under the age of 50 (OECD 2013).

In addition to the reforms of agriculture cooperatives undertaken by Shinzō Abe, there are other ways to revitalize rural areas in Japan:

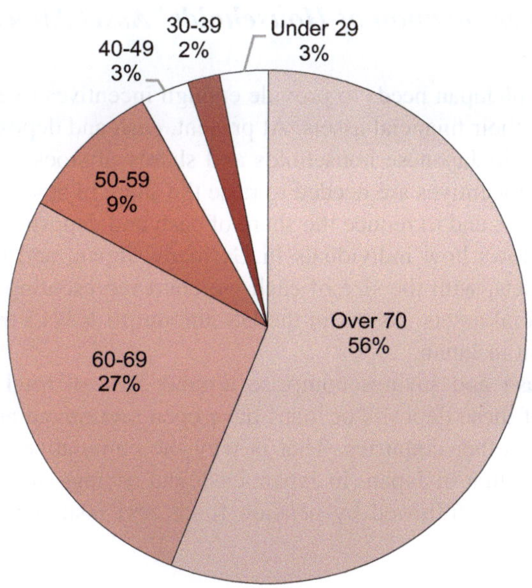

Fig. 1.11 Age distribution of rice farmers in Japan, 2010 (*Source*: Ministry of Agriculture, Forestry, and Fisheries 2010)

- The production adjustment program should be phased out over a fixed and relatively short time, thereby increasing the share of rice produced using efficient methods and reducing its production costs. The impact of lower rice prices should be mitigated by transitory income payments to large farmers (OECD 2013).
- Liberalizing border tariffs on agricultural goods, when done in conjunction with domestic reforms, will facilitate Japan's participation in comprehensive regional and bilateral trade agreements, including the Trans-Pacific Partnership.
- There should be more progress in farm consolidation. The prohibition on nonagriculture corporations owning farmland should be abolished to attract labor, capital, and technology into agriculture, while ensuring that land-use regulations limit the shift of farmland to other uses. At the same time, taxation ought to be reformed to discourage the holding of idle agricultural land near urban areas (OECD 2013).
- There should be new methods of financing, not only by banks, but also through hometown investment trust (HIT) funds and crowdfunding that can provide finance to rural small and medium-sized enterprises (SMEs) and farmers.[3]

One reform that the Government of Japan has launched under the Abe administration is to enable elderly people who own farmland to lease it to younger people. Formerly this was not allowed. In combination with the hometown investment trust fund, this means that many more people can build an agriculture business.

Remedy 5: Diversification of Households' Asset Allocation

The Government of Japan needs to provide enough incentives to encourage households to diversify their financial assets. At present, cash and deposits form the bulk of financial assets in Japanese households and shares of stocks and securities are low. Government incentives are needed to raise the share of stocks and securities in household portfolios and to reduce the share of cash and deposits.

Figure 1.12 shows how individuals in Germany, Japan, and the US distribute their financial assets, with the size of each pie chart representing the total amount of personal financial assets. Assets in the US amount to ¥3715 trillion, more than double the amount in Japan.

In the US, cash and savings comprise around 15% of total financial assets. More than half of these deposits or loans have been securitized and many of them have been sold to other countries. That is why the cumulative debt of the US is much smaller than that of Japan. In Japan, cash and savings make up the majority of total assets (55%), followed by pension funds and insurance. The number of

[3]Hometown investment trust (HIT) funds are a new form of financial intermediation that has been adopted as a national strategy in Japan. The name reflects their goal: to connect fund providers with their hometowns. Naoyuki Yoshino, coauthor of this chapter, was one of the earliest proponents of the funds.

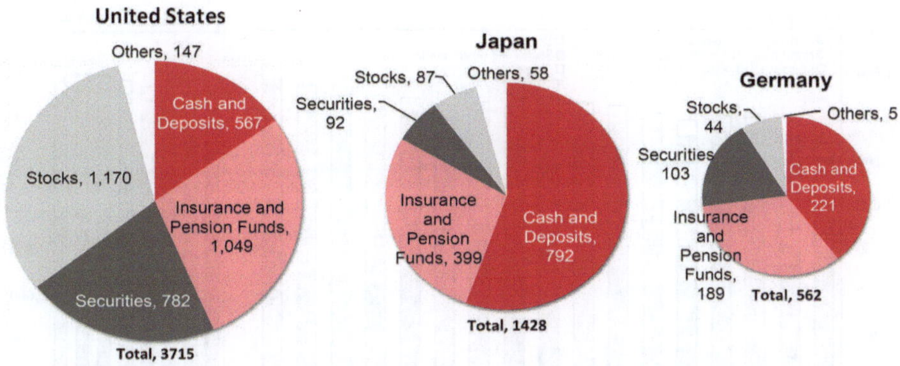

Fig. 1.12 Financial asset allocations of the United States, Japan, and Germany (¥ trillion) (*Source*: Yoshino 2013)

marketable securities and shares is extremely small and, if this falls further, could create issues over who will provide money for corporations and environmental projects in regions with possibilities for growth but that carry risk. If not handled properly, opportunities for growth could be overlooked, with the flow of funds through Japan's financial institutions going only to safe borrowers.

In contrast, individuals in the US are much less risk averse. In the US, for example, over half of all household assets are held in shares and marketable securities, and it appears that private individuals are motivated to take risks in the hope of high returns.

In this regard, Germany used to resemble Japan. However, with the emergence of investment trusts and the profitable sell-off of shares for privatization in Japan, there has been a shift to shares and investments (Yoshino and Mizoguchi 2013). In the case of privatization of companies such as Nippon Telegraph and Telephone Corporation and Japan Tobacco, shares were sold, but their prices fell. Ultimately, investors were not able to channel their investments profitably into equities (Yoshino 2013).

Figure 1.13 shows how households in Japan allocate their financial assets. After cash and deposits, insurance policies form the second-largest share of households' assets. In Japan, insurance is regarded as a long-term saving scheme. Deposits are usually held for 1 or 2 years, but insurance policies are for 10, 20, or 30 years. Many people in Japan prefer to keep their financial assets as deposits initially and then to take out insurance.

When considering the distribution of assets across the population in Japan, Table 1.6 shows that older people have the greatest number of assets and young people have the least. Older people prefer to hold deposits, insurance, and government bonds, which are perceived as safe, rather than assets that they regard as risky. This is another reason why the share of cash and savings is so high in Japanese households, and also why this share is greater than in many other countries.

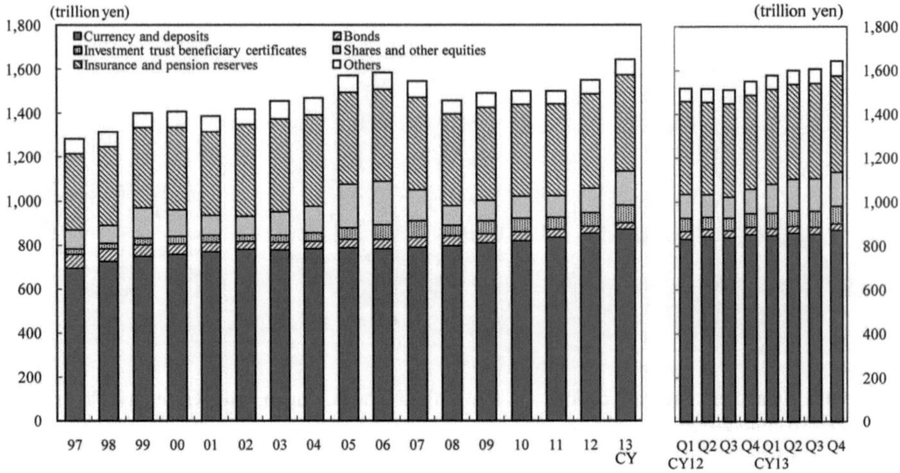

Fig. 1.13 Financial assets held by households in Japan. *CY* calendar year (*Source*: Bank of Japan 2014a)

Table 1.6 Financial assets of Japanese people by age (¥10,000)

Age	Deposits	Insurance	Securities	Others	Total
Average	635	303	179	52	1169
20 years	266	26	40	10	342
30 years	298	122	77	40	537
40 years	355	241	85	62	743
50 years	533	344	126	65	1068
60 years	811	409	276	43	1539
70 years	1035	333	287	52	1707

Source: Yoshino and Taghizadeh-Hesary (2014a)

Figure 1.14 shows a country comparison of income from interest and dividends, divided by income. Germany has the highest share while Japan has the lowest. France and Germany were major supporters of the creation of the euro, making it simple for Germany to invest in the 18 countries in the eurozone, whenever it feels this will be profitable. That is why German dividends and interest payments are very high. Japan's low rate of return is due to 20 years of slow growth and the high value of the yen, which means that Japanese investments overseas have a low rate of return in terms of yen.

Judging from Fig. 1.13, one consequence of Abenomics has been the diversification of households' asset allocations from an overconcentration of deposits to much wider asset holdings.[4] The government has introduced a new investment savings

[4]When Shinzō Abe was elected to his second term as Prime Minister in December 2012 he introduced a reform program called Abenomics. It aimed to revive the sluggish economy with

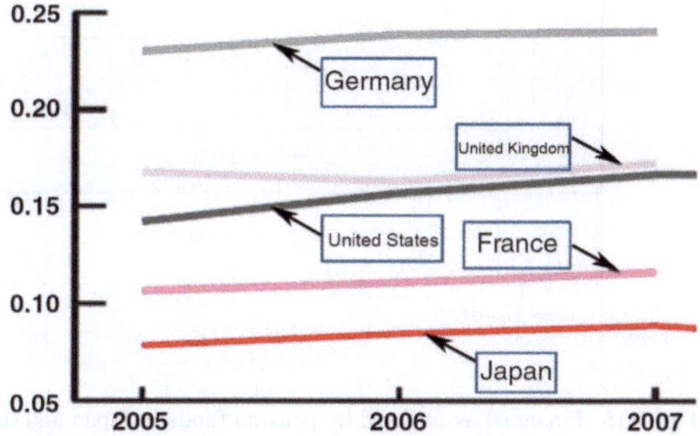

Fig. 1.14 Revenue share of financial assets in France, Germany, Japan, the United Kingdom, and the United States (income from interest and dividends divided by income) (*Source*: Yoshino 2013)

account—Nippon Individual Saving Account—which it hopes will widen the share of stocks and bonds in the financial assets of Japanese householders (Yoshino and Taghizadeh-Hesary 2014a). There is a need for more policies such as this that will accelerate the diversification of households' financial assets. This will give them an incentive to enter the stock market or raise the share of stocks and bonds in their portfolio and to reduce the share of cash and deposits.

Remedy 6: Switching Asset Allocation Pension Funds and Insurance Companies from Pay-as-You-Go to 401(k)-Style

Figure 1.15 shows the financial assets held by pension funds in Japan and the US. Unlike the US, pension funds and insurance companies in Japan mainly invest in government bonds and are very cautious about investing in stocks. The main reason for this is that Japanese pension funds are pay-as-you-go style and pension contributors cannot control how their funds are invested. Investors let the government decide how to allocate their funds to various financial products. In contrast, most US pensions are 401(k)-style and pension contributors decide what percentage can be invested in risky and safe assets, which means self-responsibility for pension management. In this case, with the contributor deciding what proportion of pension funds to be allocated to risky assets and what proportion to safe assets, the job of the asset management company is very easy. If all the funds are aggregated, x% will be invested in risky assets and 1–x% will be allocated to safe assets. In Japan, there is complete reliance on the decisions of asset managers. There

"three arrows": fiscal consolidation, more aggressive monetary easing from the Bank of Japan, and structural reforms to boost Japan's competitiveness and economic growth.

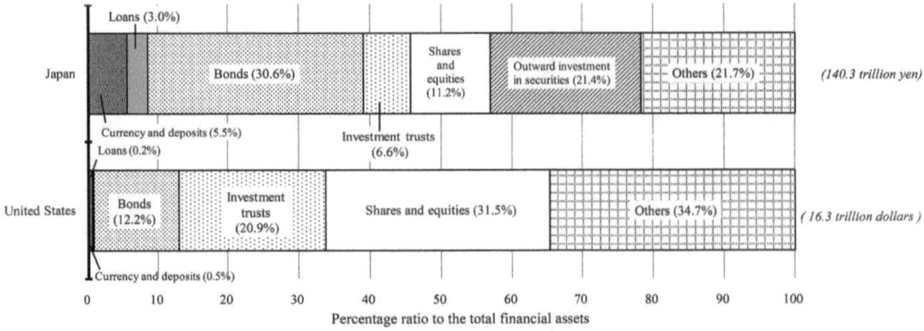

Fig. 1.15 Financial assets held by pension funds in Japan and the United States (% ratio of total financial assets) (*Note*: "Others" is the residual amount that remains after deducting currency and deposits, loans, bonds, investment trusts, shares and equities, and (for Japan) outward investment in securities, from total financial assets. The US flow of funds data includes both outward and domestic investment in securities. *Source*: Bank of Japan 2014b)

is no self-responsibility with regard to pension funds and insurance companies. Hence, asset managers want to invest in government bonds, which are the safest asset. If Japan's pension system changes to 401(k)-style and asset allocation relies on individuals' portfolio allocations, then stock market investment and overseas investment in stocks will become much easier because they will be based on individuals' decisions (Yoshino and Taghizadeh-Hesary 2014b).

Remedy 7: Review of Asset Management Fees

The sales commissions of asset management companies need to be reviewed. The discussion here refers to sales commissions for financial instruments.

In Fig. 1.16, households ("investors" in the figure) want to maximize their rates of return through dividends or interest payments. But in the middle, distributors, such as banks or securities companies who sell financial products to individual investors, are looking for trust fees and commissions rather than rates of return. In many countries, including Japan, trust fees and commissions are based on principal + dividends. So even if the dividends are negative, distributors always receive commissions and fees. That is one reason why Japanese investors have tended to lose money in recent years. To change this system, distributors' fees and commissions need to be based only on dividends so that investors and distributors are driven by the same maximization goals.

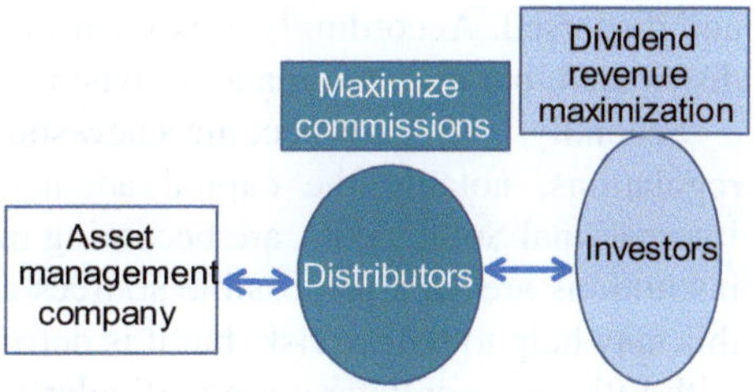

Fig. 1.16 Sales of financial products (*Source*: Yoshino and Taghizadeh-Hesary 2014a)

Remedy 8: Use of Hometown Investment Trust Funds to Finance Riskier Businesses

After the housing bubble burst in the early 1990s, Japan's unique system of financial intermediation—the "collateral principle"—was blamed. Its lending criteria were based on the amount of collateral, rather than the viability of the project. It subsequently became a national objective in Japan to adopt Anglo-American ways of finance. Two decades later, the Lehman crisis devastated the world economy and Anglo-American financial methods were discredited. Then, in March 2011, the Great East Japan Earthquake and tsunami struck Japan. During the long and painful recovery process that followed, many Japanese people had a strong desire to contribute to the recovery. They were often looking for opportunities to contribute, rather than to benefit from high returns. They also realized that local small and medium-sized enterprises (SMEs) and many startup companies needed financing. There was a clear need for a meeting place for these borrowers and lenders. Furthermore, the country's budget deficit-to-GDP ratio breached 200% in 2010, casting doubt on the efficiency and effectiveness of public investment. There was a need for private financing with transparent performance monitoring.

It was in this period that a new form of financing—the hometown investment trust (HIT) fund—was proposed to connect fund providers and their hometowns, and a committee at the Cabinet Office was created to study the proposal. There are three advantages to HIT funds. Firstly, they can reinforce financial stability by reducing information asymmetry and sharing risk. The downfall of the pre-Lehman "originate and distribute" model was that borrower IOUs were hidden deep within complicated financial instruments. This made risk difficult to calculate and track. Once markets had lost faith in the ability of borrowers to repay, nobody knew where the risks were and credit markets froze. Far from "distributing" risk to achieve financial stability, information ended up being as asymmetric as it could possibly have been. In contrast to this model, the HIT method encourages stability by reducing information asymmetry as much as possible. This is because households—and firms, if they want to invest in other companies—are keen to obtain information on the borrowing firms, mainly SMEs. The lenders are from the same "hometown" as the borrowers, or they may share a similar interest. There is also a low degree of scale and concentration, with both the lenders and borrowers being relatively small and dispersed. Accordingly, this form of financial intermediation allows risk to be distributed, but does not make it invisible in the process.

Secondly, HIT funds become a new source of much-needed risk capital. Financial regulations, notably the capital adequacy ratio requirements of the Bank for International Settlements, are becoming more stringent as banks and other financial institutions are seen as possible sources of instability. In a macroprudential sense, this may help to reduce risk, but it is detrimental to the supply of risk capital. Firms with little or no collateral are particularly affected by this change, so the provision of a new and stable source of risk capital can be especially beneficial.

Thirdly, HIT funds are project driven. Unlike other arrangements, such as the Grameen Bank, where investment destinations are determined later, HIT investors can choose their investment from a pool of projects. Investors are not necessarily seeking high returns. Instead, they are motivated to help a project they feel strongly about. This may be because the project is based in their hometown, or they may see significance in the investment's potential to reduce poverty, address environmental concerns, or assist in disaster recovery. In this way, investors may feel a level of personal satisfaction in their choice, and have the added benefit of actually being able to "see" the results. This is not possible with ordinary mutual funds, where investors are not able to track the destinations of their investments.

The drawback of these regional trust funds, however, is that they are not guaranteed by the Deposit Insurance Corporation of Japan and risks are borne by the investors. Steps must be taken to increase investor confidence to enable the HIT market to grow. This could be done by ensuring that the terms of the fund are explained in detail to investors, including information about associated risks and where the funds will be invested.

Examples of regional funds in Japan are those covering wind-power generation, startup businesses, and agriculture businesses. Around 20 wind-power generators in Japan have been constructed through private–public partnerships. For these projects, local residents invested between $1000 and $5000, and in return they receive annual dividends from the sales of electricity generated.

Project evaluations play an important role in the creation of regional funds, as some funds that have been invested in risky ventures have failed to perform well. Globally, banks are becoming increasingly concerned about their risks following the implementation of Basel III (Yoshino and Hirano 2011). Since Asia is dominated by bank loans, and capital markets are generally not well developed, it is even harder to raise venture capital and finance riskier projects. Consequently, project assessors must identify potential nonperforming investments that could lose money for investors. It should be noted, though, that some of Japan's regional funds are regarded as charities and offer an opportunity for investors to contribute to their region and support venture businesses. (for more information about evaluation of SMEs and credit rating of SMEs please see Yoshino and Taghizadeh-Hesary 2014e).

Banks are often not able to finance high-risk projects, even if the expected rates of return are high. If, however, these projects are financed through regional funds, rather than by deposits transformed into bank loans, banks can receive money though the sales of regional funds by their branch offices. They do not have to worry

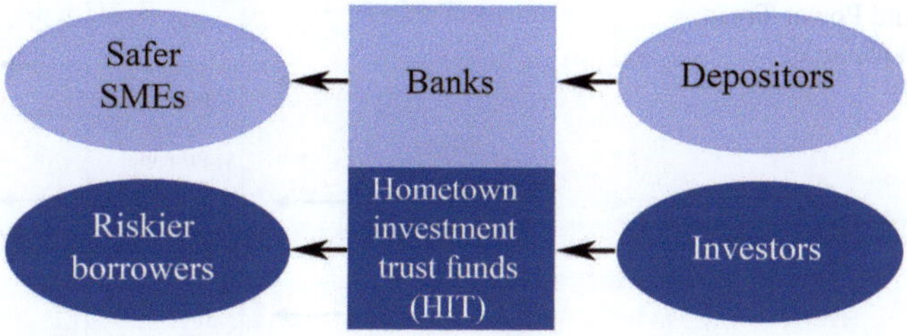

Fig. 1.17 Bank-based financing of small and medium-sized enterprise and regional financing to riskier borrowers. *SMEs* small and medium-sized enterprises (*Source*: Yoshino and Taghizadeh-Hesary 2014a)

about accumulation of nonperforming loans. Investors must be made fully aware of the risks when making their investments, but they may also receive a high rate of return, and this could increase investments in riskier projects that would otherwise not have been funded.

The success of its regional funds may help a bank to attract more investors. Conversely, if funds do not perform well, banks may lose future investors. In this way, through performance-based competition among the regional funds, the quality of projects and the risk-adjusted returns for investors can be improved (Yoshino 2012).

Figure 1.17 illustrates bank-based SME financing and regional financing to riskier borrowers. Bank loans go to relatively safe borrowers. HIT funds finance riskier projects.

With ordinary investment trusts, an outlay is made by a group of investors who provide funds to a range of borrowers, with the investors receiving dividends but not knowing what their investment will be used for. The main feature of HIT funds is that the investor knows the borrower's identity and where the investment is going. Investors can choose to support their local region and borrowers and, by doing so, to use the fund as both an investment and a donation.

Remedy 9: Optimal Mix of Public and Private Funds

Figure 1.18 shows the forms in which private and public funds may be collected to invest in wind power generator projects. It would be ideal if all the funding came from the private sector.

However, in the case of enterprises that represent a public good, such as solar panels, it is conceivable that public funds (from national or local governments) could be introduced in the form of matching funds or grants that would be combined with funds from private sector investors. In Fig. 1.18, private sector funds represent 70% and public sector funds 30% of the total. If we suppose that all the proceeds (the returns) from the project go to the private sector investors, and that, even though

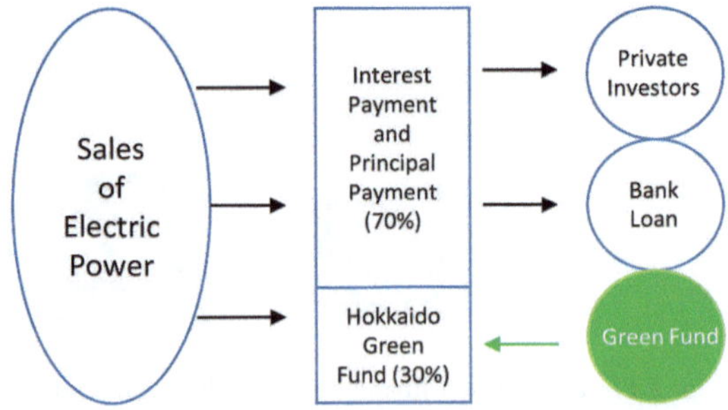

Fig. 1.18 Wind Power Trust Fund of Japan (*Source*: Yoshino 2013)

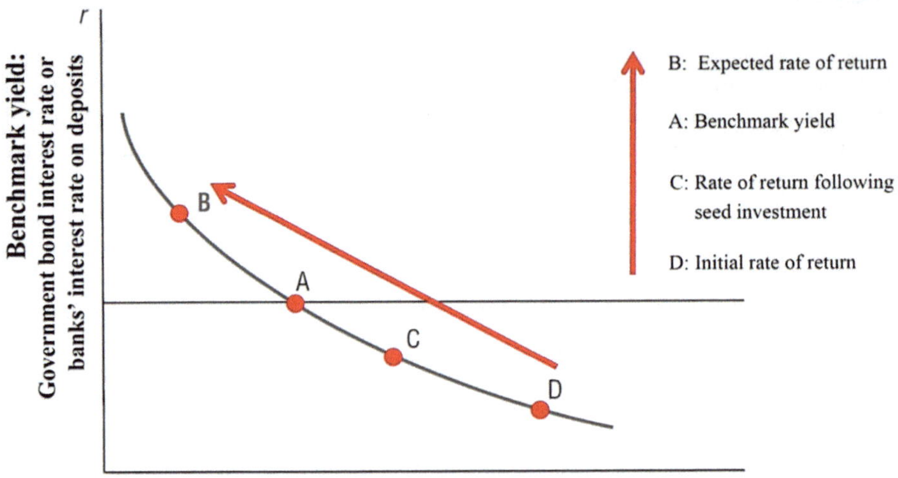

Fig. 1.19 Calculated rate of return (*Source*: Yoshino and Taghizadeh-Hesary 2014a)

the profitability for the private sector investors will not be high, it will increase if dividends do not have to be paid to the originators of the national government funds. This will make the investment attractive to private sector investors because it will offer an anticipated rate of return that is higher than the benchmark profitability shown by the horizontal line in Fig. 1.19.

If private and public sector funds are combined as described above, there may be a leveraging effect because investors can be told that the project has official government support. They can also be told that, even if the rate of return is low, since interest and dividends need not be paid to the public investors, there will be an increased rate of return for private sector investors. A further reason for combining private and public funds is that the introduction of private sector funds will enhance project efficiency. Lengthy, low-quality construction work will be avoided as projects funded solely by the private sector would usually only concentrate on generating profits as quickly as possible (Yoshino 2010).

Remedy 10: Review of Monetary Policy Goals

Monetary policy must set goals for inflation and economic growth. A rigid exchange-rate system will increase the central bank's foreign reserves and will therefore greatly increase the monetary base. Gradual adjustment of the exchange rate from a current basket to desired weights for the basket will be desirable.

In 2013 the Bank of Japan set a price stability target of 2% (year-on-year rate of change in the consumer price index). It is implementing aggressive monetary easing to achieve this target. We believe, however, that this target needs to be reviewed and reduced because of the recent drop in oil prices. After nearly 5 years of stability, oil prices began to drop rapidly in 2014 and more than halved in the 5 months following September 2014. In Europe, the price of a barrel of Brent crude oil fell from $117.15 on 6 September 2014 to $45.13 on 14 January 2015.

Oil is one of the most important production inputs. Figure 1.20 shows that in periods with cheaper oil, the aggregate demand (AD) curve shifts to the right because of higher consumption. In the supply side of the economy, the aggregate supply (AS) curve also shifts to the right because of cheaper production costs, which raises the output (Q_2). So the intercept of the price level becomes lower (P_{Q2}), and the inflation target needs to be reviewed. Because oil price is exogenously given for Japanese monetary policy, the target rate of inflation should be lower than 2% during the current period of cheap oil prices.

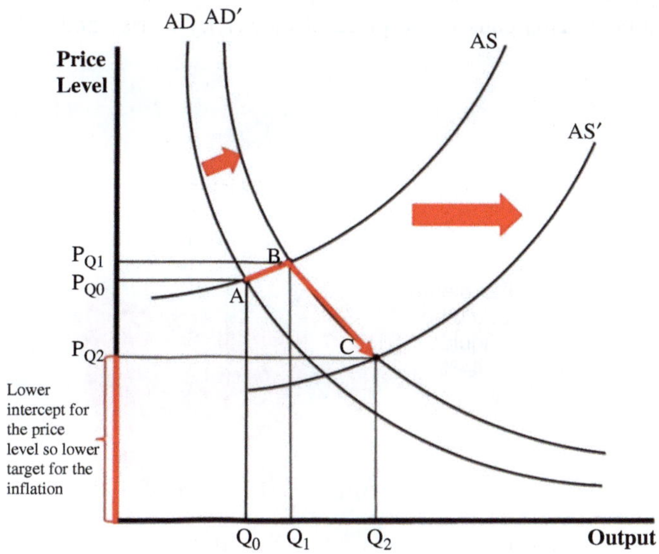

Fig. 1.20 The effect of lower oil prices on the price level intercept. *AD* aggregate demand, *AS* aggregate supply, *Q* quantity (*Source*: Authors' calculations)

Remedy 11: Diversification of the Energy Basket

Japan is the world's largest liquefied natural gas importer, the second-largest coal importer, and the third-largest net oil importer after the US and the PRC. Japan has limited domestic energy resources, meeting less than 15% of its own total primary energy use from domestic sources (Government of the United States, Energy Information Administration 2015). Figure 1.21 shows the share of each energy carrier in Japan's total energy consumption.

Oil demand in Japan has declined by nearly 15% since 2000. This decline stems from structural factors, such as fuel substitution, a declining population, and government-mandated energy efficiency targets. In addition to the industrial sector's shift to natural gas, fuel substitution is occurring in the residential sector as high prices have led to decreased demand for kerosene for home heating. Japan consumes most of its oil in the transportation and industrial sectors, and it is also highly dependent on naphtha and low-sulfur fuel oil imports. Demand for naphtha has fallen as ethylene production is gradually being displaced by petrochemical production in other Asian countries (Yoshino and Taghizadeh-Hesary 2014c).

The 9.0 magnitude Great East Japan Earthquake and tsunami that hit Japan on 11 March 2011 resulted in an immediate shutdown of about 10 gigawatts of nuclear electricity generating capacity. In the 14 months following the Fukushima disaster, Japan lost all of its nuclear capacity as a result of scheduled maintenance and lack of government approvals to return to operation. Japan replaced this significant loss of nuclear power with generation from imported natural gas, low-sulfur crude oil, fuel oil, and coal. This caused the price of electricity to rise and led to inflation.

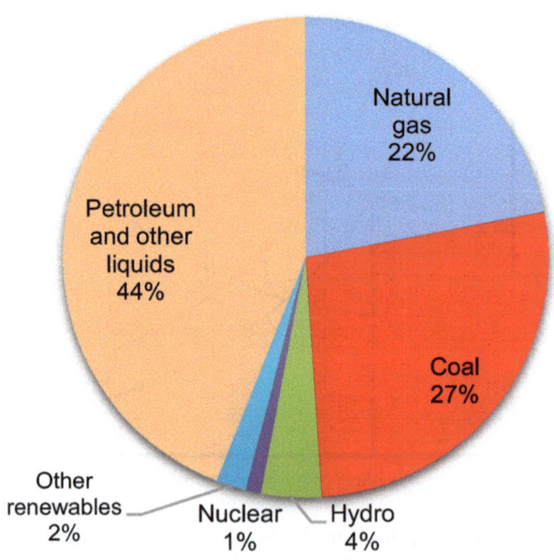

Fig. 1.21 Japan's energy consumption, 2013 (*Source*: British Petroleum 2014)

Increases in the cost of fuel imports in the 2 years since the disaster resulted in Japan's top ten utilities losing over $30 billion. In 2012, Japan spent $250 billion on total fuel imports—a third of the country's total import value—and consumed over 4.7 million barrels of oil per day (Yoshino and Taghizadeh-Hesary 2015). The increased cost of imported energy had a significant, negative impact on the Japanese economy.[5]

Because of increased imports of fossil fuels after the Fukushima disaster, the trade balance reversed from a 30-year trade surplus of $65 billion in 2010 to a deficit of $112 billion in 2013. The recent drop in oil prices in the latter part of 2014 is likely to ease the trade deficit and provide some relief to Japanese utilities.

Japan needs to diversify its energy basket away from fossil fuels to non-fossil fuels (renewable and nuclear) to reduce energy costs. This will reduce production costs for Japanese manufacturers, stimulate the economy, and raise the self-reliance on energy to help protect the economy from further shocks.

Like Japan's current government, we believe that Japan needs to use nuclear energy as a base load power source, with necessary safety measures. This will help ease current energy supply strains and reduce the high energy prices faced by Japan's industries and end users.

The government's 2014 energy policy emphasizes energy security, economic efficiency, and emissions reduction. Key goals and plans to balance the country's fuel portfolio include strengthening the share of renewable and alternative energy sources. These efforts occur in the context of the government's goals to reverse 2 decades of economic stagnation in Japan and to provide economic revitalization through public infrastructure spending, monetary easing, labor market reform, and business investment (Government of the United States, Energy Information Administration 2015).

1.6 Concluding Remarks

The empirical analysis in this chapter shows that stagnation of the Japanese economy comes from a vertical investment–saving curve. The impact of fiscal policy drastically declined from the 1990s and the Japanese economy faces structural problems rather than a temporary downturn. Our empirical findings also reject the idea proposed by Paul Krugman that the Japanese economy is in a liquidity trap.

Structural problems have arisen mainly from the aging population, ineffective fiscal policy, and the transfers from the central government to local governments that make up about 16% of total government spending. This high spending rate has kept some sectors, such as agriculture, weak. Further structural problems have

[5]For more information on the impact of higher energy prices on the economy see Taghizadeh-Hesary et al. (2013, 2016); Taghizadeh-Hesary and Yoshino (2014); and Yoshino and Taghizadeh-Hesary (2014c, d).

arisen from the Basel capital requirements that made Japanese banks reluctant to lend money to startup businesses and SMEs, thus discouraging Japanese innovation and technological progress. Economic growth was further slowed by the high appreciation of the yen in the mid-1990s, which caused Japanese manufacturing companies to move from Japan to other Asian countries. Finally, wage increases also pushed Japanese companies abroad, resulting in diminished domestic production.

The remedies for stimulating economic growth in Japan are

(i) required reforms regarding the aging population,
(ii) reduction in the transfers from central to local governments,
(iii) diversification of households' asset allocation,
(iv) reform of the agriculture sector,
(v) switching the asset allocation pension funds and insurance companies from pay-as-you-go to 401(k)-style,
(vi) a review of asset management fees,
(vii) use of HIT funds to finance riskier businesses,
(viii) optimal mix of public and private funds,
(ix) a review of monetary policy goals, and
(x) diversification of Japan's energy basket.

The experience of Japan after the "Lost Decade" should be a lesson for other countries, including the PRC, the countries of the eurozone, and the US, to prevent them falling into long-term recession and to encourage their economic growth.

References

Alvstam CG, Ström P, Yoshino N (2009) On the economic interdependence between China and Japan: challenges and possibilities. Asia Pac Viewpoint 50(2):198–214

Bank of Japan (2014a) Basic figures of the flow of funds—third quarter of 2014. 24 December. Research and Statistics Department, Tokyo

Bank of Japan (2014b) Flow of funds—overview of Japan, US, and the euro area. 24 December. Research and Statistics Department, Tokyo

Bank of Japan Foreign exchange rates. Time series database. https://www.stat-search.boj.or.jp/index_en.html. Accessed 24 Feb 2017

British Petroleum (2014) BP statistical review of world energy 2014, London

Galí J (1992) How well does the IS-LM model fit postwar U.S. data? Q J Econ 107(2):709–738

Government of Japan, Ministry of Agriculture, Forestry and Fisheries (2010) 2010 census of agriculture and forestry, Tokyo

Government of Japan, Ministry of Agriculture, Forestry and Fisheries (2012) FY2011 annual report on food, agriculture and rural areas in Japan, Tokyo

Government of Japan, Ministry of Finance (2015) Highlights of the draft budget for FY2015, Tokyo

Government of Japan, Ministry of Internal Affairs and Communications (2012) Basic survey on employment structure, Tokyo

Government of the United States, Energy Information Administration (2015) Analysis: Japan. 30 January. Washington, DC

Hall RE, Taylor JB (1988) Macroeconomics: theory, performance, and policy, 2nd edn. Norton & Co, New York

Horioka CY (2006) The causes of Japan's "lost decade": the role of household consumption, NBER working paper no 12142. National Bureau of Economic Research, Cambridge, MA

Krugman P (1998a) Japan's trap. Blog post. http://web.mit.edu/krugman/www/japtrap.html. Accessed 24 Feb 2017

Krugman P (1998b) It's Baaack! Japan's slump and the return of the liquidity trap. Brook Pap Econ Act 2:137–187

NEEDS (2014) The Nikkei Economic Electronic Databank System (NEEDS). http://www.nikkeieu.com/needs

Organisation for Economic Co-operation and Development (OECD) (2013) Economic survey of Japan. April. Paris

Revankar N, Yoshino N (2008) An empirical analysis of Japanese banking behavior in a period of financial instability. Keio Econ Stud 45:1–15

Taghizadeh-Hesary F, Yoshino N (2014) Monetary policies and oil price determination: an empirical analysis. OPEC Energy Rev 38(1):1–20

Taghizadeh-Hesary F, Yoshino N, Abdoli G, Farzinvash A (2013) An estimation of the impact of oil shocks on crude oil exporting economies and their trade partners. Front Econ China 8(4):571–591

Taghizadeh-Hesary F, Yoshino N, Abadi MMH, Farboudmanesh R (2016) The response of macro variables of emerging and developed oil importers to oil price movements. J Asia Pac Econ 21(1):91–102

Yoshino N (2010) Financing transport infrastructure development. In: OECD (ed) Southeast Asian economic outlook 2010. OECD Publishing, Paris

Yoshino N (2012) Global imbalance and the development of capital flows among Asian countries. OECD J Financ Mark Trends 1:81–112

Yoshino N (2013) The background of hometown investment trust funds. In: Yoshino N, Kaji S (eds) Hometown investment trust funds: a stable way to supply risk capital. Springer, Tokyo

Yoshino N, Hirano T (2011) Pro-cyclicality of the Basel capital requirement ratio and its impact on banks. Asian Economic Papers 10(2):22–36

Yoshino N, Mizoguchi T (2013) Change in the flow of funds and the fiscal rules needed for fiscal stabilization. Public Pol Rev 9(1):51–69

Yoshino N, Nakahigashi M (2000) Economic effects of infrastructure—Japan's experience after world war II. Jpn Bank Int Coop Rev 3:3–19

Yoshino N, Sakakibara E (2002) The current state of the Japanese economy and remedies. Asian Econ Pap 1:110–126

Yoshino N, Taghizadeh-Hesary F (2014a) An analysis of challenges faced by Japan's economy and Abenomics. Jpn Polit Econ 40(3–4):37–62

Yoshino N, Taghizadeh-Hesary F (2014b) Three arrows of "Abenomics" and the structural reform of Japan: inflation targeting policy of the central bank, fiscal consolidation, and growth strategy, ADBI working paper no 492. Asian Development Bank Institute, Tokyo

Yoshino N, Taghizadeh-Hesary F (2014c) Economic impacts of oil price fluctuations in developed and emerging economies. Inst Energy Econ Jpn 9:58–75

Yoshino N, Taghizadeh-Hesary F (2014d) Monetary policy and oil price fluctuations following the subprime mortgage crisis. Int J Monet Econ Financ 7(3):157–174

Yoshino N, Taghizadeh-Hesary F (2014e) Analytical framework on credit risks for financing SMEs in Asia. Asia Pac Dev J 21(2):1–21

Yoshino N, Taghizadeh-Hesary F (2015) Effectiveness of the easing of monetary policy in the Japanese economy, incorporating energy prices. J Comp Asian Dev 14(2):227–248

Yoshino N, Taghizadeh-Hesary (2016) Causes and remedies of the Japan's long-lasting recession: lessons for China. Chin World Econ 24(2):23–47

Yoshino N, Taghizadeh-Hesary F, Nili F (2013) Optimal premiums for the deposit insurance system: an empirical work on the deposit insurance system of Japan, Keio economic society discussion paper 13–1. Keio University, Tokyo

Chapter 2
Changes in Economic Effect of Infrastructure and Financing Methods: The Japanese Case

Masaki Nakahigashi and Naoyuki Yoshino

Abstract This chapter analyzes the economic effect of infrastructure, focusing on the productivity effect of public investment, and discusses how to promote the private sector investment in infrastructure by enhancing the rate of return to investors by utilizing part of spillover effects from the infrastructure. Traditional highway or railway investment relies on toll fees or train fees, which are often regulated to keep the price low. Private investors find it difficult to obtain an adequate rate of return. This chapter proposes the incremental tax revenues along the highway or railway should contribute a certain fraction of tax revenues (say 30%) to investors in infrastructure.

The important factors for further promoting the use of private sector resources in infrastructure development include (i) government involvement in high-risk infrastructure projects and risk sharing between government and the private sector, (ii) an earnings structure that appropriately reflects the spillover effect of infrastructure (e.g., return of some spillover tax revenues to infrastructure investors), and (iii) systems designed to increase incentives for infrastructure-operating entities.

Keywords Infrastructure • Productivity effect of public capital • Public-private partnership • Spillover effects

JEL Classification G23, G28, H54

M. Nakahigashi (✉)
Niigata University, Niigata, Japan
e-mail: m-nakahigashi@econ.niigata-u.ac.jp

N. Yoshino
Asian Development Bank Institute (ADBI), Tokyo, Japan

Keio University, Tokyo, Japan

N. Yoshino, F. Taghizadeh-Hesary (eds.), *Japan's Lost Decade*, ADB Institute Series on Development Economics, DOI 10.1007/978-981-10-5021-3_2

2.1 Introduction

Japan's cumulative public debt is higher than that of the Greek government's largely due to the expansion of social security expenditure for an aging population (Yoshino and Taghizadeh-Hesary 2015, 2016). It has become difficult to increase government spending, including for public investment. In addition, after the ceiling collapse accident in Sasago Tunnel in December 2012, measures for containing the aging and maintaining the quality of infrastructure have become a challenge. Infrastructure provides essential services for our daily lives, so we have to construct good infrastructure and maintain it, in order to keep constant services.

This chapter analyzes two aspects of infrastructure investment. Firstly, we reveal through an analysis using the trans-log production function whether the productivity effect of public investment has changed in recent years. Secondly, we propose measures to promote infrastructure investment, made necessary by infrastructure aging, by the private sector rather than by the government, and describe measures to maintain infrastructure while reducing expenditure from public funds and to promote the economic effect of infrastructure.

2.2 Changes to and Evaluation of Productivity Effect of Public Capital in Recent Years

In this section, we clarify whether the productivity effect of public capital has remained stable in recent years. Specifically, we assess contributions to productivity through infrastructure development.

In Japan, much research on the productivity effect of public capital was carried out, especially around the year 2000. More recently there has been a middling amount. Annala et al. (2008), Miyara and Fukushige (2008), and Okubo (2008) base their analyses on data from before the late 1990s. Hayashi (2009) and Miyagawa et al. (2013) carry out their analyses using recent prefectural macro data, as compared with previous research, and indicate that output elasticity of public capital has increased in recent years.[1]

We estimate the productivity effect of public capital by industry and region based on the production function, as is adopted in Yoshino et al. (1999), using the 36 years of data from 1975 to 2010. We also clarify whether the output elasticity of public capital has increased in recent years.

---

[1]See Yoshino et al. (1999), Nakahigashi (2003), and Yoshino and Nakahigashi (2004) for research on the productivity effect of public capital around 2000. See Nakahigashi (2015) for research on the productivity effect of public capital using Japanese macroeconomic data.

Estimation Model of the Economic Effect of Public Capital

In our analyses, output is the total of real private value-added. Input factors of production consist of (i) private capital, (ii) labor, and (iii) public capital. We use a trans-log production function, which is a log-linear approximation around the average of each variable.

$$\begin{aligned}\ln Y_t - \ln \overline{Y} = {} & \alpha_K \left(\ln K_{Pt} - \ln \overline{K_P}\right) + \alpha_L \left(\ln L_t - \ln \overline{L}\right) + \alpha_G \left(\ln K_{Gt} - \ln \overline{K_G}\right) \\ & + \beta_{KL} \left(\ln K_{Pt} - \ln \overline{K_P}\right)\left(\ln L_t - \ln \overline{L}\right) \\ & + \beta_{KG} \left(\ln K_{Pt} - \ln \overline{K_P}\right)\left(\ln K_{Gt} - \ln \overline{K_G}\right) \\ & + \beta_{LG} \left(\ln L_t - \ln \overline{L}\right)\left(\ln K_{Gt} - \ln \overline{K_G}\right) + \frac{1}{2}\beta_{KK}\left(\ln K_{Pt} - \ln \overline{K_P}\right)^2 \\ & + \frac{1}{2}\beta_{LL}\left(\ln L_t - \ln \overline{L}\right)^2 + \frac{1}{2}\beta_{GG}\left(\ln K_{Gt} - \ln \overline{K_G}\right)^2\end{aligned}$$

where the symmetry of second derivatives is assumed. Furthermore, it is assumed that $\beta_{KK} < 0$, $\beta_{LL} < 0$, and $\beta_{GG} < 0$ based on the law of diminishing marginal productivity.

However, in a trans-log production function, there are many cross terms of factor variables and it is likely that multicollinearity will occur. Therefore, we introduce the following two assumptions: (i) the production function is the constant returns to scale across labor and private capital, i.e., the homogeneity of degree one in labor and private capital, and (ii) the factor payment for each factor input follows the marginal productivity theory. Moreover, the factor payment is equal to marginal productivity of each input. When meeting these assumptions, income is fully distributed to labor and private capital, and the income share of private capital is equal to the output elasticity of private capital and the income share of labor is equal to the output elasticity of labor. Therefore, in order to satisfy these assumptions, we impose the following parameter constraints:

$$\begin{cases} \alpha_K + \alpha_L = 1 \\ \beta_{KK} + \beta_{KL} = 0 \\ \beta_{KL} + \beta_{LL} = 0 \\ \beta_{KG} + \beta_{LG} = 0 \end{cases} \tag{2.1}$$

where these restrictions are a sufficient condition for this assumption. Our estimated equation system is as follows:

$$
\begin{aligned}
&\left(\ln Y_t - \ln \overline{Y}\right) - \left(\ln L_t - \ln \overline{L}\right) \\
&\quad = \alpha_K \left[\left(\ln K_{Pt} - \ln \overline{K_P}\right) - \left(\ln L_t - \ln \overline{L}\right)\right] \\
&\quad + \alpha_G \left(\ln K_{Gt} - \ln \overline{K_G}\right) + \beta_{KL} \left[\left(\ln K_{Pt} - \ln \overline{K_P}\right)\left(\ln L_t - \ln \overline{L}\right) \right. \\
&\quad \left. - \frac{1}{2}\left(\ln K_{Pt} - \ln \overline{K_P}\right)^2 - \frac{1}{2}\left(\ln L_t - \ln \overline{L}\right)^2 \right] \\
&\quad + \beta_{KG}\left(\ln K_{Gt} - \ln \overline{K_G}\right)\left[\left(\ln K_{Pt} - \ln \overline{K_P}\right) - \left(\ln L_t - \ln \overline{L}\right)\right] \\
&\quad + \frac{1}{2}\beta_{GG}\left(\ln K_{Gt} - \ln \overline{K_G}\right)^2 + \epsilon_{P,t}
\end{aligned}
\tag{2.2}
$$

$$
\begin{aligned}
S_{L,t} = 1 - \alpha_K + \beta_{KL}\left[\left(\ln K_{P,t} - \ln \bar{K_P}\right)\left(\ln L_t - \ln \bar{L}\right)\right] \\
+ \beta_{KG}\left(\ln K_{G,t} - \ln \bar{K_G}\right) + \epsilon_{S,t}
\end{aligned}
\tag{2.3}
$$

where $S_{L,t}$ represents the labor share in period t, and $\epsilon_{P,t}$ and $\epsilon_{S,t}$ are the error terms of the labor share function and production function, respectively. In addition, under producers' profit maximization, the following sign conditions are necessary: $\alpha_K \geq 0$, $\alpha_G \geq 0$, $\beta_{KL} > 0$, and $\beta_{GG} < 0$.

Methods for Measuring the Productivity Effect of Public Capital

The productivity effect of public capital, in general, is represented by the output elasticity or marginal productivity by marginal increase in factor input. In this chapter, the productivity effect of public capital is the increase in output by marginal increase in factor input, including the effect of variation in factor productivity, which is same as Yoshino and Nakano (1994), Yoshino et al. (1999), and Nakahigashi (2003). Our marginal productivity of public capital from Eq. 2.2 is as follows[2]:

$$
\frac{dY}{dK_G} = \eta_{K_G}\frac{Y}{K_G} + \eta_{K_P}\frac{\eta_{K_G}\eta_{K_P} + \beta_{KG}}{\eta_{K_P}\left(1 - \eta_{K_P}\right) + \beta_{KL}}\frac{Y}{K_G} + \eta_L\frac{\eta_{K_G}\eta_L - \beta_{KG}}{\eta_L\left(1 - \eta_L\right) + \beta_{KL}}\frac{Y}{K_G}
\tag{2.4}
$$

[2]See Yoshino et al. (1999) for deriving Eq. 2.4.

where $\eta_{K_P}, \eta_L, \eta_{K_G}$ represent the output elasticity of private capital, labor, and public capital, respectively. Based on Eq. 2.2, the output elasticity of labor is the same as Eq. 2.3 and the output elasticity of private capital and public capital is expressed as follows:

$$\eta_{K_P} = \alpha_K + \beta_{KL}\left[\left(\ln L - \ln \overline{L}\right) - \left(\ln K_P - \ln \overline{K_P}\right)\right] + \beta_{KG}\left(\ln K_G - \ln \overline{K_G}\right) \quad (2.5)$$

$$\eta_{K_G} = \alpha_G + \beta_{KG}\left[\left(\ln K_P - \ln \overline{K_P}\right) - \left(\ln L - \ln \overline{L}\right)\right] + \beta_{GG}\left(\ln K_G - \ln \overline{K_G}\right) \quad (2.6)$$

The first term on the right-hand side of Eq. 2.4 is the marginal productivity of public capital (direct effect of public capital); the second term on the right-hand side of Eq. 2.4 indicates the indirect effect of private capital, which shows the level of output increase by varying the productivity of private capital through marginal increase of public capital; and the third term on the right-hand side of Eq. 2.4 is the indirect effect of labor, which represents the level of increase in output by varying labor productivity through a marginal increase in public capital.

The public capital stock used in this chapter is prefectural gross public capital stock, which is estimated by the Cabinet Office Director General for Economic, Fiscal and Social Structure (2012). Our public capital stock consists of roads, ports, airport facilities, sewerage, waste disposal, water supply, urban parks, school facilities, social education facilities, flood control, forest conservation, coastal, agriculture, forestry, fishing, national forests, and industrial water supply.

The private capital stock in our analysis is based on trial estimates by the Cabinet Office, Economic and Social Research Institute (2011). In the trial estimates, however, there are several sharp increases because the number of private companies increases whenever public enterprises are privatized. Hence, we assume that the growth rate of private capital stock remains unchanged regardless of whether privatized public enterprises exist, and the private capital stock is estimated retrospectively using the growth rate from the private capital stock at the end of FY2010.

Output by industry and region is real gross regional product (GRP), calculated by dividing the nominal GRP by the GRP deflator. The nominal GRP is the GRP at producers' prices excluding taxes on production and imports less subsidies. After FY2001, the GRP deflator by economic activity is directly used by Annual Report on Prefectural Accounts. Before FY2000, the deflator regarded as the same in all prefectures for each industry, and then we use a GDP deflator by economic activity of Annual Report on National Accounts as the deflator. Note that all the data are estimated retrospectively using the growth rate from the value of FY2010. This is because there is a possibility that the definition of System of National Account of Japan changes for each reference year.

Labor input is the product of working hours and the number of workers. The number of employed persons and the number of workers by prefecture are estimated using the Ministry of Internal Affairs and Communications' population census, which is published every 5 years as a benchmark; in the estimation of interpolate years, the ministry's labor force survey and population census are used[3]. When estimating working hours, it is assumed that there are no regional differences for workers in the same industry. Working hours of the agriculture, forestry, and fisheries industries are estimated using the labor force survey. Working hours of other industries are estimated using the Ministry of Health, Labour and Welfare's monthly labor statistics survey.

The labor income of workers is estimated using the number of workers and workers' wage per capita. In agriculture, forestry, and fisheries, it is assumed that although there are regional differences between the employees' income and other workers' income, the ratio of these is the same among regions, and then labor income is estimated using this ratio. In other industries, on the other hand, it is assumed that labor income per capita of employees and workers is the same, and labor income is estimated by multiplying the number of workers by the ratio of the number of employees to the compensation of employees. Note that all the data are estimated retrospectively using the growth rate from the value of FY2010.

Industrial and Regional Classification

Our industrial classification is reconstructed based on "economic activity" in the System of National Accounts of Japan and we classify industries into primary, secondary, and tertiary. Our "Electricity, Gas and Water Supply" industry includes "Electricity, Gas and Water Supply" of "Producers of Government Services," and our "Service" industry includes "Service Activities" of "Producers of Government Services" and "Producers of Private Non-profit Services to Households."

In our production function, it is assumed that all parameters can take a different value depending on region. This assumption considers influences of the regional allocation policy for public investment, which reflects the unequal relationship between potential supply level of the infrastructure services and actual utilization of infrastructure services among regions, and our rough industrial classification.

In addition, to internalize regional spillover effects of the productivity effect of public capital, we reaggregated 46 prefectures, excluding Okinawa, into 11 regions. Table 2.1 shows the regional segmentation in our analysis.

Specification Method of the Estimation Model

In addition to the above description, we describe four points for our estimation. Firstly, variables representing the effect of the private sector's technological progress are not included explicitly in Eq. 2.2 and Eq. 2.3. That is because we acknowledge that the technical progress of the private sector has been embedded

[3]The number of workers and number of employees do not consider the number of workers with a sideline, unlike estimates of the System of National Account of Japan.

Table 2.1 Regional segmentation in our analysis

Region	Prefecture
Hokkaido	Hokkaido
Tohoku	Aomori, Akita, Iwate, Miyagi, Yamagata, Fukushima
Northern Kanto	Ibaraki, Tochigi, Gunma, Nagano
Southern Kanto	Saitama, Chiba, Tokyo, Kanagawa, Yamanashi
Hokuriku	Niigata, Toyama, Ishikawa, Fukui
Tokai	Shizuoka, Gifu, Aichi, Mie
Kinki	Shiga, Kyoto, Osaka, Hyogo, Nara, Wakayama
Chugoku	Tottori, Shimane, Okayama, Hiroshima, Yamaguchi
Shikoku	Kagawa, Tokushima, Ehime, Kochi
Northern Kyushu	Fukuoka, Saga, Nagasaki, Oita
Southern Kyushu	Kumamoto, Miyazaki, Kagoshima

in factor inputs such as capital and labor input. Secondly, it is assumed that the error term of the production function ($u_{P,it}$) consists of a usual error term ($\epsilon_{P,it}$) and the region-specific constant value (μ_i), which represents the effect on output by elements other than factor inputs:

$$u_{P,it} = \mu_i + \epsilon_{Pit} \quad \text{for all } i\ t \tag{2.7}$$

Thirdly, the error vector $\epsilon_t = (\epsilon_{Pt}\ \ u_{St})'$ meets $E(\epsilon_t) = 0, E\left(\epsilon_t\, \epsilon_t'\right) = \Omega$ in all t. Since Eq. 2.3 is derived from the production function of Eq. 2.2, the estimation model is a simultaneous equation system and there is the possibility that ϵ_{Pt} and u_{St}, which is the error term of labor share function, are correlated.

Finally, seemingly unrelated regression (SUR) is used in estimating our simultaneous model. We can see that explanatory variables of the labor share function appear in explanatory variables in the production function. As indicated by Revankar (1974), SUR estimates of the labor share function in our system are the same as least square estimates of the labor share function, and are the best linear unbiased estimator of the labor share function. Therefore, in specifying the estimation model we give the following two steps: first, the labor share function, Eq. 2.3, is specified by ordinary least squares estimation while considering the sign condition of parameters. Secondly, we determine the parameters of production function to be estimated based on the specification of labor share function in the first step and then specify the whole estimation model.

2.3 Results of the Productivity Effect of Public Capital

Based on the specifications of the estimation model in section 2.2 we show the estimated results using the panel data of 11 regions from FY1975 to FY2010 and estimate the productivity effect of public capital. Note that the estimation model, consisting of Eq. 2.2 and Eq. 2.3, is represented by a log-linear approximation around the average, which is the average from FY1975 to FY1994.

Results for the Production Function

Tables 2.2, 2.3, and 2.4 show the estimated results of primary, secondary, and tertiary industries, respectively. Estimates shown in the first block of each table are parameter estimates that takes same value in all regions, and coefficient dummy

Table 2.2 Estimation result for production function in primary industry

Parameter	Estimate	(Std. err.)	Coefficient dummy β_{KL}		
α_K	0.440**	(0.006)	Hokkaido	–	
α_L	–		Tohoku	–	
β_{KL}	–		Northern Kanto	–	
β_{KG}	–		Southern Kanto	–	
β_{GG}	–		Hokuriku	–	
Coefficient dummy α_K			Tokai	–	
Hokkaido	0.175**	(0.011)	Kinki	–	
Tohoku	−0.083**	(0.012)	Chugoku	–	
Northern Kanto	−0.082**	(0.012)	Shikoku	–	
Southern Kanto	–		Northern Kyushu	–	
Hokuriku	0.050**	(0.012)	Southern Kyushu	–	
Tokai	−0.041**	(0.012)	Coefficient dummy β_{KG}		
Kinki	0.040**	(0.011)	Hokkaido	–	
Chugoku	−0.135**	(0.012)	Tohoku	0.046**	(0.014)
Shikoku	−0.148**	(0.011)	Northern Kanto	0.100**	(0.013)
Northern Kyushu	–		Southern Kanto	0.076**	(0.014)
Southern Kyushu	–		Hokuriku	0.057**	(0.014)
Coefficient dummy α_G			Tokai	–	
Hokkaido	−0.131**	(0.021)	Kinki	–	
Tohoku	−0.049*	(0.022)	Chugoku	−0.001	(0.028)
Northern Kanto	−0.064**	(0.021)	Shikoku	–	
Southern Kanto	−0.057**	(0.021)	Northern Kyushu	0.063**	(0.026)
Hokuriku	−0.125**	(0.023)	Southern Kyushu	–	
Tokai	−0.009	(0.024)	Coefficient of determinant		
Kinki	−0.189**	(0.024)	Production function		0.928
Chugoku	−0.005	(0.021)	Labor share function		0.748
Shikoku	0.151**	(0.021)			
Northern Kyushu	−0.172**	(0.020)			
Southern Kyushu	0.077**	(0.020)			

Notes: ** and * denote statistical significance at 1% and 5% level, respectively; in addition to variables shown in this table, the estimation model includes the regional fixed effect, but the estimated result of this effect has been omitted

Table 2.3 Estimation result for production function in secondary industry

Parameter	Estimate	(Std. err.)	Coefficient dummy β_{KL}		
α_K	0.251**	(0.004)	Hokkaido	–	
α_L	–		Tohoku	–	
β_{KL}	–		Northern Kanto	–	
β_{KG}	–		Southern Kanto	0.091**	(0.013)
β_{GG}	–		Hokuriku	–	
Coefficient dummy α_K			Tokai	–	
Hokkaido	0.026**	(0.008)	Kinki	0.121**	(0.037)
Tohoku	–		Chugoku	–	
Northern Kanto	0.080**	(0.007)	Shikoku	–	
Southern Kanto	−0.021**	(0.008)	Northern Kyushu	–	
Hokuriku	0.070**	(0.008)	Southern Kyushu	–	
Tokai	0.050**	(0.008)	Coefficient dummy β_{KG}		
Kinki	–		Hokkaido	0.019*	(0.009)
Chugoku	−0.017*	(0.008)	Tohoku	0.041**	(0.008)
Shikoku	0.077**	(0.007)	Northern Kanto	–	
Northern Kyushu	–		Southern Kanto	–	
Southern Kyushu	−0.041**	(0.008)	Hokuriku	−0.035**	(0.009)
Coefficient dummy α_G			Tokai	–	
Hokkaido	0.134**	(0.015)	Kinki	0.077*	(0.031)
Tohoku	0.107**	(0.013)	Chugoku	0.069**	(0.009)
Northern Kanto	0.235**	(0.012)	Shikoku	–	
Southern Kanto	0.236**	(0.015)	Northern Kyushu	0.056**	(0.008)
Hokuriku	0.182**	(0.015)	Southern Kyushu	0.076**	(0.009)
Tokai	0.274**	(0.016)	Coefficient of determinant		
Kinki	0.243**	(0.014)	Production function		0.971
Chugoku	0.296**	(0.014)	Labor share function		0.672
Shikoku	0.187**	(0.012)			
Northern Kyushu	0.196**	(0.013)			
Southern Kyushu	0.188**	(0.014)			

Notes: ** and * denote statistical significance at 1% and 5%, respectively; in addition to variables shown in this table, the estimation model includes the regional fixed effect and the discontinuity dummy, which is a constant dummy of each region after 2005 to take into account the discontinuity of data due to a change of industrial classification after 2005. These estimated results have been omitted

shown in subsequent blocks of the table show the difference from parameter estimates shown in the first block of the table. When an estimate shown in the first block of each table does not exist, the estimate of the coefficient dummy provides a region-specific parameter estimate.

The following describes parameters affected by public capital. Firstly, except for some regions of primary industry (agricultural sector), it can be indicated that α_G is significantly positive. At least in secondary industry (manufacturing) and tertiary industries (service sector), positive α_G appears and shows the increase in

Table 2.4 Estimation result for production function in tertiary industry

Parameter	Estimate	(Std. err.)	Coefficient dummy β_{KL}		
α_K	0.346**	(0.002)	Hokkaido	–	
α_L	–		Tohoku	–	
β_{KL}	–		Northern Kanto	–	
β_{KG}	0.104**	(0.002)	Southern Kanto	–	
β_{GG}	–		Hokuriku	–	
Coefficient dummy α_K			Tokai	–	
Hokkaido	−0.030**	(0.004)	Kinki	–	
Tohoku	−0.012**	(0.004)	Chugoku	–	
Northern Kanto	−0.027**	(0.004)	Shikoku	–	
Southern Kanto	–		Northern Kyushu	–	
Hokuriku	–		Southern Kyushu	–	
Tokai	−0.073**	(0.004)	Coefficient dummy β_{KG}		
Kinki	−0.025**	(0.004)	Hokkaido	−0.036**	(0.006)
Chugoku	–		Tohoku	–	
Shikoku	−0.047**	(0.004)	Northern Kanto	−0.019**	(0.006)
Northern Kyushu	−0.014**	(0.004)	Southern Kanto	–	
Southern Kyushu	−0.055**	(0.004)	Hokuriku	–	
Coefficient dummy α_G			Tokai	–	
Hokkaido	0.114**	(0.010)	Kinki	−0.038**	(0.006)
Tohoku	0.143**	(0.010)	Chugoku	−0.039**	(0.005)
Northern Kanto	0.176**	(0.009)	Shikoku	–	
Southern Kanto	0.225**	(0.010)	Northern Kyushu	−0.042**	(0.006)
Hokuriku	0.171**	(0.010)	Southern Kyushu	–	
Tokai	0.217**	(0.010)	Coefficient of determinant		
Kinki	0.131**	(0.011)	Production function		0.985
Chugoku	0.076**	(0.009)	Labor share function		0.904
Shikoku	0.133**	(0.010)			
Northern Kyushu	0.088**	(0.010)			
Southern Kyushu	0.096**	(0.010)			

Notes: ** denotes statistical significance at the 1% level; in addition to variables shown in this table, the estimation model includes the regional fixed effect and the discontinuity dummy, which is a constant dummy of each region after 2005 to take into account the discontinuity of data due to a change of industrial classification after 2005. However, in this table, estimated results of these have been omitted

productivity by increases in public capital. Secondly, when comparing parameter α_G among regions, it is found that the effect of public capital in Southern Kanto and Tokai regions is higher than that in other regions.

Furthermore, parameters β_{KG}, which indicate the direction of the impact of the increase in public capital on the factor share, are positive in almost all regions and industries. Thus, it can be said that public capital is a capital-using and labor-saving factor in the sense that capital share is raised by increasing the public capital.

Derivation of Point Estimates of the Productivity Effect of Public Capital

We derive point estimates of the productivity effect of public capital using the estimated results of the production function in Tables 2.2, 2.3 and 2.4, and compare point estimates from FY2010—which is the final year of our analysis—to those of FY1990, when the Japanese economy was in a favorable situation. Marginal productivity is used in deriving the point estimates of the productivity effect of public capital.

Table 2.5 denotes the productivity effect of public capital by industry and region in FY2010. When comparing the productivity effect of public capital between industries, the industry with the largest effect is tertiary industry and the industry with the smallest effect is primary industry. In primary industries, both the direct effect and the indirect effect are near zero. When looking at the indirect effect in detail, in secondary industry the indirect effect of labor is greater than that of private capital, while in tertiary industry the indirect effect of private capital is greater than that of labor. In secondary industry, under fixed factor prices, an increase in public capital will result in an increase in output via, mainly, an increase in labor productivity. In the tertiary industry, under fixed factor prices, an increase in public capital will result in an increase in output via an increase in labor productivity.

Next, we compare the productivity effect of public capital in FY2010 to that of FY1990. Table 2.5 shows the point estimate of the productivity effect of public capital in FY2010. Figures 2.1 and 2.2 show the point estimate of the productivity effect of public capital in secondary industry and tertiary industry, respectively. Both figures show that the FY2010 point estimate is lower than for FY1990. It can be seen that the effect of increasing productivity by marginal increase of public capital is smaller than in the past. Furthermore, the decrease in its effect from FY1990 to FY2010 in secondary industry is more remarkable than that in tertiary industry.

Interval Estimation of Productivity Effect of Public Capital

If the estimates of parameters to be used in deriving the productivity effect of public capital are the realization of the random variables, it is possible to derive an interval estimation of the productivity effect of public capital. Then we compare the level of the productivity effect of public capital from a statistical point of view through interval estimation for FY2010 and FY1990.

The productivity effect of public capital can be calculated from Eq. 2.4. If all factor inputs in our model are defined as non-random variables, the only estimated parameters are random variables. Then we can readily derive the direct effect of public capital because the direct effect can be represented by a linear combination of random variables. The indirect effect, on the other hand, cannot be derived

Table 2.5 Point estimates of productivity effect of public capital, FY2010

		Public capital			
				Indirect effect	
	Private capital	Direct effect		Capital	Labor
1. Primary industry					
Hokkaido	0.057	−0.005	−0.002	−0.002	−0.001
Tohoku	0.025	0.000	0.000	0.001	−0.001
Northern Kanto	0.026	0.003	0.001	0.003	−0.002
Southern Kanto	0.030	0.001	0.000	0.001	0.000
Hokuriku	0.022	−0.001	0.000	0.001	−0.001
Tokai	0.017	0.001	0.000	0.001	0.000
Kinki	0.017	−0.002	−0.001	−0.001	−0.001
Chugoku	0.010	0.000	0.000	0.000	0.000
Shikoku	0.014	0.006	0.002	0.001	0.004
Northern Kyushu	0.027	−0.002	−0.001	0.000	−0.002
Southern Kyushu	0.033	0.004	0.001	0.001	0.002
2. Secondary industry					
Hokkaido	0.083	0.028	0.008	0.005	0.016
Tohoku	0.109	0.052	0.017	0.017	0.017
Northern Kanto	0.068	0.297	0.064	0.019	0.215
Southern Kanto	0.055	0.227	0.054	0.006	0.166
Hokuriku	0.078	0.080	0.018	0.001	0.060
Tokai	0.092	0.341	0.089	0.056	0.196
Kinki	0.057	0.196	0.066	0.020	0.109
Chugoku	0.072	0.198	0.058	0.040	0.099
Shikoku	0.089	0.073	0.021	0.010	0.042
Northern Kyushu	0.091	0.119	0.036	0.027	0.056
Southern Kyushu	0.094	0.089	0.027	0.021	0.042
3. Tertiary industry					
Hokkaido	0.197	0.122	0.043	0.053	0.027
Tohoku	0.222	0.189	0.066	0.107	0.015
Northern Kanto	0.235	0.273	0.095	0.124	0.054
Southern Kanto	0.254	0.882	0.304	0.434	0.145
Hokuriku	0.220	0.217	0.075	0.117	0.024
Tokai	0.203	0.429	0.148	0.175	0.105
Kinki	0.202	0.316	0.110	0.131	0.075
Chugoku	0.212	0.121	0.044	0.068	0.010
Shikoku	0.223	0.193	0.068	0.098	0.026
Northern Kyushu	0.213	0.178	0.063	0.087	0.028
Southern Kyushu	0.228	0.156	0.057	0.090	0.009

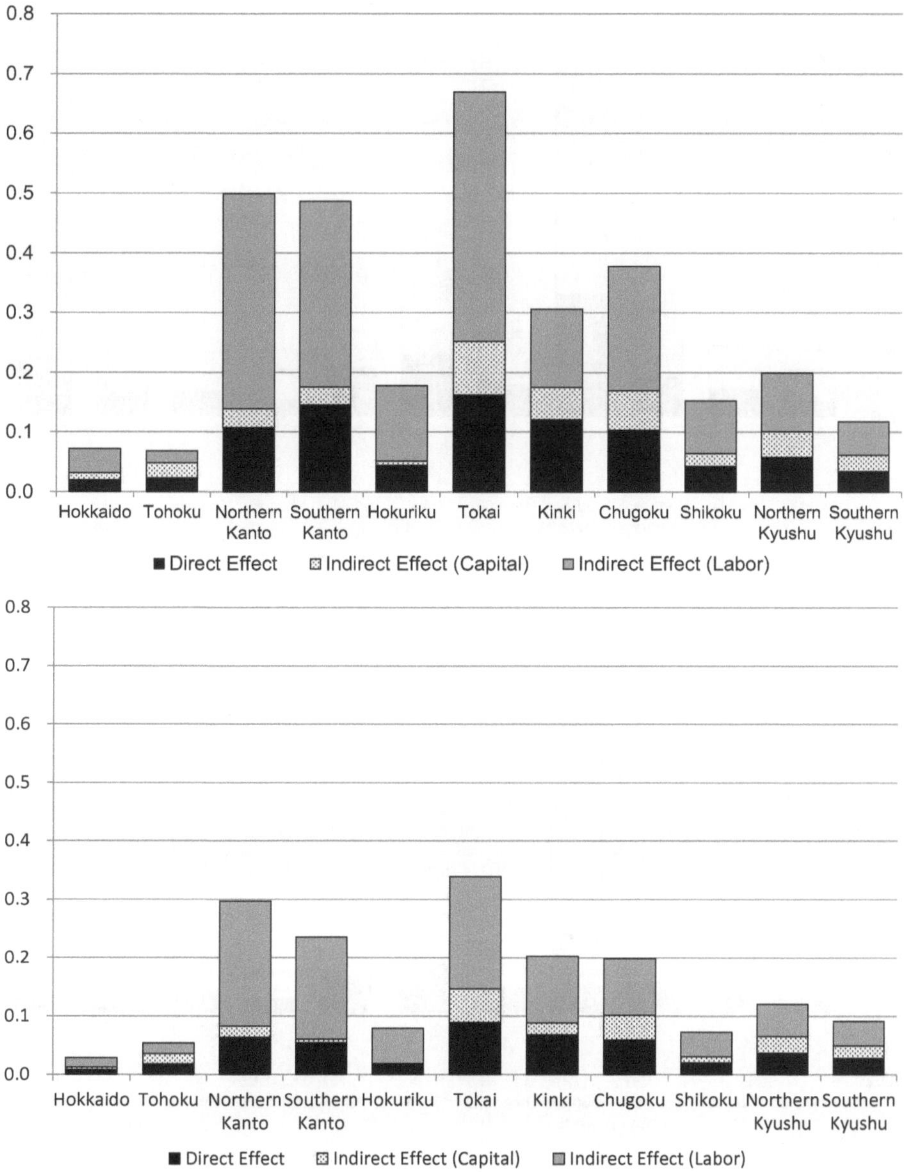

Fig. 2.1 Changes in productivity effect of public capital in secondary industry. *Black* direct effect; *dot* indirect effect (capital); *gray* indirect effect (labor)

easily because the indirect effect is the ratio of a random variable to a random variable. Therefore, in our paper, interval estimations are adopted only for the direct effect, i.e., the marginal productivity of public capital. Our interval estimation is the confidence interval at the 95% level under the assumption that error terms are normally distributed random variables.

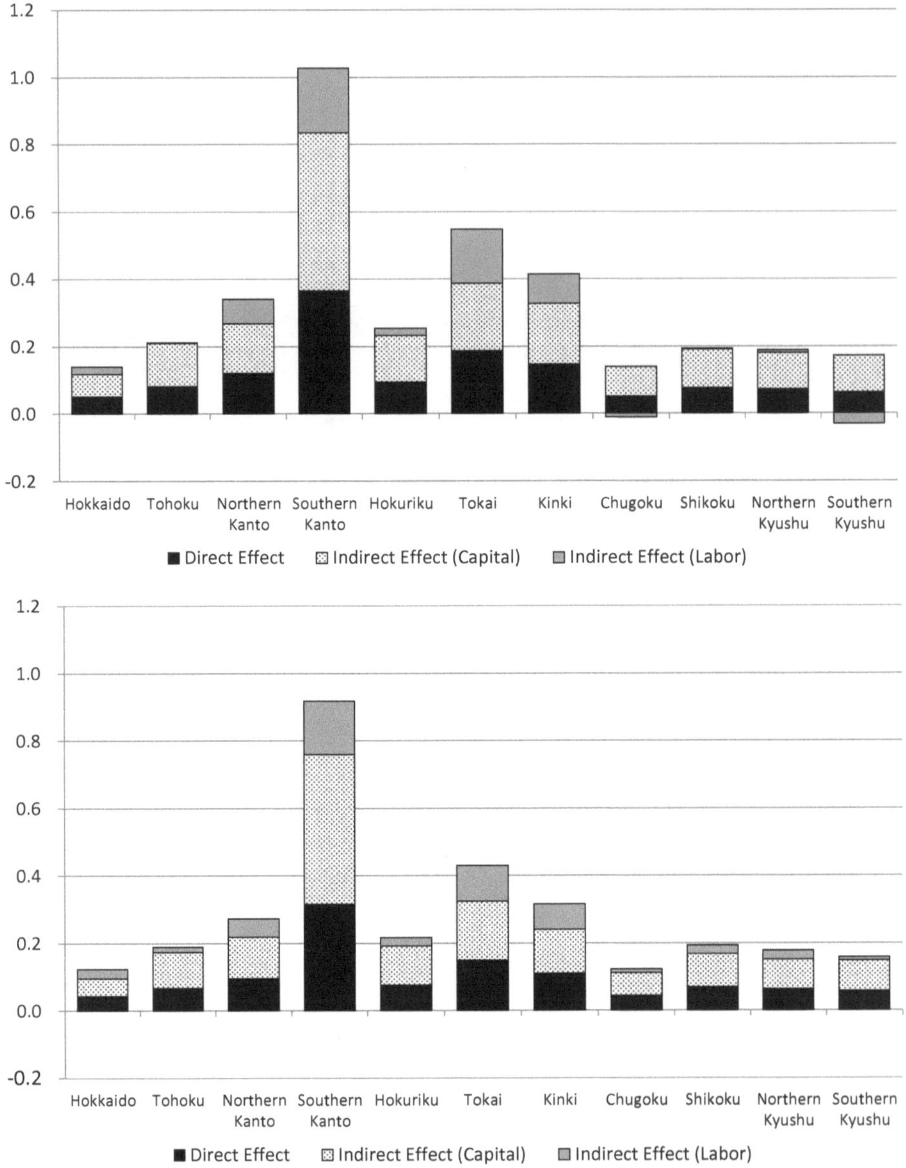

Fig. 2.2 Changes in productivity effect of public capital in tertiary industry. *Black* direct effect; *dot* indirect effect (capital); *gray* indirect effect (labor)

Tables 2.6 and 2.7 show the interval estimation of productivity effect of public capital in FY2010 and FY1990, respectively. It should be noted that the interval estimates of the productivity effect of public capital are calculated using all the estimated parameters regardless of the statistical significance and that we calculate the output elasticity as well as marginal productivity.

Table 2.6 95% confidence interval of productivity effect of public capital (FY2010)

	Output elasticity			Marginal productivity		
	Lower	Estimate	Upper	Lower	Estimate	Upper
1. Primary industry						
Hokkaido	−0.173	−0.131	−0.089	−0.002	−0.002	−0.001
Tohoku	−0.044	0.013	0.071	−0.001	0.000	0.001
Northern Kanto	0.021	0.077	0.132	0.000	0.001	0.002
Southern Kanto	−0.011	0.043	0.097	0.000	0.000	0.000
Hokuriku	−0.100	−0.037	0.025	−0.001	0.000	0.000
Tokai	−0.001	0.062	0.126	0.000	0.000	0.001
Kinki	−0.235	−0.189	−0.142	−0.001	−0.001	−0.001
Chugoku	−0.063	−0.006	0.050	0.000	0.000	0.000
Shikoku	0.109	0.151	0.192	0.001	0.002	0.002
Northern Kyushu	−0.138	−0.085	−0.033	−0.001	−0.001	0.000
Southern Kyushu	0.038	0.077	0.116	0.001	0.001	0.002
2. Secondary industry						
Hokkaido	0.120	0.154	0.188	0.006	0.008	0.010
Tohoku	0.127	0.161	0.194	0.014	0.018	0.022
Northern Kanto	0.212	0.235	0.257	0.058	0.064	0.070
Southern Kanto	0.206	0.236	0.265	0.048	0.054	0.061
Hokuriku	0.104	0.140	0.177	0.013	0.018	0.022
Tokai	0.200	0.280	0.360	0.064	0.089	0.115
Kinki	0.255	0.329	0.403	0.053	0.068	0.083
Chugoku	0.337	0.370	0.402	0.054	0.059	0.064
Shikoku	0.163	0.187	0.210	0.018	0.021	0.023
Northern Kyushu	0.223	0.253	0.284	0.032	0.037	0.041
Southern Kyushu	0.252	0.288	0.323	0.024	0.028	0.031
3. Tertiary industry						
Hokkaido	0.159	0.182	0.206	0.037	0.043	0.048
Tohoku	0.211	0.230	0.250	0.061	0.066	0.072
Northern Kanto	0.223	0.243	0.264	0.087	0.095	0.103
Southern Kanto	0.303	0.322	0.342	0.296	0.315	0.334
Hokuriku	0.243	0.263	0.282	0.069	0.075	0.081
Tokai	0.284	0.304	0.325	0.139	0.149	0.159
Kinki	0.168	0.192	0.216	0.096	0.110	0.123
Chugoku	0.114	0.134	0.155	0.037	0.044	0.050
Shikoku	0.222	0.242	0.261	0.063	0.069	0.074
Northern Kyushu	0.125	0.148	0.171	0.053	0.063	0.073
Southern Kyushu	0.177	0.196	0.216	0.052	0.057	0.063

From these tables it is found that there are industrial differences statistically in the productivity effect of public capital. The productivity effect of primary industry is very low compared with that of other industries. In primary industry, it is found that public capital does not contribute very much to productivity. In the secondary and tertiary industries, on the other hand, the productivity effect of public capital

Table 2.7 95% confidence interval of productivity effect of public capital (FY1990)

	Output elasticity			Marginal productivity		
	Lower	Estimate	Upper	Lower	Estimate	Upper
1. Primary industry						
Hokkaido	−0.173	−0.131	−0.089	−0.005	−0.004	−0.003
Tohoku	−0.073	−0.027	0.018	−0.003	−0.001	0.001
Northern Kanto	−0.059	−0.015	0.028	−0.002	−0.001	0.001
Southern Kanto	−0.063	−0.020	0.024	−0.001	0.000	0.000
Hokuriku	−0.140	−0.092	−0.043	−0.003	−0.002	−0.001
Tokai	−0.032	0.018	0.067	−0.001	0.000	0.001
Kinki	−0.235	−0.189	−0.142	−0.002	−0.002	−0.001
Chugoku	−0.049	−0.005	0.039	−0.001	0.000	0.001
Shikoku	0.109	0.151	0.192	0.003	0.004	0.005
Northern Kyushu	−0.183	−0.141	−0.100	−0.005	−0.004	−0.003
Southern Kyushu	0.038	0.077	0.116	0.002	0.004	0.005
2. Secondary industry						
Hokkaido	0.109	0.138	0.167	0.016	0.020	0.024
Tohoku	0.089	0.115	0.141	0.018	0.023	0.028
Northern Kanto	0.212	0.235	0.257	0.097	0.107	0.117
Southern Kanto	0.206	0.236	0.265	0.127	0.145	0.164
Hokuriku	0.147	0.176	0.205	0.037	0.044	0.051
Tokai	0.241	0.275	0.308	0.143	0.163	0.182
Kinki	0.226	0.256	0.285	0.107	0.121	0.135
Chugoku	0.279	0.306	0.333	0.094	0.103	0.112
Shikoku	0.163	0.187	0.210	0.038	0.043	0.049
Northern Kyushu	0.177	0.203	0.229	0.051	0.058	0.065
Southern Kyushu	0.174	0.202	0.229	0.029	0.034	0.039
3. Tertiary industry						
Hokkaido	0.110	0.131	0.151	0.044	0.052	0.060
Tohoku	0.148	0.167	0.186	0.073	0.082	0.091
Northern Kanto	0.172	0.191	0.209	0.109	0.121	0.133
Southern Kanto	0.227	0.246	0.265	0.337	0.365	0.393
Hokuriku	0.175	0.194	0.213	0.085	0.094	0.103
Tokai	0.219	0.239	0.259	0.172	0.188	0.203
Kinki	0.123	0.144	0.165	0.126	0.148	0.169
Chugoku	0.074	0.092	0.110	0.041	0.052	0.062
Shikoku	0.140	0.159	0.178	0.068	0.077	0.086
Northern Kyushu	0.082	0.102	0.122	0.058	0.073	0.087
Southern Kyushu	0.106	0.125	0.144	0.054	0.063	0.073

was significantly positive in FY2010. Even in recent years the productivity effects of public capital have existed.

Secondly, we find that the productivity effect of public capital is different between FY1990 and FY2010. In secondary industry, although output elasticity of all regions except Chugoku and Southern Kyushu regions is unchanged, marginal productivity of the productivity effect decreases in all regions except Tohoku and Southern Kyushu. In tertiary industry, although the output elasticity of public capital increases significantly in all regions, the marginal productivity of public capital decreases or is unchanged.

Some research, e.g., Hayashi (2009) and Miyagawa et al. (2013), suggests that the output elasticity of public capital may increase in recent years. Our result is the same as the conclusion in previous researches only in tertiary industry. On the other hand, marginal productivity of public capital in FY2010 is smaller than that in FY1990 in almost all regions and industry.

Finally, it can be seen that there are regional differences statistically in the productivity effect of public capital. In secondary industry, the ranking of regions based on the marginal productivity of public capital was almost the same for FY2010 and FY1990. The region with the lowest marginal productivity is Hokkaido, and the second-lowest regions are Tohoku, Hokuriku, and Shikoku. The highest marginal productivity is found in the metropolitan regions of Southern Kanto, Tokai, and Kinki. Furthermore, in tertiary industry, marginal productivity of capital in different regions are almost the same for FY1990 and FY2010. The lowest region in terms of marginal productivity is Hokkaido, and the second-lowest regions are Tohoku, Hokuriku, Shikoku, Northern Kyushu, and Southern Kyushu. On the other hand, the highest region is Southern Kanto and the second highest is Tokai. From our analysis, since 2000, although economic efficiency has become a consideration in the regional allocation of public investment, it is found that the structure of regional differences in the productivity effect of public capital has not changed significantly between FY1990 and FY2010.

2.4 Infrastructure Financing Through Private Funds

In recent years, public–private partnerships, including the use of private funds, are being emphasized. Reasons to use private funds for infrastructure development are (i) pressure to shorten the construction period and complete the infrastructure as quickly as possible, (ii) a need to minimize construction costs, and (iii) the potential for profitability and/or reducing costs after completion of the project. However, the Cabinet Office Private Financial Initiative (PFI) Promotion Office (2015) shows that the accumulated number of PFI projects—which is a major measure of the utilization of private resources, from FY1999 when the PFI Law was enacted until FY2014—is 489 and the accumulated business scale is about ¥4.5 trillion, which is not large compared with the amount of all infrastructure projects.

In this section, we will discuss the methods and conditions necessary to promote expanded use of private funds in infrastructure development.

Public–Private Cooperation in High-Risk Projects

Infrastructure projects have a variety of risks, which include (i) regime change—for example, stoppages due to change in local governor before completing the infrastructure project; (ii) cost increase—for example, creating an additional interest burden through extensions in construction period and delays in land acquisition; (iii) revenue—for example, facing unexpected decreases in revenue due to inaccurate fee setting and decreased traffic; and (iv) additional burdens—for example, compensation for noise occurring after the completion of an infrastructure project.[4]

Private investors apply various ideas to avoid possible risks and earn benefits. Some investors, however, may force the transfer of risks onto the public sector. In Japan, infrastructure projects have been carried out by third-party entities established by various regional governments, and consequently there has been a financial deficit in the public sector. In these cases, it will be essential to determine sharing of business risk between public and private sectors in advance.

A viability fund coming from tax revenues created by the spillover effects of infrastructure such as highways and railways would be an especially appropriate measure to apply to infrastructure projects that are indispensable for the public, but that are high-risk and low-earning. For example, Fig. 2.3 shows a case in which a project is supplied with 30% extra return by the tax revenues stemming from spillover effects of the infrastructure. Through the injection of the fraction of tax

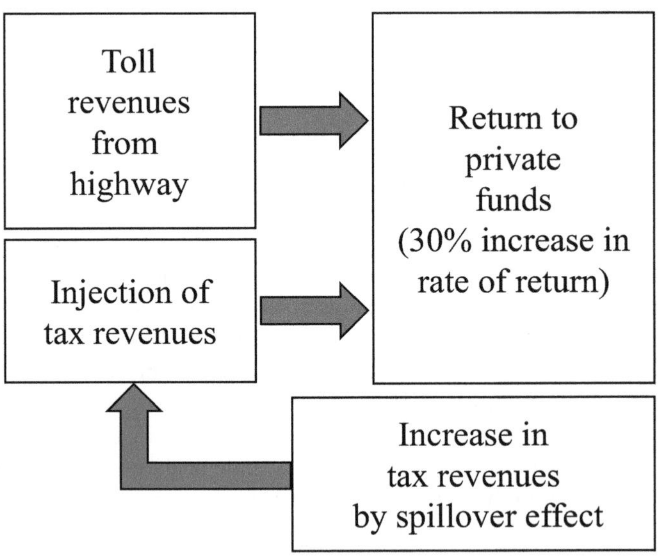

Fig. 2.3 Injection of the fraction of tax revenues gained from spillover effect

[4]See OECD (2008) concerning the classification of risk under public–private partnership projects.

revenues in the region, the rate of return in the private sector would increase. Even in projects that were not privately funded due to expectation of low revenue accrued from tolls, it is possible to introduce private funds using a viability fund. When toll revenue be too low, there is a possibility that the private sector would not put their money into the project at all.[5]

Increase in Rate of Return on Infrastructure Projects Through the Internalization of External Effects

Infrastructure projects have benefits other than revenue such as tolls. For example, a company that uses a highway could get more benefits than its usage cost from cost reduction and increase in sales through reducing the transit time of raw materials and products.

Yoshino and Pontines (2015) estimate the increase in tax revenues of regions along the Philippine highway STAR (Southern Tagalog Arterial Road). In particular, they evaluate the change rates of business tax revenue and property tax revenue due to the opening of the STAR highway. To compare the change rate of tax revenues in affected regions with that in unaffected regions they use the difference-in-differences technique, which is used in policy analysis.[6]

Estimated equation of the increase in tax revenues due to the STAR highway compared with unaffected regions is as follows. Time t is represented on the basis of the completion point of the highway. In addition, the tax revenue (logarithmic value) can be expressed by the following equations:

The tax revenue at the time t of the affected region A of the highway (T_{At}):

$$T_{At} = \alpha_A + X'_{At}\beta + \sum_t \delta_t + \epsilon_{At} \tag{2.8}$$

The tax revenue at the time t of the unaffected region N of the highway (T_{Nt}):

$$T_{Nt} = \alpha_N + X'_{Nt}\beta + \epsilon_{Nt} \tag{2.9}$$

where α is a constant term and X' is the vector of macroeconomic and microeconomic variables that affect the tax revenue, such as the number of employees and the amount of investment by private companies. δ_t in Eq. 2.8 represents the highway's effect on affected regions at the time t and ϵ is the error term. The estimated equation is as follows:

[5]Under this framework, a revenue bond is one of the measures for raising private funds. See Yoshino (2010) and Yoshino (2012) for more information about revenue bonds.

[6]Yoshino and Abidhadjaev (2015) estimate the impact on gross domestic product (GDP) from the development of Uzbekistan's railway network. They use the same estimation method as Yoshino and Pontines (2015).

Table 2.8 Increase in business tax in affected regions as compared with unaffected regions of Philippine STAR highway (million pesos)

	t_{-2}	t_{-1}	t_0	t_{+1}	t_{+2}	t_{+3}	After t_{+4}
Lipa city	134.36	173.50	249.70	184.47	191.81	257.35	371.93
Ibaan city	5.84	7.04	7.97	6.80	5.46	10.05	12.94
Batangas city	490.90	622.65	652.83	637.89	599.49	742.28	1208.61

$$T_{it} = c + \alpha D_g + X'_{it}\beta + \sum_t \delta_t D_g + \epsilon_{it} \tag{2.10}$$

where c is the constant term, and D_g is the dummy variable in which the regions affected by the highway are set as 1 and the other regions are set as 0. If δ_t is significantly positive, the tax revenue of affected areas would increase compared with that of unaffected areas.

Table 2.8 shows estimates of the increase in business tax of affected and unaffected regions before and after the completion of the STAR highway, using results for Eq. 2.10. t_0 represents the completion year of the STAR highway and its subscript shows the reference time relative to completion time (0) of the STAR highway. In other words, negative subscript represents the number of years before completion, and positive subscript represents the number of years elapsed after completion.

The results in Table 2.8 suggest that business tax in affected regions has increased in all periods compared with unaffected regions. After the highway's completion, business tax increased because of cost reductions and sales increases of companies along the highway due to the shortened transport time for materials and products. Before the highway's completion, the business tax increase was due to the increased sales of construction materials.

This increase in business tax and property tax can be said to be an external effect due to the highway. If it can be confirmed that the tax revenue increase is due to the external effects of the highway, it might be possible to return the increase in tax revenue to private investors and the public sector. This would increase the rate of return to private investors, making it easier to attract private funding for various infrastructure projects.

Incentive Mechanisms of Infrastructure-Operating Entities

To enhance efficiency of infrastructure projects and increase these rate of return, it is necessary that (i) the dividend for private investors is tied to the revenue from those infrastructure projects, and (ii) there exists an incentive for infrastructure-operating entities to generate higher income.

Table 2.9, as an example, shows the payoff table by the presence or absence of efforts by investors and an infrastructure-operating entity. If neither the entity nor the investors make efforts, the entity gains 50 in revenue and investors receive the

Table 2.9 Payoff table for infrastructure-operating entity and investors

	Normal case	Effort case
Normal case	$\begin{pmatrix} 50 & , & r \end{pmatrix}$ Operating entity Investors	$\begin{pmatrix} 50 & , & ar \end{pmatrix}$ Operating entity Investors
Effort case	$\begin{pmatrix} 100 & , & r \end{pmatrix}$ Operating entity Investors	$\begin{pmatrix} 100 & , & ar \end{pmatrix}$ Operating entity Investors

dividend income *r*. It is supposed that the entity can increase operating income by 100 through improvements in its salary system, such as by bonus payments to its staff based on the increase in revenue. Furthermore, investors make various efforts to maximize their dividends, such as reducing costs and boosting revenue through more highway turnoffs and traffic capacity, by increasing the dividend income to *ar* ($a > 1$). The lower right of the payoff table (Table 2.9) represents the revenue when both the entity and investors make various concerted efforts to increase its revenue and improve its service. The income obtained in this case is higher than in the normal case. (The income of the entity increases from 50 to 100 and the income of investors from *r* to *ar*).

In Table 2.9 we show the importance of shaping the institutional design of the dividend policy and salary system in an infrastructure-operating entity so that they lead to increased revenues for both the entity and investors.

In a public–private partnership, as described above, it is necessary to improve the efficiency of infrastructure projects through private sector participation and to introduce mechanisms to benefit the staff of an infrastructure-operating entity, for example, through paying staff bonuses tied to the increase in profit.

2.5 Conclusion

This chapter analyzes whether the productivity effect of public capital, which is one of the economic effects of public capital, has changed using a trans-log production function, and discusses how one might promote the use of private sector money for the maintenance of infrastructure and for enhancing the economic effect of infrastructure while reducing government spending.

In the secondary and tertiary industries, the productivity effect of public capital has been significantly positive throughout the estimated period and has been present in recent years. In the 2000s, although interregional allocation of public investment has changed over time, the structure of the regional differences in its productivity effect has not. When comparing the magnitude of its productivity effect in FY1990 to that of FY2010 in regard to the output elasticity of public capital, it can be seen that there are statistically different directions in some industries and regions, but marginal productivity has declined in almost all regions.

To promote investment of private funds in future infrastructure development, the following measures are required: (i) User charges alone do not give enough rate of return to infrastructure investors, and therefore the private sector does not want to invest in infrastructure; however, if the tax revenues created by spillover effects are partly returned to infrastructure investors, the rate of return will rise; and (ii) To increase incentives for infrastructure-operating entities, incentive mechanisms must be introduced for their staff; it means if the rate of return on infrastructure becomes larger, the salaries or bonuses of workers on these projects or of the operating companies should increase.

References

Annala CN, Batina RG, Feehan JP (2008) Empirical impact of public infrastructure on the Japanese economy. Jpn Econ Rev 59(4):419–437

Cabinet Office, Director General for Economic, Fiscal and Social Structure (2012) Public capital stock in Japan 2012. http://www5.cao.go.jp/keizai2/jmcs/jmcs.html

Cabinet Office, Economic and Social Research Institute (2011) Prefectural capital stock of private enterprises (at CY2000 price, SNA-based, May 2011). http://www.esri.cao.go.jp/jp/sna/data/data_list/kenmin/files/contents/main_h21stock.html

Cabinet Office, PFI Promotion Office (2015) On the current state of PFI (May 2015). http://www8.cao.go.jp/pfi/pfi_gaiyou.html (in Japanese)

Hayashi M (2009) Productivity effect of public capital: reconsideration by the dynamic panel. Public Financ Stud 5:119–140 (in Japanese)

Miyagawa T, Kawasaki K, Edamura K (2013) Re-examination of the productivity effect of public capital. RIETI Discussion Paper Series 13-J-081 (in Japanese)

Miyara I, Fukushige M (2008) Types of public capital and their productivity in Japanese prefectures. Jpn Econ Rev 59(2):194–210

Nakahigashi M (2003) Productivity effect of public capital in Japan. Mitsubishi Economic Research Institute, Tokyo (in Japanese)

Nakahigashi M (2015) Aging of public capital and the productivity effect. In: Yoshino N, Kameda K, Nakahigashi M, Nakata M (eds) Challenges and course of Japanese economy: theoretical and empirical analyses of economic policy. Keio University Press, Tokyo (in Japanese)

Okubo M (2008) Public capital and productivity: a nonstationary panel analysis. Appl Econ Lett 15:95–99

Organisation for Economic Co-operation and Development (OECD) (2008) Public-private partnership: in pursuit of risk sharing and value for money. OECD Publishing, Paris

Revankar NS (1974) Some finite sample results in the context of two seemingly unrelated regression equations. J Am Stat Assoc 69(345):187–190

Yoshino N (2010) Financing transport infrastructure investment. In: OECD (ed) Southeast Asian economic outlook 2010. OECD Publishing, Paris

Yoshino N (2012) Global imbalances and the development of capital flows among Asian countries. OECD Journal: Financial Market Trends 2012(1):81–112

Yoshino N, Abidhadjaev U (2015) An impact evaluation of investment in infrastructure: the case of the railway connection in Uzbekistan, ADBI working paper No 548. Asian Development Bank Institute, Tokyo

Yoshino N, Nakahigashi M (2004) The role of infrastructure in economic development. ICFAI J Manag Econ 2:7–24

Yoshino N, Nakano H (1994) Public investment allocations to the Tokyo metropolitan area. In: Hatta T (ed) Economic analysis of Tokyo over-concentration. Nihon Keizai Shimbun, Inc., Tokyo (in Japanese)
Yoshino N, Pontines V (2015) The highway effect on public finance: case of the STAR highway in the Philippines, ADBI working paper No 549. Asian Development Bank Institute, Tokyo
Yoshino N, Taghizadeh-Hesary F (2015) Effectiveness of the easing of monetary policy in Japanese economy, incorporating energy prices. J Comp Asian Dev 14(2):227–248
Yoshino N, Taghizadeh-Hesary F (2016) Causes and remedies of Japan's long-lasting recession: lessons to China. Chin World Econ 24(2):23–47
Yoshino N, Nakajima T, Nakahigashi M (1999) Productivity effect of public capital. In: Yoshino N, Nakajima T (eds) Economic effect of public investment. Nihon Hyoron-sha, Tokyo (in Japanese)

Chapter 3
Optimal Fiscal Policy Rule for Achieving Fiscal Sustainability: A Japanese Case Study

Naoyuki Yoshino, Tetsuro Mizoguchi, and Farhad Taghizadeh-Hesary

Abstract Japan's debt-to-gross domestic product (GDP) ratio is the highest among Organisation for Economic Co-operation and Development (OECD) countries. This chapter will answer the question of whether Japanese government debt is sustainable. While the Domar condition and Bohn's condition are often used in the literature to check whether a government's debt situation is in a dangerous zone, this chapter will show that the Domar condition is obtained only from the government budget constraint (namely the supply of government bonds) and does not take into account the demand for government bonds. A simple comparison of the interest rate and the growth rate of an economy using the Domar condition is not adequate to check the stability of a government's budget deficit. Both the interest rate and the growth rate of the economy are determined endogenously in the model. This chapter shows that Bohn's condition satisfies the stability of the government budget in the long run by imposing constraints on the primary balance. However, Bohn's condition does not achieve economic stability—even if the condition is satisfied, the recovery of the economy may not be achieved. This chapter will propose a new condition that satisfies both the stability of the government budget and the recovery of the economy. The chapter will shed light on these issues both theoretically and empirically. The empirical findings declare that in order to achieve fiscal sustainability based on the optimal fiscal policy rule provided in this chapter, both sides of the Japanese government budget (expenditure and revenue) need to be

N. Yoshino
Asian Development Bank Institute (ADBI), Tokyo, Japan

Keio University, Tokyo, Japan
e-mail: nyoshino@adbi.org

T. Mizoguchi
Faculty of Economics, Takasaki City University of Economics, Gunma, Japan
e-mail: tmizo@tcue.ac.jp

F. Taghizadeh-Hesary (✉)
Faculty of Economics, Keio University, Tokyo, Japan

Graduate School of Economics, The University of Tokyo, Tokyo, Japan
e-mail: farhadth@gmail.com; farhadth@keio.jp

N. Yoshino, F. Taghizadeh-Hesary (eds.), *Japan's Lost Decade*, ADB Institute Series on Development Economics, DOI 10.1007/978-981-10-5021-3_3

adjusted simultaneously. Moreover, the results show that the decrease in government expenditure must be more than the increase in tax revenue.

Keywords Japanese Bond Market • Fiscal Sustainability • Fiscal Policy Rule • Government Debt Management

JEL Classification E42, E63

3.1 Introduction and an Overview of the Japanese Bond Market

Japan's debt-to-gross domestic product (GDP) ratio is the highest among Organisation for Economic Co-operation and Development (OECD) countries, at more than 220% (Fig. 3.1). The interesting point is that Japan's debt is still sustainable, while the southern European countries Greece and Cyprus went bankrupt due to high government deficits, although their debt–GDP ratios were lower than Japan's.

Figure 3.1 illustrates the general government gross financial liabilities as a percentage of GDP for selected OECD countries. It is clear that the ratio for Japan is the highest, at 229.6%, in 2014. Greece and Italy have the second- and third-highest levels at 188.7% and 147.2%, respectively. The average gross debt–GDP ratio for all OECD countries is 111.1%. Estonia has the lowest ratio among OECD countries, at 13.0%.

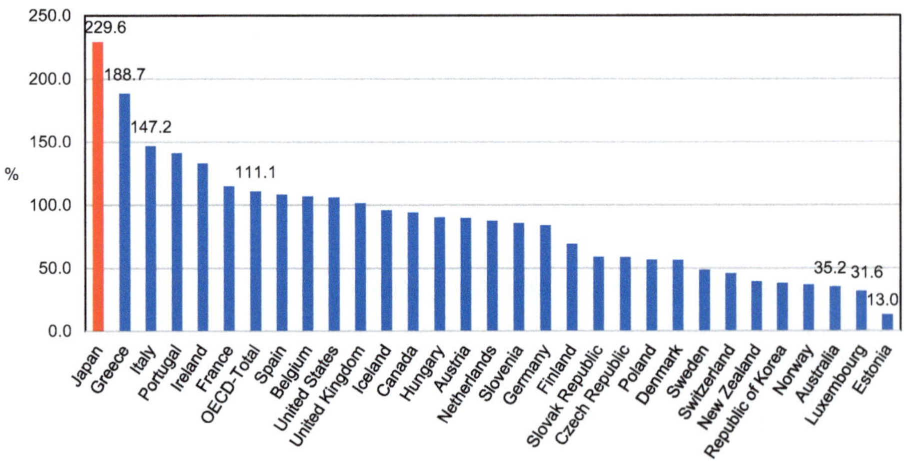

Fig. 3.1 Gross debt/gross domestic product in selected OECD countries, 2014.*Note:* General government gross financial liabilities as a percentage of gross domestic product. *OECD* Organisation for Economic Co-operation and Development (*Source:* OECD Economic Outlook No. 95 database (2014))

Accumulated government debt in Japan now amounts to more than 220% of GDP and it will be difficult to issue further bonds unless the Bank of Japan purchases Japanese government bonds (JGBs). Despite its huge budget deficit, the Japanese economy can sustain the stability of the bond market. Many Europeans ask why Japan is still stable while Greece and other European countries are in serious trouble.

The differences between Japan and Greece can be found in the demand for government debt, rather than the supply of government debt. More than 90% of the Government of Japan's debt is held by domestic investors in banks, postal savings, life insurance, and pension funds. The Japanese government issues various kinds of bonds based on demand by differing sectors, and the government bond market has been quite stable in Japan. Japanese investors continue to hold government bonds, since Basel capital requirements set the risk of government bonds at zero. On the other hand, more than 70% of investors in Greece's bond market are foreign and they have been quick to move out of the market at times of risk. (Yoshino and Mizoguchi 2013a).

Japan has achieved the highest life expectancy in the world and the Japanese economy is facing an aging population. Because of the aging population, social welfare costs have started to increase and currently one-third of government spending is allocated to social welfare, while the government budget deficit is rising every year. In the general account budget for 2015, social security accounts for 32.7% of the total budget. This is the major reason for the increase in the amount of outstanding government bonds (Fig. 3.2). The second reason for this continuous

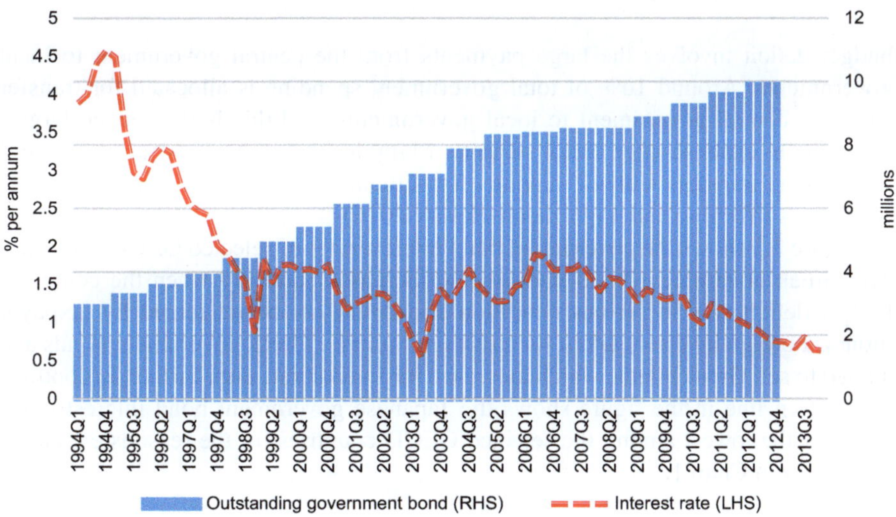

Fig. 3.2 Interest rate and government bonds outstanding. *Note:* The right-hand scale shows outstanding government bonds and other government borrowings. The annual data was converted to annual data and exponentially smoothed. The interest rate is the 10-year yield of the Japanese government bonds. *LHS* left-hand scale, *RHS* right-hand scale (Source: NIKKEI NEEDS database)

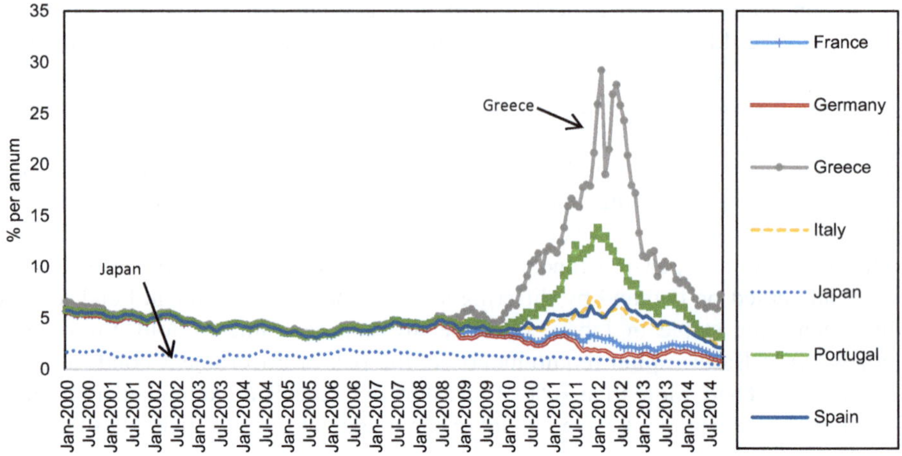

Fig. 3.3 Interest rates in selected OECD countries. *OECD* Organisation for Economic Co-operation and Development (*Note:* The rate is the 10-year government bond interest rate. Generally, the yield is calculated at the pre-tax level before deductions for brokerage costs and commissions, and is derived from the relationship between the present market value of the bond and the value at maturity, taking into account interest payments paid through to maturity. Monthly figures shown are calculated as the average of weighted or unweighted arithmetic rates relating to all days or specified days in the month, or to a day at or near the month's end. For short- and long-term interest rates, annual and quarterly data are the averages of the monthly figures, while for "overnight" rates, annual and quarterly data usually refer to the figure for the final month of the period)
Source: Monthly Monetary and Financial Statistics (MEI), OECD statistics, released 5 May 2015

budget deficit involves the large payments from the central government to local governments. Around 16% of total government spending is allocated for transfer from the central government to local governments, and this is the second-largest government expense after social security. Many local governments rely on central government transfers without making efforts themselves to revitalize their regional economies (Yoshino and Taghizadeh-Hesary 2016).

Figure 3.3 shows the government bond interest rates of selected OECD countries. The Greek government bond interest rate increased suddenly when the country's budget deficit was in serious condition and could not be redeemed by taxpayer money. Foreign investors asked for a risk premium for Greek government bonds and started to sell Greek bonds, which increased the interest rate even further. In contrast, the bottom line in the figure shows the Japanese government bond interest rate[1], which is the lowest among the selected OECD countries for the reasons explained in Fig. 1.9 in Chap 1.

[1]In Feb 2016, the BOJ took further steps, and started a negative interest rate policy, by increasing massive money supply through purchasing long-term Japanese government bonds (JGB), Previously the BOJ only purchased short-term government bonds. This policy has flattened the yield curve of JGBs. Banks started to reduce purchasing government bonds, because the yield of short-term government bonds' became negative, and even for long-term government bonds up to 15 years the interest rates became negative. for more information see: Yoshino, Taghizadeh-Hesary, Miyamoto (2017) and Yoshino, Taghizadeh-Hesary, Tawk (2017)

Japan's demand for government bonds is increasing and the demand curve for government bonds is shifting to the right, since banks, insurance companies, pension funds, etc. are looking to encourage investment. Banks have continued to receive deposits and are looking for investment in government bonds. Insurance and public pension funds in Japan are inclined to invest in government bonds, as they are regarded as safe assets. Therefore, the demand curve for government bonds has been increasing and has kept the Japanese interest rate low.

Regarding the government bond markets, the Domar condition and Bohn's condition are often used in the literature to check whether an economy is in a dangerous zone. Domar suggests that an economy should make its interest rate lower than the growth rate of the economy Domar (1944). Domar suggests that an economy should make its interest rate lower than the growth rate of the economy. Bohn proposes that a primary balance be maintained so that the debt–GDP ratio does not diverge from its original level.

The purpose of this chapter is twofold. The first point we will argue is that the Domar condition is obtained only from the government budget constraint (namely the supply of government bonds) and does not take into account the demand for government bonds. A simple comparison of the interest rate and the growth rate of the economy is not adequate to check the stability of the government budget deficit as both the interest rate and the growth rate of the economy are determined endogenously in the model.

The second point is that Bohn's condition satisfies the long-run stability of the government budget in by imposing constraints for the primary balance. However, it does not achieve economic stability. Even if Bohn's condition is satisfied, the recovery of the economy may not be achieved. This chapter will propose the new condition that can be satisfied with both the stability of the government budget and the recovery of the economy.

The chapter is organized as follows. Section 3.2 provides the related literature. Section 3.3 shows the revised Domar condition and Bohn's condition combined with the bond market. Section 3.4 provides the mathematical model. Section 3.5 provides the fiscal policy rule and tax rule to achieve sustainability of the budget, Sect. 3.6. provides growth dividend the empirical survey and Sect. 3.7 contains the concluding remarks.

3.2 Related Literature

There is substantial research concerning the fiscal sustainability conditions derived from the government budget constraint. The sustainability of public debt can be examined only from the government budget constraint, supply side of the public debt, in the fiscal policy literature. Bohn (1998) proposed a different fiscal sustainability test to estimate the transversality condition. He found that an increase in the ratio of government deficit to GDP increased the ratio of the primary surplus to GDP from 1916 to 1995 in the United States (US). He concluded that US fiscal policy sustained an intertemporal budget constraint. Bohn (2005) also examined the sustainability of US fiscal policy by using data from the US fiscal records from 1792–2003 and critically reviewed the sustainability conditions and their testable implications, applying them to US data to emphasize the ramifications of economic growth dividend. A "growth dividend" has historically covered the entire interest bill on US debt. Unit root tests on real series, unscaled by GDP, are distorted by the series' severe heteroscedasticity. The most credible evidence in favor of sustainability is the robust positive response of primary surpluses to fluctuations in the debt-to-GDP ratio.

For Japanese cases, there are also substantial empirical studies on this issue. A study by Yoshino and Mizoguchi (2010) investigates the role of the Liberal Democratic Party on the field of public expenditure. The study shows that spending initially fueled Japan's rapid postwar growth and kept the Liberal Democratic Party in power for most of the last half-century. However, after the economic bubble burst in 1990, the country fell into a long economic malaise, called the "Lost Decade." Considering the current Japanese government bond (JGB) circumstances, we introduce the stability condition for the government bond market by taking into account both the government supply of government bonds and financial institutions' demand for government bonds. McNelis and Yoshino (2012) applied Bayesian estimation to an open-economy dynamic stochastic general equilibrium (DSGE) model of Japan. They found that the emergence of even a small risk premium on government debt will trigger significant instability in the real and nominal variables. Yoshino and Mizoguchi (2013b) investigated the features of the flow of funds in Japan across time. They demonstrated that an increased volume of corporate savings was deposited as liquid savings and used to purchase Japanese government bonds through financial institutions from the perspectives of the flow of funds. They also show that the demand for JGBs plays an important role in the stability of the market. Recently, Yoshino and Vollmer (2014) compared Greece with Japan to explain why Japan has not yet suffered from a debt crisis even though its gross government debt–GDP ratio is much larger than Greece's. In Japan, a large share of government debt is being held domestically, there are substantial central bank holdings of government debt, and autonomous monetary policy can be used to ease financial crisis. Based on their model analysis, they show why Japanese domestic investors hold such huge amounts of JGBs. Hoshi and Ito (2014) used a simulation method to see whether Japan's budget deficits are sustainable and concluded that Japan's fiscal situation is in a dangerous zone. Yoshino and Taghizadeh-Hesary (2014a) show that although currently the Japanese government budget and the debt market are sustainable, there is no guarantee that this market will be sustainable in the future; therefore, fiscal consolidation, which is one of the three arrows of "Abenomics," is essential for the sustainability of the Japanese economy.[2]

[2]"Abenomics" refers to the economic policies advocated by Shinzo Abe, who became Prime Minister of Japan for a second time when his Liberal Democratic Party won an overwhelming majority in the general election in December 2012. Abenomics is distinguished by a set of policies comprising "three arrows": (1) aggressive monetary policy, (2) fiscal consolidation, and (3) a growth strategy. For more information, see Yoshino and Taghizadeh-Hesary (2014b).

Previous analysis, such as that by Bohn (1998, 2005), only used the government budget constraint for the stability of the government bond market. In our model, the fiscal sustainability of government bonds in Japan can be explained by the demand for government bonds rather than the supply. We consider this to be representative of reality. This chapter presents a new stability condition for the bond market. We also present some rules for fiscal stabilization and explain the fiscal rules corresponding to Taylor's rule for monetary policy.

3.3 The Revised Domar Condition and Bohn's Condition Combined with the Bond Market

The Domar condition and Bohn's condition are often used to determine whether budget deficits are sustainable.

The Domar condition is obtained from the government budget constraint as follows:

Government Budget Constraint

$$G_t + r_t B_{t-1} = \Delta B_t + T_t \tag{3.1}$$

Equation (3.1) states that government spending (G_t) + interest payments ($r_t B_{t-1}$) = new issue of government bonds (ΔB_t) + tax revenue (T_t).

Dividing Eq. (3.1) by GDP (Y_t) and rewriting Eq. (3.1), we get.

Domar Condition

$$b_t - b_{t-1} = \frac{(r_t - \eta_t)}{1 + \eta_t} b_{t-1} + g_t - t_t \tag{3.2}$$

where $b_t = B_t/Y_t$ *and* $\eta_t = \Delta Y_t/Y_t$and $g_t = G_t/Y_t$ and $t_t = T_t/Y_t$.

Equation (3.1) denotes the government budget constraint, which describes the supply of government bonds. Dividing Eq. (3.1) by Y_t and with a few transformations, the Domar condition in Eq. (3.2) is obtained. If the interest rate is higher than the growth rate of the economy, the budget deficit will increase rapidly. On the other hand, if the interest rate is lower than the growth rate of the economy, the budget deficit will converge in a stable manner. However, the Domar condition focuses only on the supply of government bonds and does not consider the demand.

3.4 Mathematical Model

This chapter describes the equations of both the government bond supply and the government bond demand based on the model set out by Yoshino and Mizoguchi (2010, 2013a). Our model is summarized as follows:

Government Budget constraint = Supply of Government Bonds

$$G_t + r_t^B B_{t-1} = \Delta B_t^S + T_t + \Delta M_t \tag{3.3}$$

Demand for Government Bonds

$$\Delta B_t^D = b_0 + b_1 r_t^B \tag{3.4}$$

From Eqs. (3.3) and (3.4), we obtain the equilibrium interest rate of government bonds:

$$r_t^{B*} = \frac{G_t - T_t - b_0 - \Delta M_t}{b_1 - B_{t-1}} \tag{3.5}$$

A simple macro model that includes the demand side of the government bond can be constructed as follows:

Equation (3.3) is the disposable income, showing wage income, transfer payments from the government, and interest received from government bonds, minus tax payments. The disposable income is distributed into consumption and savings. Savings are allocated for the purchase of government bonds, for money demand, and to increase domestic deposits.

Disposable income is defined as income (Y_t) plus the interest received from government bonds by households ($r_t^B B_{t-1}$), minus the tax payment (T_t) as it follows:

The disposable income is divided into consumption (C_t) and savings (S_t)

$$YD_t = Y_t - T_t + r_t^B B_{t-1} = C_t + S_t \tag{3.6}$$

where $S_t = \Delta B_t + \Delta M_t + \Delta W_t^D$.

Savings (S_t) = Government bonds(ΔB_t) + Money demand (ΔM_t) + Domestic deposits(ΔW_t^D).

Investment Function

$$I_t = i_0 - i_1 r_t \tag{3.7}$$

Consumption Equation[3]

$$C_t = c_0 + c_1 YD_t \tag{3.8}$$

Deposit Equation

$$\Delta W_t^D = d_0 + d_1 YD_t + d_2 r_t \tag{3.9}$$

[3]We assume that the consumption function is a Keynesian consumption function, non-Ricardian type.

Consumption depends on disposable income, for simplicity. The deposit market is expressed as the supply of deposits and the demand for deposits in Eq. (3.9). The demand for deposits is explained by disposable income and the interest rate of government bonds. If the interest rate for government bonds increases, households will want to buy more government bonds and reduce the amount of deposits. All deposits are used for bank loans to satisfy investment.

From Eqs. (3.6), (3.7), (3.8) and (3.9), we have the investment–saving (IS) balance equation:

IS-balance

$$(1 - c_1) Y_t - c_1 r_t^B B_{t-1} + i_1 r_t = c_0 + i_0 + G_t - c_1 T_t \tag{3.10}$$

We assume that investment in the private sector will be financed by deposits in the banking sector. For convenience, with regard to the banking sector's behavior, it is simply assumed that savings are used for investment.

Saving–Investment Equilibrium

$$\Delta W_t^D = I_t \tag{3.11}$$

By using Eqs. (3.10) and (3.11), we obtain income and the interest rate in the short-run equilibrium as follows:

$$Y_t^* = \frac{1}{\Delta} \Big\{ (d_1 + i_1) c_0 + d_1 i_0 + i_1 d_0 + (d_1 + i_1 + d_1 i_1) G_t - ((d_1 + i_1) c_1 + d_1 i_1) T_t + ((d_1 + i_1) c_1 + d_1 i_1) r_t^{B*} B_{t-1} \Big\} \tag{3.12}$$

$$r_t^* = \frac{1}{\Delta} \Big\{ (1 - c_1)(i_0 - d_0) - d_1 (c_0 + i_0) - d_1 G_t + d_1 T_t - d_1 r_t^{B*} B_{t-1} \Big\} \tag{3.13}$$

where $\Delta = (1 - c_1)(d_2 + i_1) - d_1 i_1$ and $r_t^{B*} = \frac{G_t - T_t - b_0 - \Delta M_t}{b_1 - B_{t-1}}$.

In the next section, we use the equilibrium interest rate and income to derive the optimal fiscal rule.

Revised Domar Condition Combined with the Bond Market

Figure 3.4 shows the trends of the long-term interest rate (10-year Japanese government bond yield) and nominal GDP growth rate of Japan. As the figure shows, particularly during 2003–2009, the long-term interest rate and nominal GDP growth rate are approximately co-moving. The figure also shows that the growth rate of the interest rate exceeds the growth rate of the economy. This suggests that the

Fig. 3.4 Real GDP growth rate and long-term interest rate in Japan. *Note:* The GDP growth rate for each quarter is compared with the previous year and seasonally adjusted. The interest rate is the 10-year Japanese government bond yield. *DP* gross domestic product (*Source:* Quarterly estimates of GDP, Economic and Social Research Institute (ESRI), Cabinet Office of Japan; Nikkei NEEDS).

Japanese budget is on an unstable path, based on the Domar condition. Applying the Domar condition and the case studies of Polito and Wickens (2007), the data show the instability of bond financing in Japan. In contrast to the stability condition analyzed in Bohn (1998) and other studies, our model considers the structure of the bond market. Since both the interest rate and bond supply and demand are endogenous in our model, we can investigate the stability condition based on each economic variable in the economy.

3.5 Fiscal Policy Rule and Tax Rule to Achieve Sustainability of the Budget

The fiscal policy rule can be obtained as follows.

The objective function of the government is set as:

$$L(B_t, Y_t, G_t, T_t, \Delta B_t) = \frac{1}{2}w_1\left(B_t - B_t^*\right)^2 + \frac{1}{2}w_2\left(Y_t - Y_t^f\right)^2 + \frac{1}{2}w_3(G_t - G_{t-1})^2 + \frac{1}{2}w_4(T_t - T_{t-1})^2 + \frac{1}{2}w_5\left(\Delta B_t - \Delta B_t^*\right)^2 \tag{3.14}$$

The government aims to stabilize government debt (B_t) as close as possible to its desired level ($B_t{}^*$), with GDP (Y_t) close to the full employment level of GDP (Y_t^f), and with a smooth change of government spending (G_t), smooth change of taxation (T_t), and smooth change of the flow of bonds (ΔB_t). Here w_i ($i = 1, \cdots, 5$) are the policy weights the government can set.

We minimize the loss from the government's objective function by means of government spending (G_t) and the smooth change of taxation (T_t).

$$\min_{G_t, T_t} L(B_t, Y_t, G_t, T_t, \Delta B_t) = \frac{1}{2} w_1 (B_t - B_t^*)^2 + \frac{1}{2} w_2 \left(Y_t - Y_t^f\right)^2 + \frac{1}{2} w_3 (G_t - G_{t-1})^2 + \frac{1}{2} w_4 (T_t - T_{t-1})^2 + \frac{1}{2} w_5 (\Delta B_t - \Delta B_t^*)^2$$

The first-order conditions[4,5] are:

$$\frac{\partial L}{\partial G_t} = w_1 (B_t - B_t^*) \left(\frac{\partial B_t}{\partial G_t}\right) + w_2 \frac{\partial Y_t}{\partial G_t} \left(Y_t - Y_t^f\right) + w_3 (G_t - G_{t-1}) + w_5 (\Delta B_t - \Delta B_t^*) \left(\frac{\partial \Delta B_t}{\partial G_t}\right) = 0 \tag{3.15}$$

$$\frac{\partial L}{\partial T_t} = w_1 (B_t - B_t^*) \left(\frac{\partial B_t}{\partial T_t}\right) + w_2 \frac{\partial Y_t}{\partial T_t} \left(Y_t - Y_t^f\right) + w_4 (T_t - T_{t-1}) + w_5 (\Delta B_t - \Delta B_t^*) \left(\frac{\partial \Delta B_t}{\partial T_t}\right) = 0 \tag{3.16}$$

From Eq. (3.15), we obtain our government spending rule.

Government Spending Rule

$$G_t - G_{t-1} = \alpha_1 (B_t - B_t^*) + \alpha_2 (\Delta B_t - \Delta B_t^*) + \alpha_3 \left(Y_t - Y_t^f\right) \tag{3.17}$$

where $\alpha_1 = \frac{w_1}{w_3}\left(\frac{B_{t-1}}{b_1 - B_{t-1}} + 1\right)$, $\alpha_2 = \frac{w_5}{w_3}\left(\frac{B_{t-1}}{b_1 - B_{t-1}} + 1\right)$, $\alpha_3 = -\frac{w_2}{w_3}\left(\frac{(d_1 + i_1) + d_1 i_1}{\Delta}\right)$

Taxation Rule

$$T_t - T_{t-1} = \beta_1 (B_t - B_t^*) + \beta_2 (\Delta B_t - \Delta B_t^*) + \beta_3 \left(Y_t - Y_t^f\right) \tag{3.18}$$

where $\beta_1 = -\frac{w_1}{w_4}\left(\frac{B_{t-1}}{b_1 - B_{t-1}} + 1\right)$, $\beta_2 = -\frac{w_5}{w_4}\left(\frac{B_{t-1}}{b_1 - B_{t-1}} + 1\right)$, $\beta_3 = \frac{w_2}{w_4}\left(\frac{(d_1 + i_1)c_1 + d_1 i_1}{\Delta}\right)$.

4 $\frac{\partial B_t}{\partial G_t} = \frac{B_{t-1}}{b_1 - B_{t-1}} + 1$, $\frac{\partial Y_t}{\partial G_t} = \frac{(d_1 + i_1) + d_1 i_1}{\Delta}$, $\frac{\partial \Delta B_t}{\partial G_t} = \frac{B_{t-1}}{b_1 - B_{t-1}} + 1$

5 $\frac{\partial B_t}{\partial T_t} = -\left(\frac{B_{t-1}}{b_1 - B_{t-1}} + 1\right)$, $\frac{\partial Y_t}{\partial T_t} = -\frac{(d_1 + i_1)c_1 + d_1 i_1}{\Delta}$, $\frac{\partial \Delta B_t}{\partial T_t} = -\left(\frac{B_{t-1}}{b_1 - B_{t-1}} + 1\right)$

From these two first-order conditions, we can find the relationship between $G_t, T_t, \left(B_t - B_t^*\right), \left(\Delta B_t - \Delta B_t^*\right)$ and the primary balance.

$$PB_t - PB_{t-1} = (\alpha_1 - \beta_1)\left(B_t - B_t^*\right) + (\alpha_2 - \beta_2)\left(\Delta B_t - \Delta B_t^*\right) + (\alpha_3 - \beta_3)\left(Y_t - Y_t^f\right) \tag{3.19}$$

Equation (3.19) implies that the government should not only check the desirable changes between GDP and the primary balance, but also set up the rule for the changes in both government expenditure and taxation. It should also not only check the difference between the GDP–debt ratio and desirable GDP–debt ratio (Bohn's condition), but also implement the policy by checking the changes in government expenditure and taxation in the previous year and the trend in the business cycle. From Eqs. (3.17) and (3.18), when the government simultaneously implements structural reforms and policies to reduce government spending, such as social security for the aging population, these policies will smooth the GDP gap and the level of government expenditure. Therefore, these will reduce the likelihood of default. Our proposed fiscal policy rules, an expansion of Bohn's condition, imply that governments should implement policies by checking (i) the strict control of issuing government bonds and (ii) the business cycle for fiscal sustainability.

3.6 Empirical Survey

We used quarterly data from 1994Q1 to 2014Q4, a period that includes the post-bubble era of the Japanese economy, the 1997–1998 Asian financial crisis, the 2008–2009 global financial crisis, and the 2011 Great East Japan Earthquake and tsunami.

The government expenditure used in our empirical survey is the total public demand and tax is the total government tax revenue, both seasonally adjusted. Money demand is M^2, the average amount of outstanding money stock based on the year-on-year change. For the outstanding bonds we used the total outstanding Japanese government bonds and other borrowings of the Japanese government. Consumption is private consumption, income is GDP, and investment is private investment, all seasonally adjusted and in real terms, deflated by the GDP deflator ($2009 = 100$). The newly issued bonds are the new issues of public bonds and new issues of government bonds. The sources of the data are time series data from the Bank of Japan, International Financial Statistics of the International Monetary Fund, the Economic and Social Research Institute, the Japanese Cabinet Office, Nikkei NEEDS, and OECD Economic Outlook.

To evaluate the stationarity of the series, we used an augmented Dickey–Fuller test. The results suggest that variables for outstanding government bonds, investment, interest rate, and private deposits are non-stationary in level. However, when we applied the unit root test to the first difference of the variables, we were able to reject the null hypothesis of unit roots for each variable. These results suggest

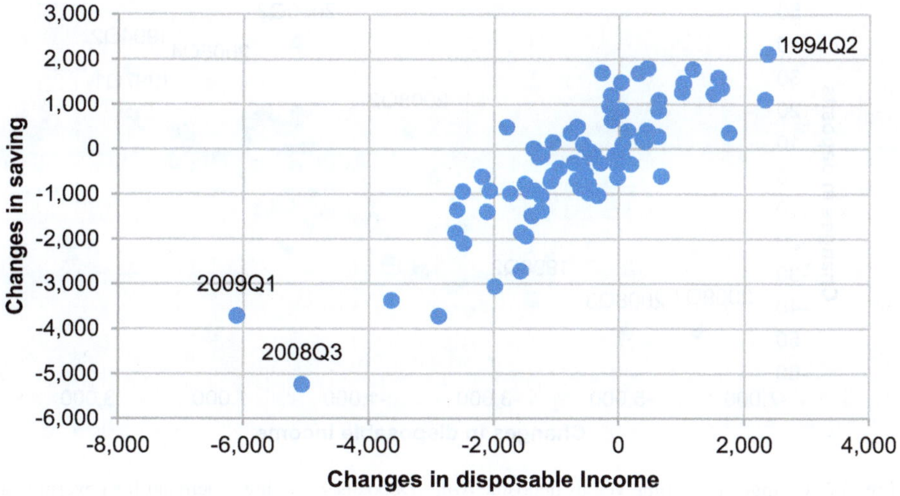

Fig. 3.5 Changes in income versus saving (*Source*: Nikkei NEEDS)

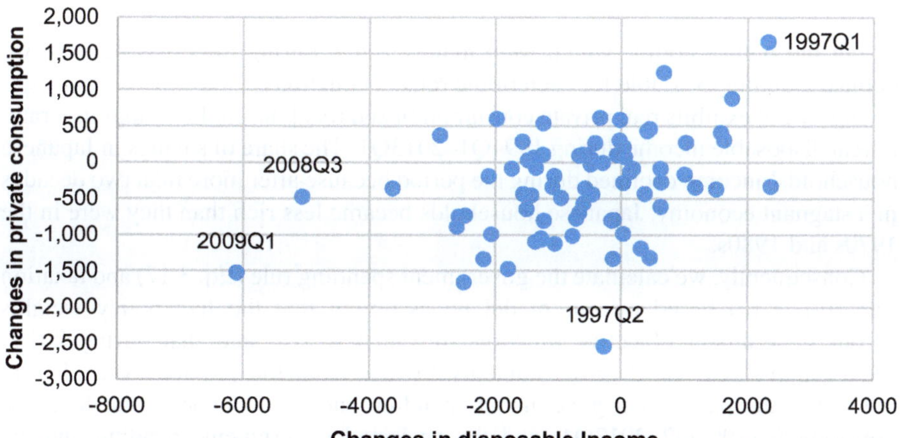

Fig. 3.6 Changes in income versus private consumption (*Source*: Nikkei NEEDS)

that each government bond, investment, interest rate, and private deposit variable contains a unit root. Once the unit root test was performed and it was discovered that the variables were non-stationary in level and stationary in the first differences, they were integrated of order 1 or I(1). Hence, variables will appear in the econometric model in first differences. We used ordinary least squares to run the regressions for each equation. We used the Akaike information criterion to select the lag orders.

Prior to running the regressions, we plotted Figs. 3.5, 3.6 and 3.7 to identify any outlier points.

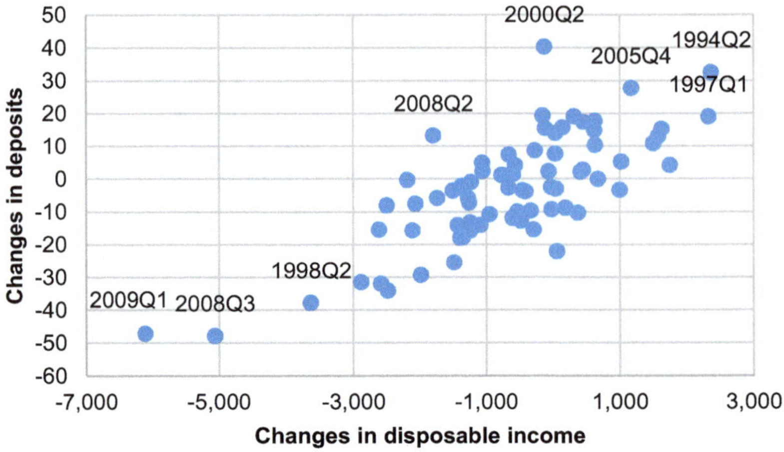

Fig. 3.7 Changes in income versus deposits. *Note:* Deposits = saving – demand for government bonds. Data points for 2000Q1 and 2001Q1 are not shown as they are outside the figure (*Source*: Nikkei NEEDS)

For the outlier points, which were mainly found during the crisis periods, we defined a dummy variable for each of the related equations.[6]

Figure 3.8 exhibits real private consumption and real household savings as a ratio of real disposable income during 1994Q1–2013Q1. The share of savings in Japanese households' income declined during the period because after more than two decades in a stagnant economy, Japanese households became less rich than they were in the 1970s and 1980s.

Consequently, we calculate the government spending rule (Eq. 3.17) and taxation rule (Eq. 3.18) based on our model by assuming that the five policy weights in our government objective function are equal to 0.2, and that during 2014–2030 Japan's real GDP grows annually by 2% from the previous year. Figure 3.9 shows the past actual government spending and tax revenue of the Japanese government (1994Q2–2013Q4) and the projected government spending and tax revenue (2014Q1–2030Q4) based on our model.

As illustrated in Fig. 3.9, to follow the optimal fiscal policy rule provided in this chapter and reduce the national debt from its present high level, Japanese government expenditure needs to be reduced drastically and the government tax

[6]Below are the results of the regressions:

Equation 3.4: Demand for government bonds: $\Delta(B_t) = 8444390 + 1336455(r_t)$
Equation 3.7: Investment function: $\Delta(I_t) = 85153 - 2125[\Delta(r_t)]$
Equation 3.8: Consumption equation: $C_t = 9445 + 0.53(YD_t)$
Equation 3.9: Deposit equation: $\Delta\left(W_t^D\right) = -10828237 + 0.22\,(YD_t) - 675616\,(r_t)$
Equation 3.8 shows the marginal propensity to consume to be 0.53, and Fig. 3.8 empirically shows this fact.

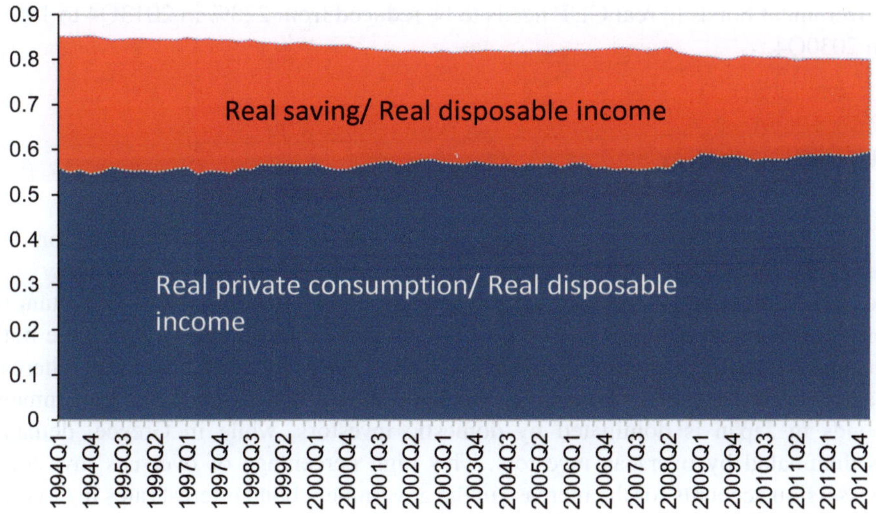

Fig. 3.8 Japanese real private consumption and real household savings as a percentage of real disposable income, 1994Q1–2013Q1. (*Source:* Nikkei NEEDS)

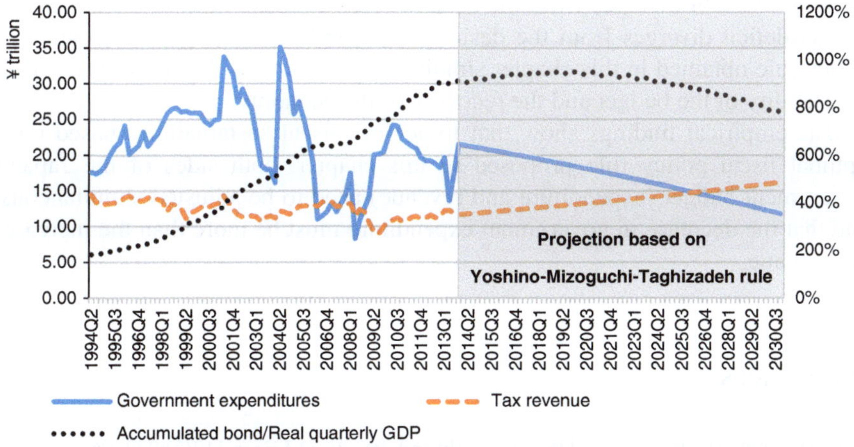

Fig. 3.9 Government expenditure and tax revenue (quarterly data) (*Note:* The *gray shaded area* indicates the projected values based on the Yoshino–Mizoguchi–Taghizadeh rule. The left-hand axis indicates government expenditures (primary expenses) and tax revenue, both quarterly values; the right-hand axis indicates the accumulated bonds/real quarterly GDP. *GDP* gross domestic product. *Source:* Raw data are from Nikkei NEEDS; projection values are compiled by the authors)

revenue needs to increase. This means that both sides of the budget need to be adjusted simultaneously (expenditure and revenue) to achieve fiscal sustainability. Further, as is apparent from this figure, the decrease in expenditure needs to be more than the revenue increase. According to our calculations for 2014–2030, the Japanese government needs to cut expenditure by 45% and raise tax revenue by 38% to achieve fiscal sustainability. To accomplish this, the ratio of accumulated government bonds to real GDP needs to be reduced from 228% in 2013Q4 to 196% in 2030Q4.

3.7 Conclusion

This chapter addresses a constraint of the conventional Domar condition for assessing the stability of the budget—that it is obtained only from the supply side for government bonds, namely the government budget condition. It is important to also consider the demand side of government bonds. Japan and Greece have both accumulated a large amount of government debt, but Greece went bankrupt whereas Japan's debt has been sustainable. We have shown that demand for government bonds in Japan is dominated by domestic investors, while in Greece, demand is dominated by overseas investors. This high percentage of overseas investors' possession accounts for the increase in the government bond interest rates in Greece.

As Bohn's condition does not satisfy economic recovery and only gives the condition to retain the budget balance, the optimal government spending rule and tax revenue rule must be obtained. The optimal fiscal policy rule must examine how government debt diverges from the desired level, how the flow of the government budget deficit diverges from the desired level, and the GDP gap. The new fiscal policy rule obtained in this chapter simultaneously satisfies the conditions for both the stability of the budget and the recovery of the economy.

The empirical findings show that to achieve fiscal sustainability based on the optimal fiscal policy rule proposed in this chapter, both sides of the Japanese government budget (expenditure and revenue) need to be adjusted simultaneously, and that the decrease in government expenditure must be more than the increase in tax revenue.

References

Bohn H (1998) The behavior of US public debt and deficits. Q J Econ 113(3):949–963

Bohn H (2005) The sustainability of fiscal policy in the United States, CESifo working paper no 1446. Center for Economic Studies and Ifo Institute, Munich

Domar ED (1944) The burden of the debt and the national income. Am Econ Rev 34(4):798–827

Hoshi T, Ito T (2014) Defying gravity: can Japanese sovereign debt continue to increase without a crisis? Econ Policy J 29(7):5–44

McNelis P, Yoshino N (2012) Macroeconomic volatility under high accumulation of government debt: lessons from Japan. Adv Complex Syst 15 Suppl No (2):1250057-1–1250057–29

Polito V, Wickens M (2007) Measuring the fiscal stance. Discussion paper in Economics, No. 2007/14. The University of York, York

Yoshino N, Mizoguchi T (2010) The role of public works in the political business cycle and the instability of the budget deficits in Japan. Asian Econ Pap 9(1):94–112

Yoshino N, Mizoguchi T (2013a) Optimal fiscal policy rule to achieve fiscal sustainability: comparison between Japan and Europe. Presented at Singapore economic review conference, Singapore, August 2013

Yoshino N, Mizoguchi T (2013b) Change in the flow of funds and the fiscal rules needed for fiscal stabilization. Public Policy Rev 8(6):775–793

Yoshino N, Taghizadeh-Hesary F (2014a) Three arrows of "Abenomics" and the structural reform of Japan: inflation targeting policy of the central bank, fiscal consolidation, and growth strategy, ADBI working paper no 492. Asian Development Bank Institute, Tokyo

Yoshino N, Taghizadeh-Hesary F (2014b) An analysis of challenges faced by Japan's economy and Abenomics. Jpn Polit Econ 40(3–4):37–62

Yoshino N, Taghizadeh-Hesary F (2016) Causes and remedies of the Japan's long-lasting recession: lessons for China. Chin World Econ 24:23–47

Yoshino N, Taghizadeh-Hesary F, Miyamoto H (2017) The effectiveness of the negative interest rate policy in Japan. Credit Cap Markets – Kredit und Kapital 50(2):189–212

Yoshino N, Taghizadeh-Hesary F, Tawk N (2017) Decline of oil prices and the negative interest rate policy in Japan. Econ Pol Stud 5(2):233–250

Yoshino N, Vollmer U (2014) The sovereign debt crisis: why Greece, but not Japan? Asia Eur J 12(3):325–341

Chapter 4
Macroeconomic Volatility Under High Accumulation of Government Debt: Lessons from Japan

Paul D. McNelis and Naoyuki Yoshino

Abstract This chapter applies Bayesian estimation to an open-economy dynamic stochastic general equilibrium (DSGE) model of Japan to assess the effects of expanding government debt on interest rates, real exchange-rate dynamics, and real sector performance. We find that the emergence of even a small risk premium on will trigger considerable instability in the real and nominal variables. We show that a switch to an exchange-rate rule for monetary policy would considerably moderate the instability induced by a rising risk premium.

Keywords Risk premium • Bayesian estimation • Financial instability

JEL Code E62, E61

4.1 Introduction

The overall debt–GDP ratio in Japan was approaching 200% in 2010 and 220% in 2011, much larger than highly indebted Organisation for Economic Co-operation and Development (OECD) countries like Greece and Italy (Fig. 4.1). Unlike the United States and other heavily indebted OECD countries, domestic Japanese residents hold more than 94% of Japanese government debt. Despite these high

---

Another version of this chapter is available as McNelis and Yoshino (2012).

P.D. McNelis (✉)
Department of Finance, Graduate School of Business Administration, Fordham University, New York, NY, USA
e-mail: mcnelis@fordham.edu

N. Yoshino
Asian Development Bank Institute (ADBI), Tokyo, Japan

Keio University, Tokyo, Japan
e-mail: nyoshino@adbi.org

N. Yoshino, F. Taghizadeh-Hesary (eds.), *Japan's Lost Decade*, ADB Institute Series on Development Economics, DOI 10.1007/978-981-10-5021-3_4

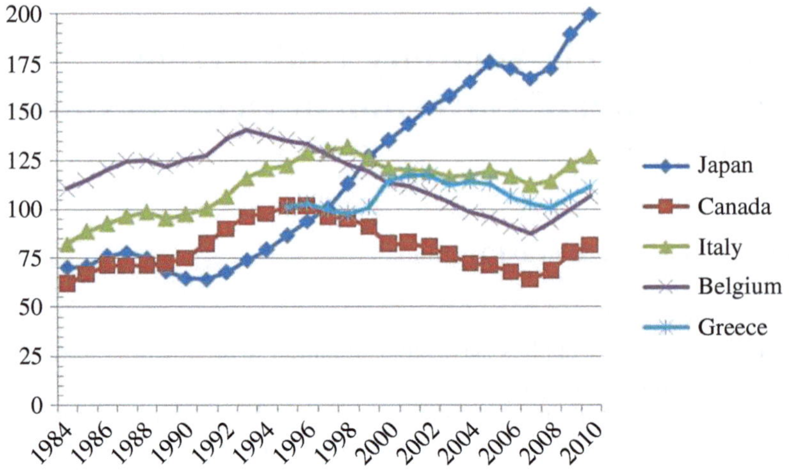

Fig. 4.1 Domestic debt to gross domestic product ratios, 1984–2010 (*Source:* Government of Japan, Ministry of Finance database)

ratios, the government bond market in Japan remains relatively tranquil, with little or no risk premium being demanded by financial institutions purchasing this debt.

This chapter investigates the implications for macroeconomic adjustment and volatility when financial markets apply a risk premium to this debt. In this case, a wedge between the bond yield and the risk-free rate has emerged, with the bond yield rising as debt continues to mount. While the central bank manages the risk-free rate, this rate will become less and less relevant for interest parity and exchange rate adjustment. Hypothetically, in a period of recession, trivial inflation, and zero interest rates, rising bond rates will trigger heightened volatility of the domestic currency.

This scenario has not yet come to fruition. Yen-denominated government bonds continue to remain attractive to overseas investors because of higher euro-bond riskiness in the wake of the crisis in Greece and European debt markets. In addition, Japanese banks are holding more government bonds because the demand for bank loans by Japanese firms has declined due to worldwide recession. With the central bank adopting an easy zero-interest-rate monetary policy, deposits are continuously flowing into Japanese banks, facilitating the purchase of government bonds by the banking sector. Thus, there is little or no immediate pressure for government bond yields to rise relative to the risk-free rate.

By contrast, in the Greek bond market, about 60% of investors are foreign investors. Not surprisingly the risk premium increased.

The large budget deficits in Japan are due to three factors. First, the aging population necessitates increased spending on social welfare and medical care. Secondly, there are large central government transfers to local governments intended to equalize the standard of living throughout the country. Finally, there are significant nonzero interest rate payments on long-term Japanese government bonds, and the continuing redemption of these government bonds. In addition, there has been a marked decline in tax revenue due to the sluggish economy (Yoshino, 2011).

The majority of public attention has been focused on the tsunami and the fallout from the subsequent damage to the nuclear energy facilities in Japan in 2011. Given that most foreign trade is part of a global supply chain with Asian neighbors, recent literature on Japan has focused on the disruptive effects of this tragedy to overall production in the People's Republic of China (PRC) and economies along its coastal rim (see Escaith et al., 2011).

However, a political tsunami of no less magnitude happened in September 2009 with the defeat of the Liberal Democratic Party, which had ruled in Japan more or less continuously since 1955. Yoshino and Mizoguchi (2010) argue that one reason why the Liberal Democratic Party held power for so long was because it was able to use public works in government spending to manipulate the business cycle in politically opportunistic ways. However, during the past decade, the payoffs for government spending projects have been declining in terms of politically effective ways to affect the business cycle. Early use of public spending for mitigating the political business cycle was documented by Ito (1990).

Figure 4.2 shows the persistent stable wedge between the bond yield and the short-term risk-free call money rate since 1994. As Fig. 4.1 shows, it was in 1994 that the debt–GDP ratio in Japan crossed the 100% threshold. But how long can this

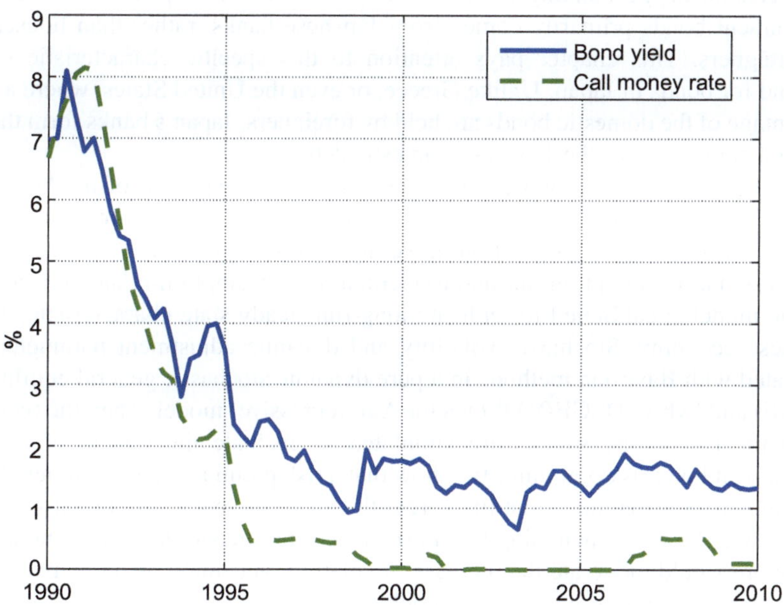

Fig. 4.2 Bond yield and risk-free call money rate in Japan, 1990–2010 (*Source*: Nikkei NEEDS Database)

scenario hold? If world demand increases, and there is increased demand for loans by firms, then government bonds will not be as attractive to the financial institutions. In this case, the government will be forced to pay a risk premium to the banks.

Two scenarios can play out. One is that despite the increasing interest rates, foreign investors may go away, leading to depreciation of the currency, as has happened in Iceland. The second scenario is that as world interest rates remain low, with increasing uncertainty about the euro, foreign investors will increase their yen deposits, thus appreciating the exchange, and thwarting recovery in the real sector. Furthermore, as interest payments increase due to the risk premium, fiscal deficits will rise even further. In this case the government will be forced to raise taxes and reduce spending, further dampening economy-wide recovery.

This chapter analyzes the transmission mechanism of these scenarios on consumption, investment, inflation, the real exchange rate, financial market volatility, and welfare. We make use of a standard new Keynesian dynamic stochastic general equilibrium framework, with a traded and nontraded sector, a financial sector, and government spending.

The model is not meant to be innovative. On the contrary, it is consistent with the canonical New Keynesian open economy framework with a representative household. But within this framework, key assumptions are made to capture specific features of the Japanese economy, which, on the surface, may appear to be unnecessary complications. In particular, we include a banking sector, which takes in deposits from households and buys government bonds. The reason for the inclusion of the banking sector is straightforward. In Japan, the demand for government bonds primarily comes from Japanese banks, rather than households or foreigners. This chapter pays attention to this specific characteristic of the demand for bonds in Japan. Unlike Greece, or even the United States, where a large percentage of the domestic bonds are held by foreigners, Japan's banks form the key demand component of the Japanese domestic debt.

In addition, we model government spending as a component of the household utility function. Again, this may seem to be an unnecessary complication. But in Japan, with its aging population, government spending is increasingly directed toward social welfare programs and to facilitating consumption-related services.

The model is calibrated to replicate long-run steady state characteristics of the Japanese economy. Stochastic volatility and dynamic adjustment parameters are estimated with Bayesian methods in a pure dynamic stochastic general equilibrium (DSGE) and hybrid DSGE/VAR (Vector Autoregressive) model. Then the recurrent government spending shocks are simulated to evaluate the effects of a rising government bond risk premium. We show that a risk premium on government bonds increases macroeconomic volatility across the board, in real and nominal variables. Finally, we show that switching to an exchange-rate rule similar to the one used in Singapore would moderate the increase in volatility generated by an increased risk premium on the Japanese government debt.

Our results come from analysis of kernel estimation of volatility distributions based on repeated simulations of the estimated model. This method, to our knowledge, has not been widely used for assessing the consequences of counterfactual policy regimes relative to the de facto regime.

4.2 The Model

This model represents quarterly adjustment and follows many assumptions with sticky prices commonly used in the New Keynesian framework. We also add financial frictions and real frictions (in the form of adjustment costs for investment and habit persistence for consumption). These are standard assumptions in the New Keynesian framework. The reason why we adopt this framework for Japan and not, for example, a real framework based on adjustment at longer frequencies is that we are comparing the effects of alternative monetary regimes. At longer frequencies, with full price flexibility, the choice of monetary regime is a moot point.

Household Preferences and Endowments

Households own capital for rental and supply labor to firms. Capital depreciates at the rate δ. When households accumulate or decumulate capital K_t through investment I_t beyond the steady state level of investment, $\overline{\delta K}$, they pay adjustment costs. The following law of motion is specified for capital, with adjustment costs given by AC_t. The parameter φ is the adjustment cost parameter for investment and δ is the depreciation rate:

$$K_t = (1 - \delta)K_{t-1} + I_t \tag{4.1}$$

$$AC_t = \left(\frac{\phi(I_t - \overline{\delta K})^2}{2K_t} \right) \tag{4.2}$$

Grüne and Semmler (2008) point out that the adjustment cost model of investment is needed to reduce the elasticity of the supply of capital to replicate observed high equity premia (as well as Sharpe ratios) in this class of models.

We assume that investment goods are imported from abroad, and that the price P^f is the relevant price for these goods. The variable $\overline{K}$ is the steady state level of the capital stock. While this assumption may seem strong, it should be remembered that well over 80% of trade among OECD countries is trade in intermediate goods and component parts, as the supply chain for production becomes increasingly globalized.

The representative household consumption at time t, C_t, is a constant elasticity of substitution (CES) bundle of both domestic consumption goods, C_t^d and imported goods, C_t^f:

$$C_t = \left[(1 - \gamma_1)^{\frac{1}{\theta_1}} (C_t^d)^{\frac{\theta_1 - 1}{\theta_1}} + (\gamma_1)^{\frac{1}{\theta_1}} (C_t^f)^{\frac{\theta_1 - 1}{\theta_1}} \right]^{\frac{\theta_1}{\theta_1 - 1}} \tag{4.3}$$

The demand for each component of consumption is a function of the overall consumption index and the price of the respective component relative to the general price level, P:

$$C_t^d = (1-\gamma_1)\left(\frac{P_t^d}{P_t}\right)^{\theta_1} C_t \tag{4.4}$$

$$C_t^f = \gamma_1\left(\frac{P_t^f}{P_t}\right)^{-\theta_1} C_t. \tag{4.5}$$

The parameters γ_1 and $(1-\gamma_1)$ are the relative shares of foreign and domestic goods in the overall consumption index. The parameter θ_1 is the intertemporal elasticity of substitution for each consumption component.

Domestically produced goods include both nontraded home goods and services, and traded goods (some of which are consumed domestically). The following constant elasticity of substitution (CES) aggregator is used for domestically produced consumption goods:

$$C_t^d = \left[(1-\gamma_2)^{\frac{1}{\theta_2}}(C_t^h)^{\frac{\theta_2-1}{\theta_2}} + (\gamma_2)^{\frac{1}{\theta_2}}(C_t^x)^{\frac{\theta_2-1}{\theta_2}}\right]^{\frac{\theta_2}{\theta_2-1}}. \tag{4.6}$$

The relative demands for the home nontraded goods and the export goods are given by the following equations:

$$C_t^h = (1-\gamma_2)\left(\frac{P_t^h}{P_t^d}\right)^{-\theta_2} C_t^d, \tag{4.7}$$

$$C_t^x = \gamma_2\left(\frac{P_t^x}{P_t^d}\right)^{-\theta_2} C_t^d, \tag{4.8}$$

where the parameters γ_2 and $(1-\gamma_2)$ are the shares of the export and nontraded goods in domestic production of consumption goods, and θ_2 is the intertemporal elasticity of substitution.

The domestically produced price index is given by the following CES aggregator:

$$P_t^d = \left[(1-\gamma_2)(P_t^h)^{1-\theta_2} + \gamma_2(P_t^x)^{1-\theta_2}\right]^{\frac{1}{1-\theta_2}}. \tag{4.9}$$

In the same manner, the overall price index, of course, is a CES function of the price of foreign and domestic consumption goods:

$$P_t = \left[(1-\gamma_1)(P_t^d)^{1-\theta_1} + \gamma_1(P_t^f)^{1-\theta_1}\right]^{\frac{1}{1-\theta_1}}. \tag{4.10}$$

In addition to buying consumption goods, households put deposits M_t in the bank, which pay a net return R_t^m, and receive dividends from Π_t from firms, as well as returns R_t^k from its capital stock. The household pays taxes on labor income $\tau W_t L_t$ and on consumption $\tau_c C_t$. The following equation gives the household budget constraint (P_t^f is the price of imported investment goods):

$$W_t L_t + (1 + R_{t-1}^m)M_{t-1} + \Pi_t + R_t^k K_t$$
$$= P_t C_t (1 + \tau_c) + M_t + \tau W_t L_t + P_t^f I_t + P_t^f \left(\frac{\phi (I_t - \delta \overline{K})^2}{2K_t} \right). \tag{4.11}$$

We assume that government spending G is bundled with consumption for utility in the CES aggregator. We do this to indicate that there is a reason for government spending to take place, that such spending creates externalities for consumption:

$$\widetilde{C}_t = \left[\phi C_t^{-\varkappa} + (1 - \phi) G_{t-1}^{-\varkappa} \right]^{-\frac{1}{\varkappa}}. \tag{4.12}$$

We make this assumption, rather than having government spending affect productivity in the traded and nontraded sectors, for several reasons. One, cited above, is that government spending in Japan has been less and less effective in mitigating the business cycle, which led to the loss of power by the Liberal Democratic Party in 2009. The second reason is that the aging population has put greater demand on government spending in the form of health care and social services. Such expenditures are thus characterized as activities complementing the utility of consumption in the representative household utility function.

However, household utility does not simply come from the current consumption bundle. Rather, habit persistence applies to this consumption index when it enters the specific utility function, so that the relevant consumption index is deflated by the habit stock, H_t. The habit stock is a function of the lagged average consumption bundle, raised to the power ρ, the habit persistence parameter:

$$H_t = \overline{\widetilde{C}}_{t-1}^{\rho} \tag{4.13}$$

The habit stock is widely used in these DSGE models for smoothing consumption response to exogenous shocks. Without such an assumption, impulse response functions jump too fast, and fail to match impulse response functions based on vector autoregressive (VAR) estimation of actual data. However, as Grüne and Semmler (2008) point out, habit persistence is also able to increase the equity premium by producing a time-varying risk aversion arising from the change in consumption.

Overall utility is a positive function of the consumption bundle, deflated by the habit stock, and a negative function of labor:

$$U(\widetilde{C}_t / H_t, L_t) = Z_t^C \frac{(\widetilde{C}_t / H_t)^{1-\eta}}{1 - \eta} - \gamma \frac{L_t^{1+\varpi}}{1 + \varpi}. \tag{4.14}$$

Again, this is the standard utility specification in the open-economy new Keynesian framework. Grüne and Semmler (2008) point out that alternative utility specifications, based on loss aversion from prospect theory, can take us much further in replicating key features of asset return.

The parameter η is the relative risk aversion coefficient, while γ is the disutility of labor, and ϖ the Frisch Labor Supply Elasticity. The variable Z_t^C is a shock to the utility of consumption and evolves according to the following law of motion:

$$\ln(Z_t^C) = \rho_C \ln(Z_{t-1}^C) + (1-\rho_C)\ln(\overline{Z}^C) + \epsilon_{Z^C,t} \tag{4.15}$$

$$\epsilon_{Z^C,t} \sim N(0, \sigma_{\epsilon_{Z^C}^2}). \tag{4.16}$$

The household chooses the paths of consumption, labor, deposits, investment, and capital to maximize the expected present value of its utility function subject to the budget constraint and the law of motion for capital. Thus, the objective function of the household is given by the following expression:

$$\underset{\{C_t, L_t, M_t, I_t, K_t\}}{\text{Max}} \mathbf{E}_t \sum_{\iota=0}^{\infty} \beta^{\iota} U(\widetilde{C}_{t+\iota}/H_{t+\iota}, L_{t+\iota}), \tag{4.17}$$

where the parameter β represents the constant, exogenous discount factor.

This optimization is subject to the two constraints, one for income and the other for the accumulation of capital. Each of these constraints is associated with a Lagrangean multiplier. The first is Λ_t, the familiar marginal utility of income or wealth, associated with the budget constraint, while Q_t, known as Tobin's Q, is the shadow price of capital for the export-goods sector, and is associated with the accumulation equation for K_t.

$$W_t L_t + (1 + R_{t-1}^m) M_{t-1} + \Pi_t + R_{t-1}^k K_{t-1} \tag{4.18}$$

$$= P_t C_t (1 + \tau_c) + M_t + \tau W_t L_t + P_t^f I_t + P_t^f \left(\frac{\phi (I_t - \delta \overline{K})^2}{2 K_{t-1}} \right),$$

$$K_t = (1-\delta) K_{t-1} + I_t. \tag{4.19}$$

Optimizing t with respect to the decision variables C_t, L_t, M_t, I_t, K_t yields the following set of first-order conditions for the representative household:

$$\Lambda_t P_t = [\widetilde{C}_t / H_t]^{-\eta} \frac{1}{H_t} (\widetilde{C}_t)^{1-\varkappa} \phi (C_t)^{-\varkappa-1} Z_t^C, \tag{4.20}$$

$$\gamma L_t^{\varpi} = \Lambda_t (1 - \tau^w) W_t, \tag{4.21}$$

$$\Lambda_t = \mathbf{E}_t [\beta \Lambda_{t+1} (1 + R_t^m)], \tag{4.22}$$

$$Q_t = \mathbf{E}_t \left\{ \beta\Lambda_{t+1}R^k_{t+1} + \beta\Lambda_{t+1}P^f_{t+1}\frac{(\phi[I_{t+1} - \delta\overline{K}])^2}{2(K_t)^2} + \beta Q_{t+1}(1-\delta) \right\} \quad (4.23)$$

$$I_t = \delta\overline{K} + \frac{K_t}{\phi}\left(\frac{Q_t}{\Lambda_t} - P^f_t\right). \quad (4.24)$$

The first equation, Eq. 4.20, simply tells us that the marginal utility of wealth is equal to the marginal utility of consumption divided by the price level. Equation 4.21 states that the marginal disutility of labor is equal to the marginal utility of consumption provided by the after-tax wage. Equation 4.22 is the Keynes–Ramsey rule for optimal saving: the marginal utility of wealth today should be equal to the discounted marginal utility tomorrow, multiplied by the gross rate of return on saving (in the form of deposits).

The equation for Tobin's Q (Eq. 4.23) tells us that the value of capital today is the discounted marginal utility of capital tomorrow, multiplied by the return to capital, in addition to the reduced value of adjustment costs in the future (due to the higher level of capital) and the discounted value of capital tomorrow, net of depreciation.

Finally, the investment equation tells us that investment will be equal to the steady state investment, $\delta\overline{K}$, when $\frac{Q_t}{\Lambda_t} = P^f_t$. Any increase in Tobin's Q_t, relative to the marginal utility of income and the price of investment goods, will trigger increases in investment.

Production and Technology

Nontraded Services

The nontraded goods and service sector is a function of labor and a productivity shock Z^h_t:

$$Y^h_t = Z^h_t L^h_t. \quad (4.25)$$

The technology shock to nontraded services (including health care and social services) follows the autoregressive process:

$$\ln(z^h_t) = \rho_{Z^h}\ln(Z^h_{t-1}) + (1-\rho_{Z^h})\ln(\overline{Z}^h) + \epsilon_{Zh,t} \quad (4.26)$$

$$\epsilon_{Z^h,t} \sim N(0, \sigma^2_{Z^h}). \quad (4.27)$$

The demand for the nontraded home goods-services can be for both domestic consumption services and government-provided services:

$$Y^h_t = C^h_t + G_t. \quad (4.28)$$

We assume that the firm faces a liquidity constraint and must borrow an amount from banks each quarter to pay a fraction μ_h of its wage bill, at the borrowing rate R_t^n.

The total profits (or dividends) of the export firm is given by the following identity:

$$\Pi_t^h = P_t^h Y_t^h - (1 + \mu h R_t^n) W_t L_t^h. \tag{4.29}$$

Traded Goods

The firm producing traded goods uses a CES production function:

$$Y_t^x = A^x[(1-\alpha)(L_t^x)^{-\kappa} + \alpha(K_t)^{-\kappa}]^{-\frac{1}{\kappa}}. \tag{4.30}$$

The parameter α is the share of capital in production, while κ is the CES aggregator, while A^x is a scale parameter.

Export demand by foreigners, C_t^*, depends on its own lag, as well as to the deviation of the real exchange rate from its steady state. It is also subject to a stochastic shock, ϵ_{C^*}, t at time t:

$$C_t^* = \rho_{C^*} C_{t-1}^* + (1-\rho_{C^*})\overline{C^*} + (1-\rho_{C^*})\rho_{C*S}[S_t/P_t^h - \overline{S}/\overline{P}^h] + \epsilon_{C^*,t} \tag{4.31}$$

$$\epsilon_{C^*,t} \sim N(0, \sigma_{C^{*2}}). \tag{4.32}$$

Under an open economy setting we also assume that the price of the export good in domestic currency is simply equal to the exchange rate S_t multiplied by the world export price, P_{t*}^x. We assume that the world export price follows the following exogenous stochastic process:

$$\ln(P_t^{x^*}) = \rho_{Px^*} \ln(P_{t-1}^{x^*}) + (1-\rho_{Px^*}) \ln(\overline{P}_t^{x^*}) + \epsilon_{Px^*,t} \tag{4.33}$$

$$\epsilon_{Px^*,t} \sim N(0, \sigma_{P^*}^2). \tag{4.34}$$

Total demand for the export good is composed of the local demand (for consumption purposes) as well as the foreign demand:

$$Y_t^x = C_t^x + C_t^*.$$

These firms also facing a liquidity constraint for meeting their wage bill:

$$N_t^x = \mu_x W_t + L_t^x. \tag{4.35}$$

The profits of the export-goods firms are given by the following relation:

$$\Pi_t^x = P_t^x Y_t^x - (1 + \mu_x R_t^n) W_t L_t^x - R_t^k K_t. \tag{4.36}$$

Optimizing profits implies the following first-order condition for cost minimization:

$$\frac{\partial Y_t^x}{\partial L_t^x} = (1 + \mu_x R_t^n)\frac{W_t}{P_t^x}, \tag{4.37}$$

$$\frac{\partial Y_t^x}{\partial K_t} = \frac{R_t^k}{P_t^x}. \tag{4.38}$$

Labor Mobility

We assume that labor can move between the nontraded goods and traded-goods sectors.

Calvo Pricing for Home Goods

The pricing for home-goods and service-providing firms is different from that of traded-goods-producing firms. We assume sticky monopolistically competitive firms in the home goods and services market.

Let the marginal cost at time t be given by the following expression:

$$A_t = \frac{(1 + \mu_h R_t^n) W_t}{(A^h Z_t^h)}. \tag{4.39}$$

In the Calvo price setting world, there are forward-looking price setters and backward-looking setters. Assuming at time t a probability of persistence of the price at ξ, with demand for the product from firm j given by $Y_t^h(P_t^h)^{\zeta}$, the expected marginal cost, in recursive formulation, is presented by the expression for $A^{mc}{}_t$. The expected demand, for the given price, is given by the variable $A^{dmd}{}_t$.

$$A_t^{mc} = Y_t^h(P_t^h)^{\zeta} A_t + \beta\xi A_{t+1}^{mc}, \tag{4.40}$$

$$A_t^{dmd} = Y_t^h(P_t^h)^{\zeta} + \beta\xi A_{t+1}^{dmd}, \tag{4.41}$$

$$P_t^o = \frac{A_t^{mc}}{A_t^{dmd}}, \tag{4.42}$$

$$P_t^{h,b} = P_{t-1}^h \left(\frac{P_{t-1}}{P_{t-2}}\right)^{\kappa^i} (1 + \widetilde{\pi}_t)^{\kappa^{\pi}}, \tag{4.43}$$

$$P_t^h = \left[\xi (P_t^{h,b})^{1-\zeta} + (1-\xi)(P_t^o)^{1-\zeta}\right]^{\frac{1}{1-\xi}} \tag{4.44}$$

The backward-looking price setters do not keep the price fixed. They will set their price equal to the price at the previous period, P_{t-1}^h multiplied by the previous period's inflation, $\left(\frac{P_{t-1}}{P_{t-2}}\right)$ raised to an indexation parameter κ^i, and by the gross inflation target announced by the central bank, $(1 + \widetilde{\pi}_t)$, representing monetary policy statements, relative to inflation targets, raised to a parameter κ^π.

Imported Goods

Importers provide goods for investment in domestically produced traded-goods firms (some of which are exported as part of a global supply chain), as well as for final consumption (in the form of materials such as fuel):

$$Y^f = C^f + I. \tag{4.45}$$

We assume importers must borrow a fraction μ_f of the cost of these imported goods in order to bring them to the home market for domestic consumers and investors:

$$N_t^f = \mu_f(S_t P_t^{f*} Y_t^f), \tag{4.46}$$

where P_t^{f*} is the world price of the import goods and S_t is the exchange rate. The domestic cost of the imported goods is given by:

$$\begin{aligned} P^f &= [\mu_f(1 + R_t^n) + (1 - \mu_f)](S_t P_{t^*}) \\ &= [1 + \mu_f R_t^n] S_t P_t^*. \end{aligned} \tag{4.47}$$

We thus introduce financial friction in the pricing of imported goods, in the form of the borrowing by firms or consumers to finance the imported goods.

The Financial Sector

Banks lend to all three types of firms:

$$N_t = N_t^x + N_t^h + N_t^f. \tag{4.48}$$

In addition to these firms, the banks lend to the government B_t^g and receive a risk-free interest rate R_t.

They borrow from foreign financial centers the amount B^f and pay a risk premium above the domestic interest rate when such foreign debt exceeds a steady-state level $\overline{B^f}$:

$$\Phi_t = \max\{0, \varphi[e^{(|B_{t-1}^f - \overline{B^f}|)} - 1]B_{t-1}^f\}. \tag{4.49}$$

The banks thus pay a gross interest rate $R_{t^*} + \Phi_t$ on their outstanding dollar-denominated debt B^f_{t-1} to foreign financial centers.

We used endogenous risk premium on foreign borrowing in one device, as pointed out by Schmitt-Grohé and Uribe (2003) for closing open-economy models. Of course, this specification is an approximation. In this specification, the risk premium can be enlarged or decreased by the size of the coefficient φ. In practice, this parameter will depend on expectations of political commitment to debt reduction and expectations of recovery. Below, with this simplified framework, we take up interactions between macroeconomic variables and the risk premium, for given large or small values of the parameter ϕ.

In addition to paying deposits the interest rate R^m_t, we assume that banks are also required to set aside a required ratio of reserves on outstanding deposits, $\phi_M M_t$. The relevant opportunity cost of holding these reserves is of course the amount the banks can earn by holding risk-free government bonds, $\phi_M R_t M_t$. In addition, banks are required to set aside a fraction of capital against their outstanding loans, $\phi_N N_t$. As in the case of the required reserves against deposits, the opportunity cost is given by $\phi_N R_t N_t$. We also assume that there is a cost in the form of risk to holding government bonds above the steady state, given by $\phi_B(B_{t-1} - \overline{B})$.

The following balance-sheet identity gives the gross profit of the banking sector:

$$\begin{aligned}\Pi^B_t &= \left(1 + R^g_{t-1}\right) B^g_{t-1} + \left(1 + R^{ff}_{t-1}\right) FF_{t-1} + \left(1 + R^n_{t-1}\right) N_{t-1} \\ &\quad - (1 + R^*_{t-1} + \Phi_{t-1}) B^f_{t-1} S_t - (1 + R^m_{t-1}) M_{t-1} - B^g_t - FF_t \\ &\quad - N_t + S_t B^f_t + M_t - \phi_M R^{ff}_{t-1} M_{t-1} - \phi_N R^{ff}_{t-1} N_{t-1} - \phi_B (B_{t-1} - \overline{B}) \qquad (4.50)\end{aligned}$$

where FF_t represents returns on bank lending or borrowing from the central bank, and R^{ff}_t is the risk-free rate of return on these loans or debts.

The bank maximizes the present discounted value of its profits, given by V^B_t, with respect to its portfolio of assets (loans to the government, to the federal funds market, and to firms, B^g_t, FF_t and N_t) and liabilities (deposits from households and borrowing from foreign financial centers M_t and B^f_t).

$$\underset{\{B^g_t, N_t, M_t, B^f_t\}}{\text{Max}} \quad V^B_t = \Pi^B_t + \beta V^B_{t+1}.$$

The set of first-order conditions leads to the familiar set of spreads for interest rates, as well as the interest-parity equation:

$$R^g_t = R^{ff}_t + \phi_B, \qquad (4.51)$$

$$R^n_t = R^{ff}_t + \phi_N, \qquad (4.52)$$

$$R^m_t = R^{ff}_t - \phi_M, \qquad (4.53)$$

$$(1 + R^g_t) S_t = (1 + R^*_t + \Phi_t + \Phi'_t B^f_t) S_{t+1} \qquad (4.54)$$

The foreign interest rate evolves according to the following law of motion:

$$R_t^* = \rho_{R^*} R_{t-1}^* + (1 - \rho_{R^*})\overline{R}^* + \epsilon_{R^*t}$$
$$\epsilon_{R^*} \sim N(0, \sigma_{R^*}^2).$$

We assume an inflation-targeting Taylor rule for setting the risk-free rate for banks borrowing or lending to the central bank:

$$R_t^{ff} = \rho_r R_{t-1}^{ff} + (1 - \rho_r)\rho_\pi \pi_t + (1 - \rho_r)\rho_y y_t + (1 - \rho_r)\overline{R}^{ff} + \epsilon_{Mt}. \tag{4.55}$$

$$\epsilon_{M,t} \sim N(0, \sigma_M^2). \tag{4.56}$$

The coefficients ρ_r and ρ_π are the smoothing parameter and inflation coefficient, with $0 < \rho_r < 1$ and $\rho_\pi > 1$. $\overline{R}$ is the steady state interest rate, equal to the steady state foreign interest rate R^* and $\widehat{\pi}_t$ is the deviation of actual inflation from the target rate of inflation, and $\widehat{y}_t$ is the deviation of output from the target (steady- state) output in log-levels. Again, we assume a shock to monetary policy given by $\epsilon_{M,t}$, normally distributed with variance $\sigma_M{}^2$. Given that the central bank sets the risk-free interest rate, it provides reserves (or takes out reserves) to the banking sector through open market operations to insure a balance-sheet equilibrium:

$$\begin{aligned} \Delta FF_t = {} & N_t + B_t - R_{t-1}^{ff} FF_{t-1} - (1 + R_{t-1}^{ff} + \phi_N - \phi_N R_{t-1}^{ff}) N_{t-1} \\ & + (1 + R_{t-1}^{ff} - \phi_M - \phi_M R_{t-1}^{ff}) M_{t-1} - M_t - (1 + R_{t-1}^{g}) B_{t-1} \\ & + (1 + R_{t-1}^* + \Phi_{t-1}) B_{t-1}^f S_{t-1} - B_t^f S_t. \end{aligned} \tag{4.57}$$

Fiscal Policy

The government takes in taxes from the households and engages in spending on traded goods. We assume that spending may be either procyclical or countercyclical depending on the value of ρ_{GY}, that there is smoothing in government consumption, and there is a stochastic component to spending:

$$G_t = (1 - \rho_G)\overline{G} + \rho_G G_{t-1} + (1 - \rho_G)\rho_{GY}(Y_{t-1} - \overline{Y}) + \epsilon_G t \tag{4.58}$$

$$\epsilon_{G,t} \sim N(0, \sigma_G^2). \tag{4.59}$$

Given its source of labor and consumption tax revenue, the fiscal borrowing requirement is given by the following identities:

$$TAX_t = \tau W_t L_t + \tau_c P_t C_t, \tag{4.60}$$

$$B_t^g = (1 + R_{t-1}) B_{t-1}^g + P_t^h G_t - TAX_t. \tag{4.61}$$

Foreign Assets and Interest Rates

The aggregate foreign borrowing or asset accumulation evolves through the following identity:

$$S_tB_t^f = [1 + R_{t-1}^* + \Phi_{t-1}]S_tB_{t-1}^f + P_t^f(C_t^f + I_t) - P_t^x(C_t^*). \tag{4.62}$$

It should be noted that the risk premium embedded in the accumulation of foreign debt effectively closes this open economy model, so that the domestic consumption and foreign debt levels do not become indeterminate. There are other ways to close the open economy model, such as adjustment costs on foreign debt accumulation, or an endogenous discount factor (see Schmitt-Grohé and Uribe, 2003). We feel that the incorporation of a time-varying endogenous risk premium is a more intuitive way to close this model. Schmitt-Grohé and Uribe (2003) have shown that the choice to close an open economy makes little difference for the dynamics of the model.

4.3 Calibrated Parameters and Bayesian Estimation

Before turning to Bayesian estimation, we first calibrate the parameters that determine the steady state. Following Christiano et al. (2007), we calibrate parameters that control the steady state, and estimate with Bayesian methods those parameters that affect the dynamics and stochastic properties of the model (Table 4.1). The reason we simply calibrate and do not estimate the first set of parameters is that computation of the steady state is very time intensive.

The parameters are set for a quarterly model. The discount parameter, β, is similar to most other models for quarterly data. The habit persistence parameter *is* within range of most models, such as that of Smets and Wouters (2003). The depreciation rate for capital, δ, is relatively high. We assume that the capital in our model is specific to the nontraded sector. Since investment goods in this sector are imported goods, we assume that the depreciation is high, while the adjustment cost parameter, φ_K, would be relatively low.

The ratios of consumption of foreign goods in the total consumption basket, γ_1; the share of export-goods consumption in the total domestic consumption basket, γ_2; and the tax parameters for labor income and consumption, τ, τ_C, all come from national income accounts. The relative risk aversion coefficient, η; the labor supply elasticity; and the disutility of labor, γ_L, are commonly used. We assume a higher intertemporal elasticity between consumption of home and foreign goods in the total consumption index than the elasticity of intratemporal substitution between consumption of export and home goods in the domestic consumption index. Hence, $\theta_1 > \theta_2$.

Table 4.1 Calibrated parameters

Symbol	Definition	Values
β	Discount factor	0.99
ϱ	Habit parameter	0.8
δ	Capital depreciation	0.06
ϕ_{K^h}	Adjustment cost	0.005
γ_1	Foreign cons. in total cons. index	0.3
γ_2	Con of export good in dom.cons. index	0.1
η	Relative risk aversion parameter	5.0
ϖ	Labor supply elasticity	0.5
γ_L	Disutility of labor	0.5
ϕ_C	Consumption in CES utility	0.95
$\varkappa$	CES utility coefficient	−0.1
θ_1	Intratemporal substitution elasticity, total cons	2.5
θ_2	Intratemporal substitution elasticity, domestic cons	1.5
τ, τ_C	Tax rates on labor income and consumption	0.2,0.1
μ_x, μ_h, μ_f	Financial friction parameters	1,1,1
ζ	Substitution elasticity for differentiated goods	6
κ	CES substitution parameter in production	−0.1
α	Capital coefficient in export goods	0.4
ϕ_M, ϕ_N	Deposit and lending costs for banks	0.1, 0.15
ϕ_B	Risk coefficient for government bonds	0, 0.3

The financial friction parameters representing the borrowing needs of export, home-goods, and importing firms were all set equal at a value of one. We assume in such a financially developed economy as Singapore that firms in any of the sectors would have easy access to short-term credit. The capital coefficient in the export production function, α_1, is set to replicate the shares of capital and labor in the economy. Finally, the banking reserve and lending cost parameters, ϕ_M *and* ϕ_N, are set to replicate observed low spreads in the financial sector.

For the risk parameter on government bonds, in our base simulation, we assume that it is equal to zero. Thus, the government bond yield and the risk-free rate are identical. In our counterfactual simulation we set the parameter at 3, with the assumption that for a percentage increase of government bonds above the steady state, the bond risk increases by 33 basis points.

Table 4.2 shows the prior distributions with the means and standard errors as well as values for the infima and suprema of the distributions. We make use of relatively flat priors for the standard deviations for the volatilities of the shocks in the model. The coefficients we estimate relate to stochastic process for government spending,

Table 4.2 Bayesian priors: parameters and distributions

Volatility	Name	Distribution	Mean	Std Dev	Inf	Sup
σG	Gov. spending	Inv. Gamma	0 01	2	0.005	0.5
σZ_x	Export prod.	Inv. Gamma	0 01	2	0.005	0.5
$\sigma PX*$	Terms of trade	Inv. Gamma	0 01	2	0.005	0.5
$\sigma R*$	For. interest	Inv. Gamma	0 01	2	0.005	0.5
$\sigma C*$	Exports	Inv. Gamma	0 01	2	0.005	0.5
σC	Consumption	Inv. Gamma	0 01	2	0.005	0.5
σM	Monetary rule	Inv. Gamma	0 01	2	0.005	0.5
σ_{Z^h}	Home goods prod	Inv. Gamma	0 01	2	0.005	0.5
Coefficient						
Λ	DSGE weight	Uniform	—	—	0	2
ρR	Taylor lag	Beta	0.5	0.2	0.1	0.9
P_π	Taylor inflation	Normal	1.5	0.2	1.1	2
P_y	Taylor output	Beta	0.5	0.5	0.01	0.95
ρG	Gov. spending	Beta	0.5	0.5	0.01	0.95
ρGY	Gov. spending	Normal	0.0	0.1	-0.3	0.3
$\rho PX*$	Terms of trade	Beta	0.5	0.2	0.01	0.95
$\rho R*$	For. interest	Beta	0.5	0.2	0.01	0.95
$\rho C*$	Export	Beta	0.5	0.2	0.01	0.95
$\rho C * S$	Export Ex. Rate	Beta	0.25	0.2	0.01	0.95
ρ_{Z^h}	Home goods	Beta	0.5	0.2	0.01	0.95
ξ	Calvo pricing	Beta	0.5	0.2	0.01	0.95

DSGE dynamic stochastic general equilibrium

and the persistence coefficient for exports, export prices, and markup pricing shocks. We allow the government spending coefficient with respect to output to be positive or negative, thus allowing the data to determine if spending is pro or countercyclical. We make a similar assumption for the coefficient of exports with respect to the real exchange rate. The coefficients for the Taylor rule are standard.

Parameter and Volatility Estimates

We estimated the models for the period 1988–2007 for the following observables: consumption, government, exports, terms of trade, foreign interest rate, inflation, and the exchange rate. Except for the foreign interest rate, the data are log first differed. The model is estimated in a pure DSGE framework as well as in a DSGE/VAR framework, following Del Negro and Schorfheide (2004), Adjemian et al. (2008), and An and Kang (2009).

Table 4.3 Fit of DSGE models

		Marginal likelihood	
Specification	λ	Laplace	Harmonic mean
DSGE	Inf	815.589	882.359
DSGE/VAR	1.406	817.623	893.453

DSGE dynamic stochastic general equilibrium, *VAR* Vector Autoregressive

We estimate the model for a DSGE framework and a DSGE/VAR framework. The combined DSGE/VAR framework starts with the premise that the DSGE framework is unspecified and needs to be supplemented with a VAR, in our case with four lags. The question is, what is the relative weight for the VAR and DSGE for the best fit? In a Bayesian context, the relative weight for the VAR is the value $1/(1+\lambda)$. For the pure DSGE model, with no weight given to the VAR, $\lambda = \infty$ while for a pure VAR model, $\lambda = 0$.

We estimated the DSGE model under the restriction $\lambda = \infty$ and for the optimal λ within an interval $[0, 2]$. The best fit gives $\lambda = 1.406$ by both the Laplace and harmonic mean measurements of the marginal likelihood (Table 4.3).

Volatility and Parameter Estimates

Table 4.4 pictures the results for Japan under the pure DSGE and the DSGE/VAR framework for the mean $\lambda = 1.406$.

The table contains the mean of the Bayesian estimates for 200,000 simulations in four blocks. We also show the infimum and supremum of each estimate for a 95% confidence interval.

We see that the highest persistence is in the markup pricing behavior under both methods. The major difference in the estimates given by the two methods is in the persistence coefficient for the shock to adjustment costs, ρ_A. The pure DSGE method gives a relatively low value while the DSGE/VAR a relatively high one. Under both methods, government spending can be either counter or procyclical.

The effect of the real exchange rate on exports, given by $\rho_C * S$, is relatively small but positive in both the DSGE and DSGE/VAR methods. The Calvo price stickiness coefficient, ξ, is also small, relative to commonly accepted specifications of 0.75 or 0.8 for the US and the euro Area, under both methods. The estimated volatilities are all relatively small, but somewhat larger in the pure DSGE than in the DSGE/VaR, with the shock to nontraded goods production and consumption demand having the largest values in both frameworks.

We also see that the response of export demand to the exchange rate, given by the parameter $\rho_C * S$, at 0.009, is much smaller than the prior mean of 0.25, indicating that there is learning from the data, in the sense that the posterior mean departs quite a bit from the prior mean. The message from this estimation is that Japanese exports are not very sensitive to exchange-rate changes. This finding is consistent, of course,

Table 4.4 Parameter and volatility estimates, DSGE and DSGE/VaR models DSGE DSGE/VAR

	DSGE			DSGE/VaR		
	Mean	Inf	Sup	Mean	Inf	Sup
Coefficient						
λ	∞	—	—	1.406	1.134	1.576
ρR	0.046	0.016	0.079	0.131	0.108	0.185
$\rho\pi$	1.504	1.501	1.506	1.490	1.488	1.491
ρy	0.333	0.236	0.415	0.146	0.063	0.204
ρC	0.609	0.547	0.648	0.151	0.108	0.197
ρG	0.933	0.918	0.949	0.573	0.542	0.598
ρGY	0.094	0.081	0.111	0.151	0.132	0.170
$\rho PX*$	0.834	0.810	0.854	0.411	0.323	0.468
$\rho R*$	0.942	0.935	0.949	0.915	0.889	0.948
ρZx	0.130	0.104	0.154	0.170	0.138	0.205
$\rho C*$	0.878	0.848	0.910	0.574	0.557	0.592
$\rho C * S$	0.094	0.067	0.139	0.032	0.018	0.047
ξ	0.592	0.505	0.637	0.523	0.480	0.576
Volatility						
σG	0.010	0.009	0.011	0.009	0.007	0.010
σM	0.072	0.045	0.089	0.020	0.014	0.026
σ_{Z^h}	0.140	0.118	0.156	0.036	0.026	0.047
σ_{PX*}	0.045	0.040	0.051	0.018	0.014	0.022
σ_C^*	0.042	0.036	0.048	0.023	0.017	0.027
σ_{C^*}	0.009	0.008	0.010	0.008	0.007	0.009
σ_C	0.100	0.085	0.114	0.044	0.035	0.054

DSGE dynamic stochastic general equilibrium, *VAR* Vector Autoregressive

with the assumption that most of the Japanese trade, both in imports and exports, is in intermediate goods, as part of a global supply chain, and thus less sensitive to short-term exchange rate fluctuations.

Similarly, for government spending, we see a small but significant procyclical component in the estimation results. While the prior mean is 0, the DSGE/VAR gives a posterior mean of 0.151. This result is consistent with the political business cycle theory of government spending.

When times are good, politicians have every incentive to spend more, to ensure more votes. Lim and McNelis (2012) have shown how such procyclical spending behavior can reduce income inequality in an open economy framework.

We also see that the volatility posterior mean estimates depart quite a bit from the prior mean values. Significant learning (in the form of differences between prior and posterior means) takes place in the estimation of the shock volatility to nontraded goods and services and to the Taylor rule. Not surprisingly, these sources of volatility play important roles in the overall variances of inflation, consumption, and the exchange rate.

Table 4.5 Variance decomposition

DSGE variable		Volatility						
		σG	$\sigma R*$	σM	σ_{Z^h}	$\sigma_P X^*$	σC^*	σC
	$\hat{\pi}$	0.018	0.001	0.504	0.042	0.325	0.096	0.014
	$\hat{c}$	0.019	0.001	0.436	0.048	0.323	0.087	0.085
	$\hat{s}$	0.004	0.000	0.195	0.457	0.265	0.076	0.003
DSGE/VAR								
	$\hat{\pi}$	0.040	0.003	0.364	0.028	0.127	0.434	0.005
	$\hat{c}$	0.047	0.002	0.256	0.032	0.119	0.324	0.221
	$\hat{s}$	0.007	0.001	0.087	0.230	0.269	0.405	0.001

DSGE dynamic stochastic general equilibrium, *VAR* Vector Autoregressive

Variance Decomposition

Of course, these estimates tell us nothing about the relative importance of each of the exogenous shocks for key endogenous variables of the model. Table 4.5 gives the mean variance decomposition of the Bayesian estimation under both the DSGE and DSGE/VAR frameworks.

We see a number of expected results—for example, that the shock to consumption explains more than 20% of the variance in consumption, the shock to terms of trade and production are important for the exchange rate, and the shock to export demand accounts for more than 30% of consumption in the DSGE/VAR model. The shock to the Taylor rule accounts for more than 50% of the variance of inflation in the DSGE and 36% in the DSGE/VAR approaches, while the shock to home-goods production explains quite a bit of the variation of the exchange rate.

4.4 Counterfactual Simulations

The results come from 500 simulation experiences for a sample size of 100. The model is solved with a second-order perturbation method. At each simulation, we calculate the volatility of key variables and then use the Epanechnikov kernel for evaluating the distribution of these volatilities for alternative seeds for the random shocks to government spending, with $\sigma_G = 0.01$. All other shocks are set to zero.

We first compare the behavior of key variables under the base "no risk" and counterfactual risk scenario. Then, under the high-risk assumption, we evaluate the gains or losses from switching to an exchange-rate rule for monetary policy.

No-Risk Versus High-Risk Scenarios

Figure 4.3 pictures the kernel estimates of the volatility measures of consumption, investment, and employment under the no-risk base scenario on government bonds, and a counterfactual risk premium on government bonds. This figures shows that the risk premium on bonds leads to a jump in volatility of all three variables by more than a factor of three.

Figure 4.4 pictures the volatility distributions for inflation, the exchange rate, the interest rate, and Tobin's Q under the base and counterfactual risk scenarios. Again, there is a jump in volatility by factors of three or more when the risk premium on bonds comes into play.

Figure 4.5 pictures the distributions of liquidity provision by the central bank, as well as deposit and loan volatility in the financial sector. The distribution of liquidity provision by the central bank is slightly more diverse in the counterfactual simulation. However, volatility in deposits and loans increased by factors of 2 or more.

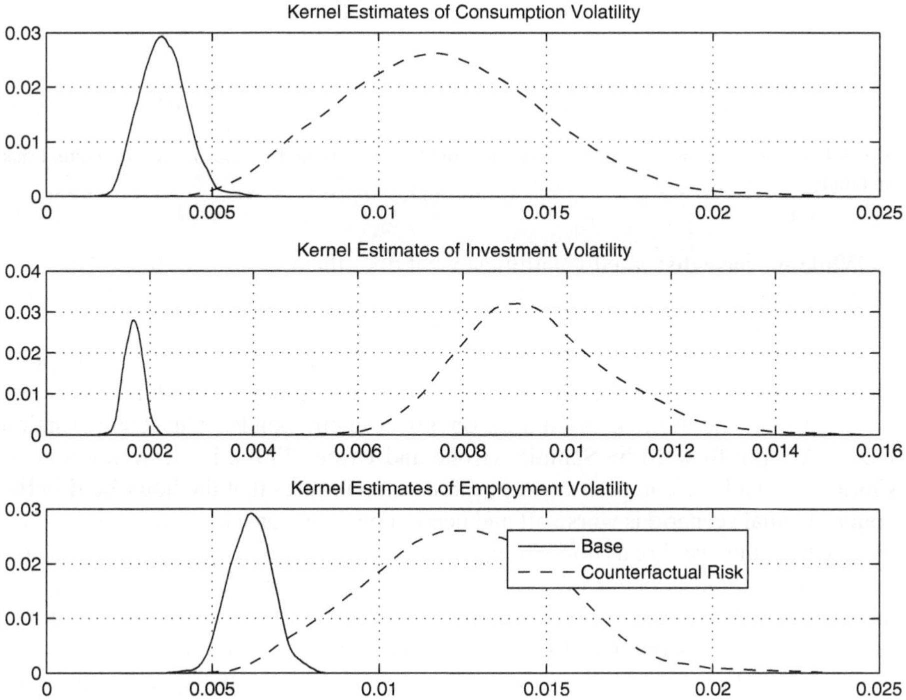

Fig. 4.3 Consumption, investment, and employment volatility under base and counterfactual risk on bonds

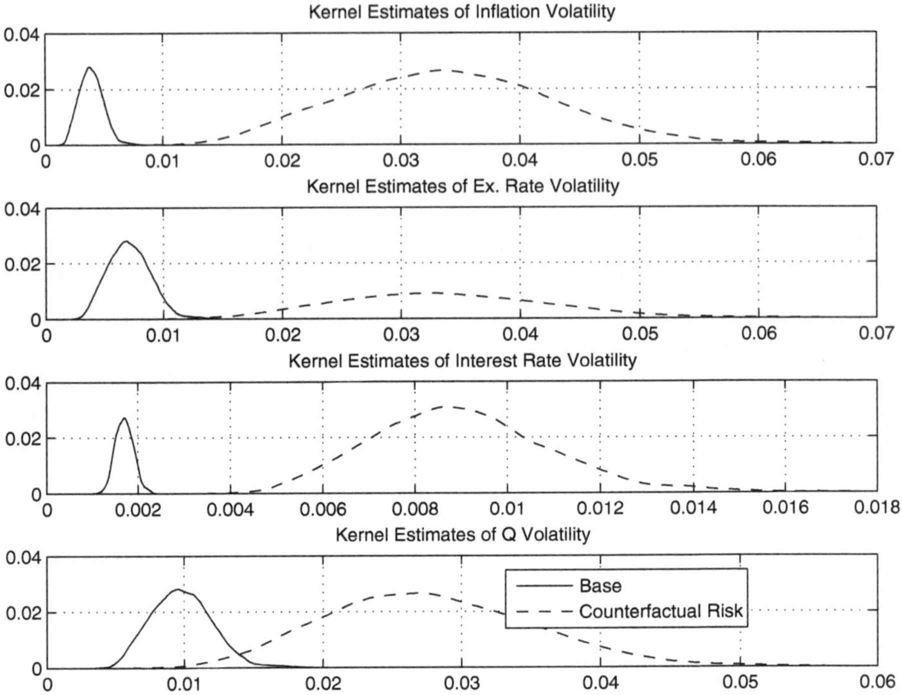

Fig. 4.4 Inflation, exchange rate, interest rate, and Q volatility under base and counterfactual risk on bonds

While we have discussed volatilities, what does this mean for welfare? One way to evaluate welfare gains or losses between two scenarios is to calculate the percent compensation one would need to equalize welfare in the two scenarios.

Figure 4.6 pictures the distribution of the implied percentage consumption compensation needed to make the representative household indifferent between the high-risk and no-risk premiums on government bonds. This compensation factor, Δ_C, put forward by Schmitt–Grohé and Uribe (2007), is a commonly used shortcut for welfare comparison. A positive value implies that the household in the counterfactual scenario is worse off and needs a positive consumption compensation to have the same welfare as households in the base scenario. A negative value means that the household is better off in the counterfactual scenario, and would have to have consumption reduced to be equal to the welfare realized in the base scenario.

Figure 4.6 shows that the distribution is skewed: 75% of the time the compensation would be positive, with a mean value of 0.31%, entailing expectation of continuing welfare losses.

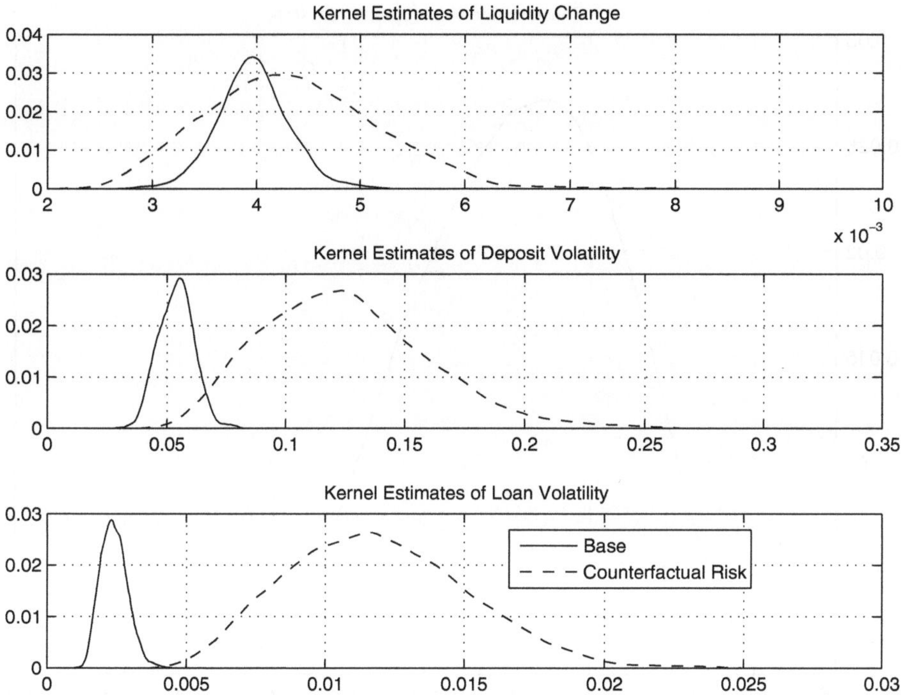

Fig. 4.5 Liquidity, deposit, and loan volatility under base and counterfactual risk on bonds

Interest Rate Versus Exchange-Rate Rule for Monetary Policy

Given the large welfare losses entailed by a risk premium on domestic debt, would a change in the monetary policy regime make any difference? Specifically, if the increased risk premium under an inflation-targeting framework leads to higher real exchange-rate volatility, would a switch to an exchange-rate targeting framework reduce overall macro volatility and improve welfare, relative to staying with the base Taylor rule inflation-targeting framework?

East Asia has many different examples of monetary regimes. While Japan, the Republic of Korea, and the Philippines follow an interest-based exchange-rate targeting framework based on a Taylor rule, Taipei,China follows a monetary aggregate rule for targeting inflation, while Singapore makes use of the exchange rate as its policy instrument for targeting inflation (see Teo (2009) for a fuller discussion of the regime in Taipei,China; for Singapore, see Yip 2002, 2005; Chow 2005; McCallum 2006).

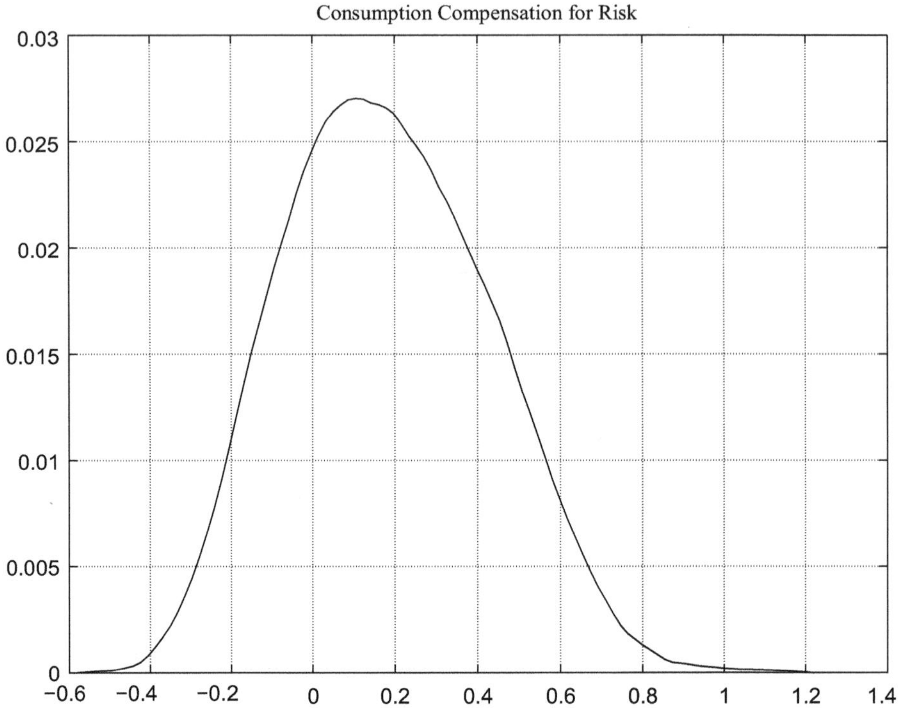

Fig. 4.6 Percentage of consumption compensation for equalizing welfare between base and counterfactual bond risk

Dropping the Taylor rule, we assume that the Bank of Japan follows a rule similar to that used by the Monetary Authority of Singapore (see McCallum, 2006):

$$\begin{aligned}[\ln(S_{t+1}) - \ln(S_t)] = \rho_S[\ln(S_t) - \ln(S_{t-1})] + (1 - \rho_s)[\ln(P_{t+1}) - \ln(P_t)] \\ - (1 - \rho_s)\rho_\pi[\ln(P_{t+1}) - \ln(P_t) - \tilde{\pi}]], \qquad (4.63)\end{aligned}$$

where π is the target rate of inflation, ρ_S is the depreciation persistence parameter, and ρ_π is the inflation coefficient.

This rule implies that in the absence of deviations from the target inflation rate, the monetary authority will follow a purchasing power parity approach to exchange-rate depreciation or appreciation. However, if inflation exceeds its target, there will be real appreciation.

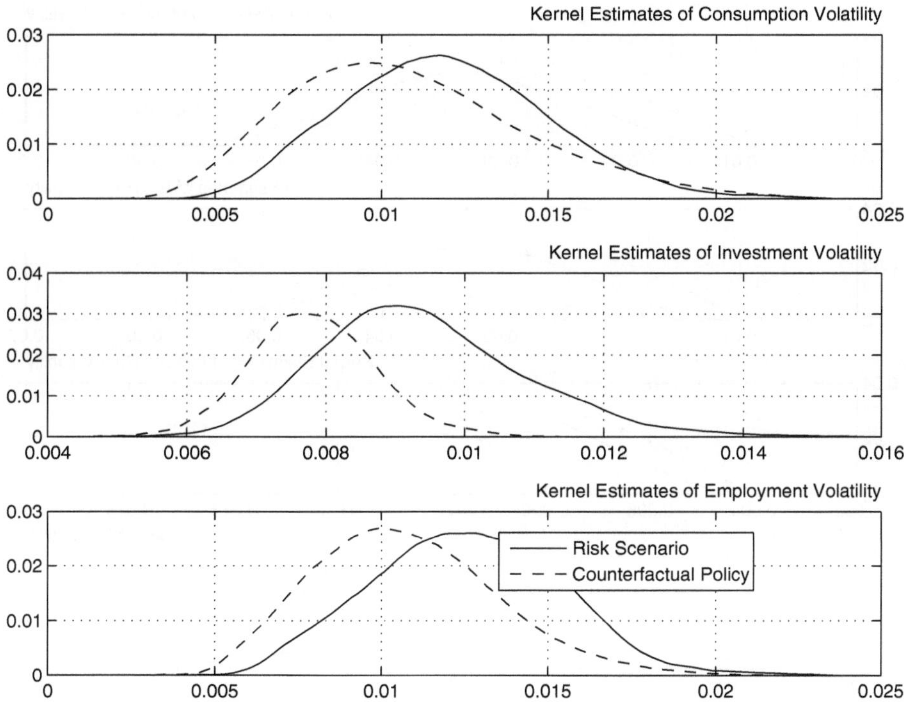

Fig. 4.7 Consumption, investment, and employment volatility under risk and counterfactual exchange-rate policy

We cannot estimate the parameters of this rule since Japan followed a Taylor rule. Instead, we specify the same persistence parameters and inflation target parameters to this rule, which were obtained from the estimated Taylor rule under the more accurate DSGE/VAR framework. Hence, $\rho_S = 0.131$ and $\rho_\pi = 1.49$.

We simulate the model with the actual Taylor rule and high risk premium as the base, and the high risk premium with exchange-rate rule as the counterfactual, again for the same set of recurrent government spending shocks.

Figure 4.7 pictures the distribution of consumption, investment, and employment volatility in the two scenarios. We see that the adoption of an exchange-rate rule reduces the volatilities of all three variables by factors of 2 or more.

Figure 4.8 shows that a similar pattern emerges for the distribution of the volatility of inflation, the exchange rate, the interest rate, and Tobin's Q.

Figure 4.9 pictures the distributions of the volatility of liquidity provision to banks, deposits, and loans. There is little change in the volatility of liquidity provision by the central bank, but there is a reduction by more than a factor of 2 for deposits and loans.

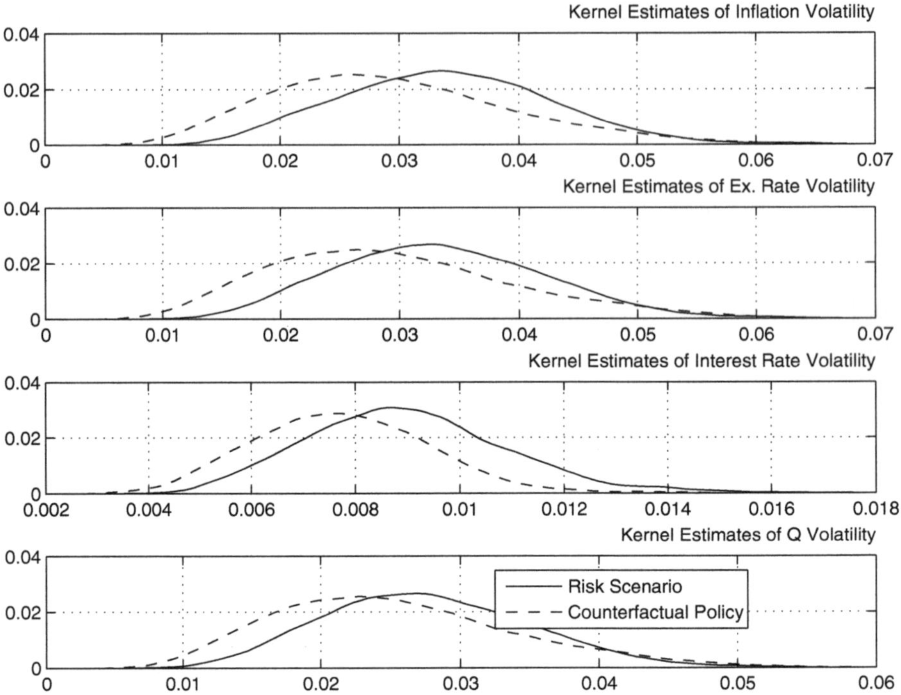

Fig. 4.8 Inflation, exchange rate, interest rate, and Q volatility under risk and counterfactual exchange-rate policy

Figure 4.10 pictures the distribution of the consumption compensation to equalize welfare between the two scenarios. Not surprisingly, the distribution is more likely to be negative, meaning that the welfare of the household in the counterfactual exchange-rate targeting regime is 66% more likely to be better off than in the base high-risk inflation-targeting regime. The mean consumption differential would be 0.4%.

Taylor Rule with Exchange-Rate Targeting

What if Japan were to adopt an expanded Taylor rule with an exchange-rate depreciation target as well as inflation and output growth targets? In this case we use the following policy rule:

$$R_t^f = \rho_r R_{t-1}^{ff} + (1-\rho_r)\rho_\pi \widehat{\pi}_t + (1-\rho_r)\rho_y \widehat{y}_t (1-\rho_r)\overline{R^{ff}} + (1-\rho_r)\rho_s \widehat{s}_t, \quad (4.64)$$

$$s_t = \ln(S_t) - \ln(S_{t-1}). \quad (4.65)$$

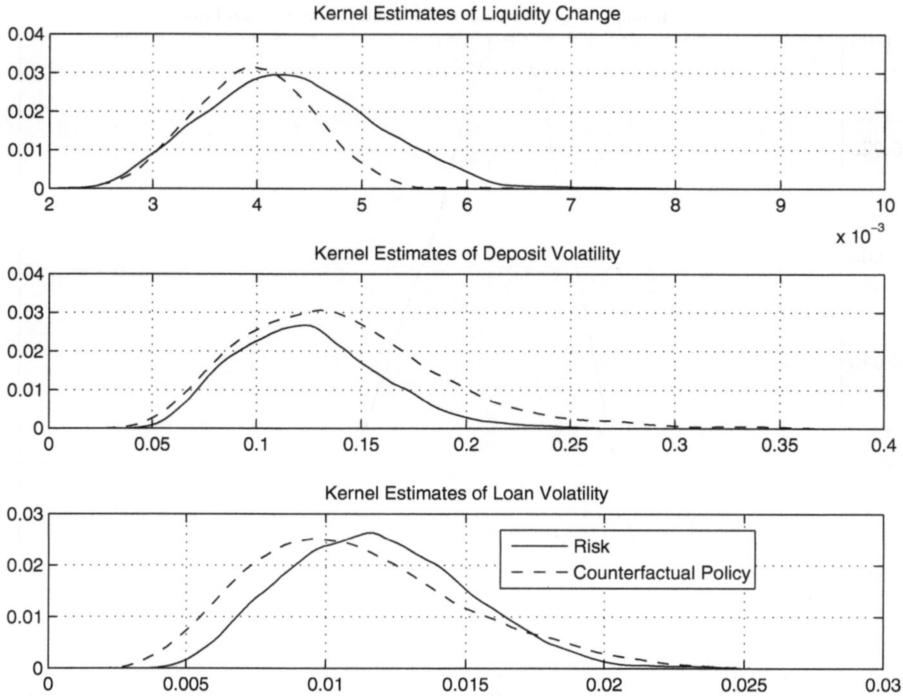

Fig. 4.9 Liquidity, deposit, and loan volatility under risk and counterfactual exchange-rate policy

We use the estimated values for ρ_r, ρ_π, and ρ_y. We calibrate a high value, with $\rho_s = 0.75$, relative to the weight on inflation, to indicate that the exchange rate plays a nearly as important role in the monetary decision. As in the previous experiment, we simulate the model with recurring shocks to government spending only, under the high-risk scenario for government debt.

We see that adopting an expanded Taylor rule, with a relatively high weight on depreciation, slightly reduces consumption, investment, and employment volatility (Fig. 4.11).

Figure 4.12 shows the corresponding volatility distributions for inflation, the exchange rate, the interest rate, and Tobin's Q. Again, using the expanded Taylor rule shifts the distribution to the left.

Figure 4.13 pictures the volatility distributions of liquidity provision by the central bank, as well as deposit and loan volatility in the financial sector. We see that there is little or no difference in these distributions.

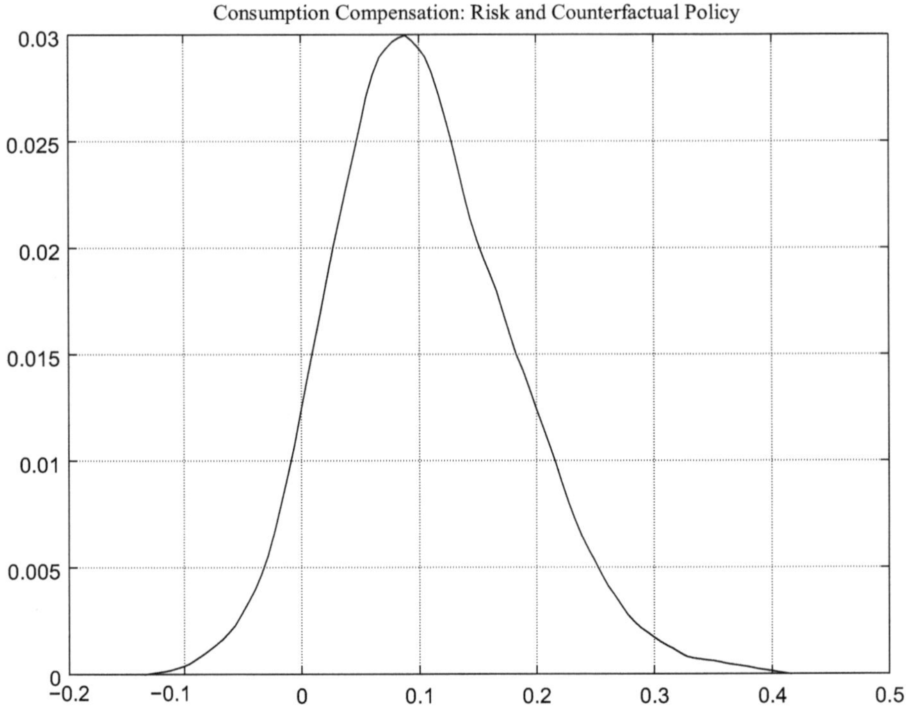

Fig. 4.10 Percentage of consumption compensation for equalizing welfare between risk and counterfactual exchange-rate policy

Figure 4.14 pictures the distribution of the consumption compensation needed to equalize welfare in the two regimes. We see that the distribution of this compensation is similar to that in Fig. 4.10, implying that there is an expected positive compensation for households in the base scenario, to equalize welfare under the expanded Taylor rule.

The results of this sector show that adding the exchange rate depreciation in the Taylor rule can achieve similar effects on volatility distributions and welfare as targeting the exchange rate itself, as a function of inflation. The only drawback to the use of the Taylor rule is the zero lower band on the interest rate. The results indicate that the exchange-rate depreciation weight in the Taylor rule must be relatively strong for the Taylor rule to work as effectively as the direct exchange-rate instrument in the counterfactual monetary regime.

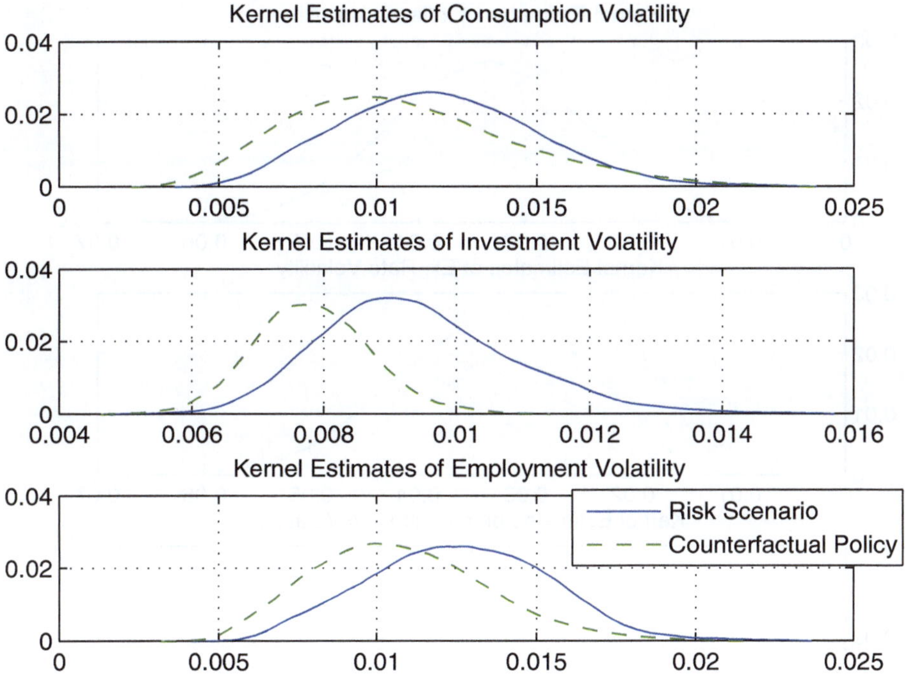

Fig. 4.11 Distribution of consumption, investment, and employment volatility under Taylor rule and counterfactual extended Taylor rule

4.5 Conclusion

Our Bayesian analysis for Japan suggests reasons for abandoning the traditional Taylor rule framework in favor of either an exchange-rate targeting framework such as that used by the Monetary Authority of Singapore, or an expanded Taylor rule that includes the exchange rate. Of course, the direct use of an exchange-rate instrument, in place of a Taylor rule with an exchange rate argument, opens the monetary authority of a large country like Japan, much more than Singapore, to criticism of currency manipulation by major trading partners. While the Taylor rule suffers from the drawback of a zero lower bound, the exchange-rate alternative suffers from the threat of political backlash.

Of course, this result should not be so surprising at first bounce. Given that Japan has been operating at the zero lower bound, an exchange-rate rule would give the Bank of Japan, at the very least, a more symmetrical instrument for stabilizing the economy. However, in our model simulations, we did not impose the zero lower bound, and thus did not stack the deck in favor of the exchange-rate rule.

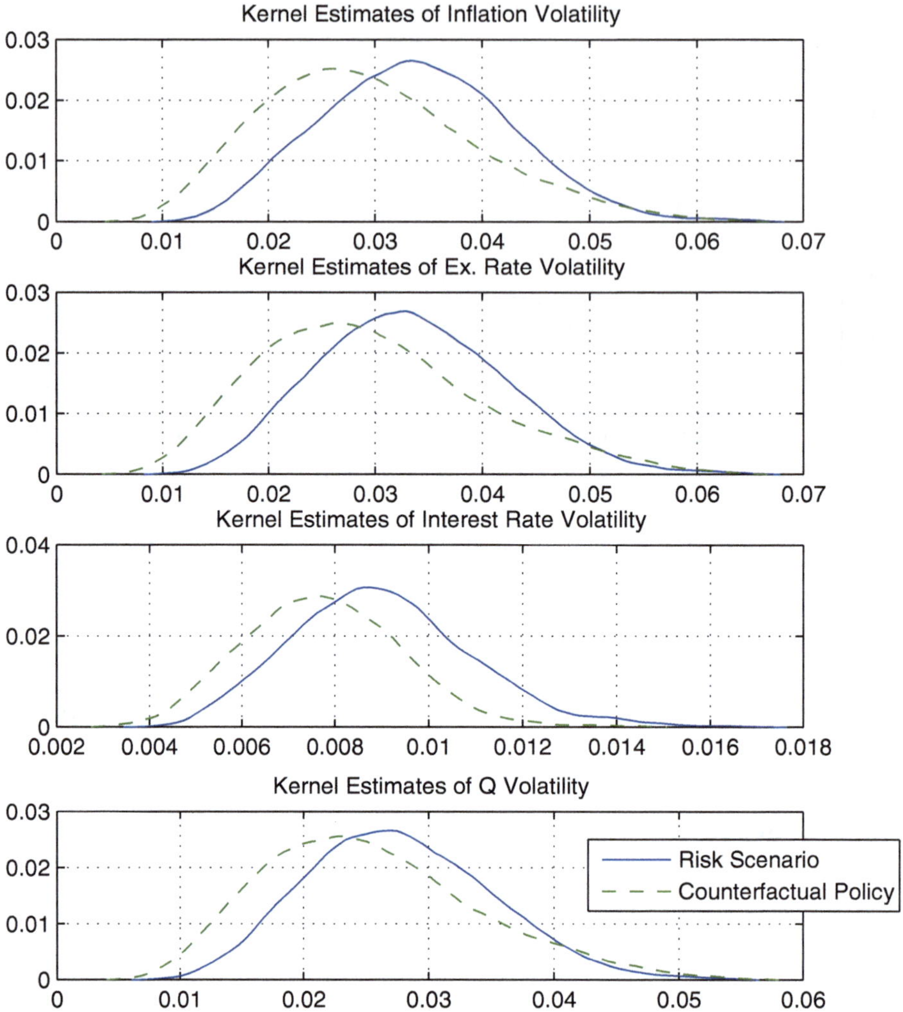

Fig. 4.12 Inflation, exchange rate, interest, and Q volatility under Taylor rule and counterfactual Taylor rule

Of course, many factors are responsible for the strong appreciation of the Japanese yen. Given the capital controls in the People's Republic of China (PRC), and the fragility of the euro zone and the US economy, significant amounts of liquid assets have been to Japan as a "safe haven," for lack of alternatives elsewhere in Asia. Given the highly open nature of the Japanese economy and its supply chain links and real-sector integration with many economies that do not have flexible exchange rates (for example, the PRC and Thailand), a more controlled exchange rate, based on a Singapore-like policy rule, may be more appropriate.

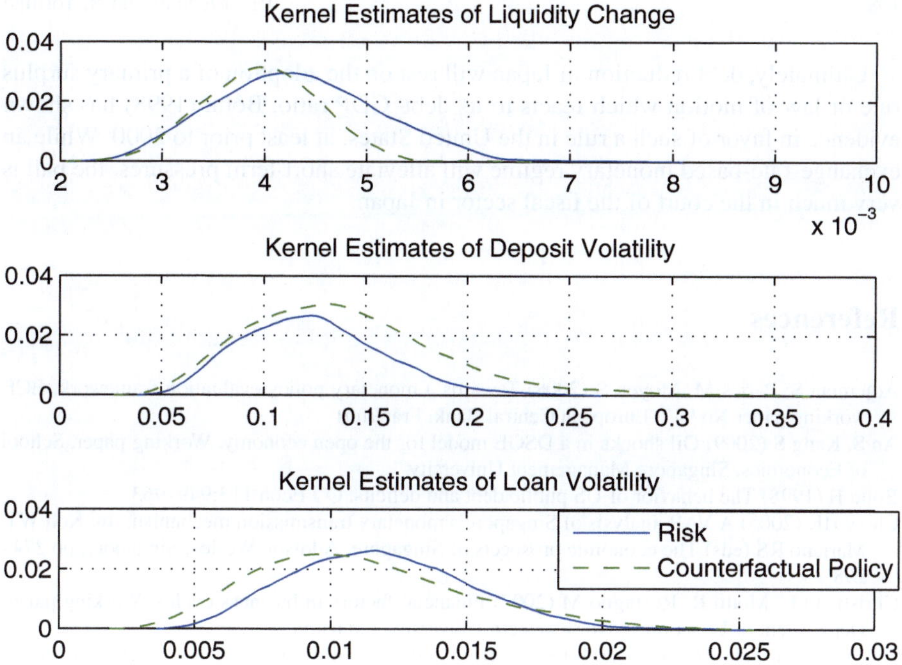

Fig. 4.13 Distribution of liquidity, deposits, and loans under Taylor rule and expanded Taylor rule

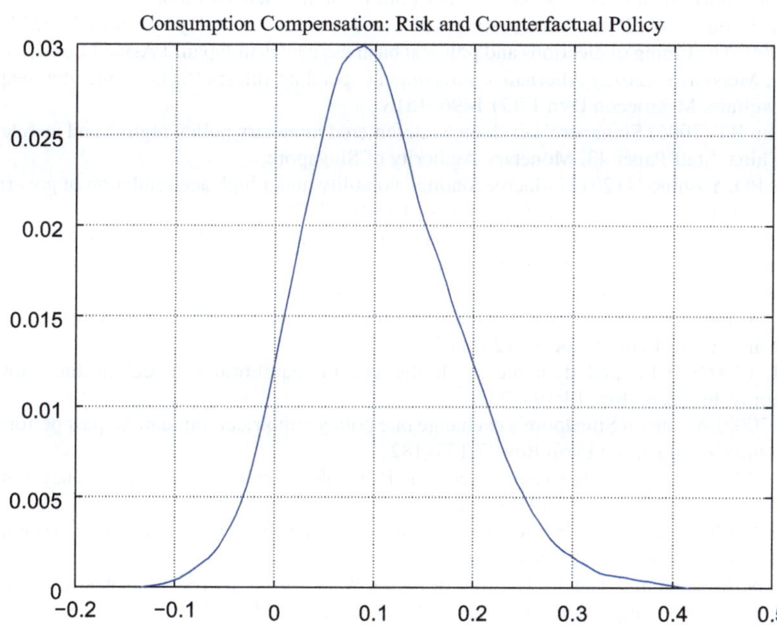

Fig. 4.14 Consumption compensation for equalizing welfare under Taylor rule and counterfactual amended Taylor rule

Ultimately, debt reduction in Japan will rest on the adoption of a primary surplus rule or law of motion which reacts to its debt–GDP ratio. Bohn (1998) has shown evidence in favor of such a rule in the United States, at least prior to 2000. While an exchange-rate-based monetary regime will alleviate short-term pressures, the ball is very much in the court of the fiscal sector in Japan.

References

Adjemian S, Paries M, Moyen S (2008) Towards a monetary policy evaluation framework. ECB working paper No 942. European Central Bank, Frankfurt

An S, Kang S (2009) Oil shocks in a DSGE model for the open economy. Working paper, School of Economics, Singapore Management University

Bohn H (1998) The behavior of US public debt and deficits. Q J Econ 113:949–963

Chow HK (2005) A VAR analysis of Singapore's monetary transmission mechanism. In: Koh WT, Mariano RS (eds) The economic prospects of Singapore. Addison Wesley, Singapore, pp 274–298

Christiano L, Motto R, Rostagno M (2007) Financial factors in business cycles. Working paper, Department of Economics, Northwestern University, Evanston

Del Negro M, Schorfheide F (2004) Priors from general equilibrium models for VARS. Int Econ Rev 45:643–673

Escaith H, Kek A, Nee C, Teh R (2011) Japan's earthquake and tsunami: international trade and global supply chain effects. VOX: CEPR's Policy Portal. www.voxeu.org

Grüne L, Semmler W (2008) Asset pricing with loss aversion. J Econ Dyn Control 32:3253–3274

Ito T (1990) The timing of elections and political business cycles in Japan. J Asian Econ 1:135–156

Lim GC, McNelis P (2012) Alternative government spending rules: effects on income inequality and welfare. Macroecon Dyn 17(7):1496–1518

McCallum BT (2006) Singapore's exchange rate-entered monetary policy regime and its relevance for China. Staff Paper 43, Monetary Authority of Singapore

McNelis PD, Yoshino N (2012) Macroeconomic volatility under high accumulation of government debt: lessons from Japan. Adv Complex Syst 15(Su):1–29

Schmitt-Grohé S, Uribe M (2003) Closing small open-economy models. J Int Econ 61:163–185

Schmitt-Grohé S, Uribe M (2007) Optimal simple and implementable monetary and fiscal rules. J Monet Econ 54:1702–1725

Smets F, Wouters R (2003) An estimated dynamic stochastic general equilibrium model of the Euro area. J Eur Econ Assoc 1:1123–1175

Teo WL (2009) Estimated dynamic stochastic general equilibrium model of the Taiwanese economy. Pac Econ Rev 14:194–231

Yip SL (2002) A note on Singapore's exchange rate policy: empirical foundation, past performance and outlook. Singapore Econ Rev 47:173–182

Yip SL (2005) The exchange rate systems in Hong Kong and Singapore, currency board vs monitoring band. Prentice Hall, Singapore

Yoshino N (2011) Growing budget deficits and sustainability: why is Japan still sustainable? APEC: SME Economic Crisis Monitor 5–6

Yoshino N, Mizoguchi T (2010) The role of public works in the political business cycle and the instability of the budget deficits in Japan. Asian Econ Pap 9:94–112

Chapter 5
Japan's Postwar Monetary Policies: Taylor Rules or Something Else?

James R. Rhodes and Naoyuki Yoshino

Abstract This brief chapter investigates postwar Japanese monetary policies through the lens of the Taylor equation and the associated Taylor rule. We break from previous studies in extending the investigation back to the early postwar period and by examining the stability of the Taylor specification in various subperiods. In general, we find little support for the Taylor equation in the Japan case. A possible exception is the period from 1980–1997, but this was a period of the "bubble economy" and subsequent "Lost Decade." We see this as setting the stage for a more detailed description and assessment of Japan's postwar monetary policies.

Keywords Monetary policy • Bank of Japan • Taylor rule

JEL Classification E42, E52, E51

5.1 Introduction

The return to power of Japan's Liberal Democratic Party and the birth of "Abenomics" has rekindled interest in Japan's monetary policy. Monetary policy is the first of three arrows in the Abe administration's policy quiver. Prime Minister Abe has expressed confidence that a combination of monetary, fiscal, and structural policies can restore the 4–5% real gross domestic product (GDP) growth path that prevailed in the two decades leading up to the collapse of the "bubble economy."

This chapter looks at Japanese monetary policy through the lens of the Taylor rule. The Taylor rule is a formula for setting the central bank's policy interest rate. In its original and conventional form, the policy rate is a positive function of the

J.R. Rhodes
National Graduate Institute for Policy Studies (GRIPS), Tokyo, Japan
e-mail: rhodes@grips.ac.jp

N. Yoshino (✉)
Asian Development Bank Institute (ADBI), Tokyo, Japan

Keio University, Tokyo, Japan
e-mail: nyoshino@adbi.org

N. Yoshino, F. Taghizadeh-Hesary (eds.), *Japan's Lost Decade*, ADB Institute Series on Development Economics, DOI 10.1007/978-981-10-5021-3_5

inflation and GDP gaps. There have been relatively few studies of the Japanese experience, but most find that a Taylor rule specification fits the data reasonably well.[1] The implication is that Japanese monetary policy can be adequately described by a Taylor rule. This chapter is motivated by the belief that such a conclusion is misinformed and, more importantly, misleading. Over the postwar period, actual monetary policy in Japan has been far more interesting and complicated than can possibly be described by a simple rule. The purpose of this chapter is to investigate the credibility of the Taylor rule specification for the Japan case. We view the Taylor rule as a convenient foil to raise questions about the true nature of Japan's postwar monetary policies.

5.2 The Taylor Rule Framework

The beauty of the Taylor rule is its simplicity, intuitive appeal, and presumed generality. In what follows, we distinguish between the Taylor equation and Taylor rules. The original Taylor equation postulates a linear relationship between the central bank's policy interest rate and the inflation and output gaps. Taylor rules may be either descriptive or prescriptive. A descriptive rule is an assertion about the policy behavior actually followed by central banks. Central banks may be said to follow a Taylor rule if they adjust policy rates in response to changes in inflation and output gaps. A prescriptive rule, in contrast, is a statement about optimal policy responses.

In the prescriptive version, the Taylor rule requires central banks to adjust the policy interest rate when inflation deviates from the central bank target and when output deviates from potential output. The policy rate should be increased whenever inflation or output increase above their desired levels. An opposite and symmetric response is called for in the case of a negative inflation or output gap. The intended goal of the prescriptive form of the Taylor rule is to keep inflation and output gaps near zero.

A Taylor equation is simply a reaction function that describes the response of the central bank's policy instrument to changes in the inflation and output gaps. In the simplest version, it assumes stable policy targets and policy response coefficients.

Taylor and others recognize that this need not, and perhaps should not, be the case. It would be very surprising if Japan's monetary policy reaction function were stable over the postwar period given the dramatic changes over time in the policy environment. In what follows, however, we wish to maintain the simplicity of the Taylor approach. We make only one modest change in the Taylor equation: we introduce the deviation of the exchange rate from the central bank target (the exchange rate gap) as a potential explanatory variable. Japan is an open economy and the exchange rate is often an important variable in macroeconomic policy deliberations.

[1] See Miyazawa (2011) and the references therein.

The Taylor equations to be estimated take the form:

$$i_t = \pi_t + r_t^* + \alpha_\pi \left(\pi_t - \pi_t^*\right) + \alpha_y \left(y_t - y_t^*\right) - \alpha_e \left(e_t - e_t^*\right)$$

where

i is the policy interest rate,
r* is the equilibrium real interest rate (natural rate),
π is the rate of change of the price level,
π* is the target rate of growth of the price level,
y is the real GDP growth rate,
y* is the potential growth rate,
e is the nominal yen exchange rate (yen relative to foreign currency),
e* is the target yen exchange rate,
and $\alpha_e = 0$ under the original Taylor specification.

In Japan, the short-term monetary policy interest rate is the call rate on loans in the overnight interbank money market. The call rate is comparable to the Unites States (US) Federal Reserve's federal funds rate. We used the uncollateralized call rate in all of our regression equations. The inflation rate is measured as the percent change in the consumer price index from the previous period. Real GDP growth is the conventional measure provided in the national accounts. We used two measures of the yen exchange rate: the yen–US dollar rate based on a comparison with the US dollar and a yen effective exchange rate based on a weighted-average calculation of exchange rates with major trading partners. We used simple, forward-looking measures of potential output growth and the target inflation and exchange rates. For the target rates, we simply used an average of the period-to-period growth rates over the entire sample period under investigation. Data was obtained from official Japanese government sources.

Two questions motivate this research. One question is whether Japanese monetary policy can be adequately described by a simple descriptive rule of the Taylor variety. A second question is whether Japan's monetary authority has followed a prescriptive rule of the Taylor form. Under a strict interpretation of the Taylor rule, the alpha coefficients would be considered time invariant. More generally, the coefficients are considered "guidelines" based on historical or theoretical simulations of optimal policy responses to inflation and output gaps. Strictly speaking, the optimal policy responses are those which maintain the inflation and output gaps consistently near zero. In what follows, we examine the stability of policy coefficients to provide indirect evidence on whether such prescriptive policies were consistently followed.

5.3 Preliminary Empirical Investigations

Table 5.1 presents the results of Taylor regressions over two relatively long periods. Model 1 uses quarterly data over the period 1980Q1–2012Q3. Model 2 uses annual data over the period 1961–2011. In both models the estimated coefficients in the

Table 5.1 Taylor rule regressions

	Model 1		Model 2
	1980Q1–2012Q3 (quarterly data)		1961–2011 (annual data)
	Call rate	Call rate	Call rate
Inflation gap	255.8***	164.5***	44.5***
	(9.3)	(6.4)	(5.07)
GDP growth gap	46.4***	25.8**	16.7*
	(3.86)	(2.49)	(1.71)
Yen/US dollar gap	−0.0332***		−0.0112**
	(10.47)		(2.2)
Yen effective exchange rate gap		−0.102***	
		(−14.51)	
Constant	2.73***	2.73***	4.55***
	(20.94)	(25.08)	(17.6)
Number of observations	130	130	50
Adjusted R^2	0.7735	0.8415	0.7492

Notes: *** 1% significance, ** 5% significance, * 10% significance. Values in parentheses are t-values. Gap variables are defined as the difference between the variable and its average over the period. Increase in the yen/US dollar or yen effective exchange rate means appreciation. *GDP* gross domestic product. The first column in the Model 1 shows the results by including yen/US dollar gap and the second column in this model is showing the results by including the yen effective exchange rate gap

Taylor equation are correctly signed and statistically significant. These results might be interpreted as evidence that the Japanese monetary authorities consistently followed a Taylor rule over the postwar period; however, they were based on strong and implausible assumptions about the target values of the three variables. We assumed that target values were constant at their respective mean values over the entire two periods. These variables all experienced profound changes in their trends over these periods. For example, when compared with the sample mean, GDP growth was consistently high in the early "high-growth" period of the 1960s and consistently low in the post-1990 period of the "Lost Decade." Likewise, inflation and exchange rates were consistently higher than average in the early years and consistently below average in the later years. Since the call rate was also higher than average in the early years and lower than average in the later years, the correlations between the call rate and the gap variables are all positive. The estimated coefficients in the Taylor regressions are likely to be spurious. (See Yoshino and Taghizadeh-Hesary 2016 for more info on Japan's Lost Decade.)

Table 5.2 reports the results of Taylor regressions using quarterly data for various subperiods. These periods are quite distinctive in their characteristics. Model 3 spans the period of Japan's "bubble economy." Model 4 roughly covers the period from the collapse of the economic bubble up to the Asian financial crisis. Model 5 includes the years of the Japanese financial crisis and the period of Prime Minister Koizumi when the output growth rate doubled. Model 6 is the most recent period of financial and economic turmoil.

Table 5.2 Taylor rule regressions by period, quarterly data

	Model 3	Model 4	Model 5	Model 6
	1980Q1–1991Q4	1992Q1–1997Q2	1997Q3–2003Q1	2003Q2–2012Q3
	Call rate	Call rate	Call rate	Call rate
Inflation gap	212.4***	−61.9	23.8**	−1.6
	(5.54)	(−0.70)	(2.52)	(−0.25)
GDP growth gap	15.5	−21.0	−1.9	−2.9
	(0.84)	(−0.60)	(−0.47)	(−1.45)
Yen effective exchange rate gap	−0.098***	−0.112***	−0.016***	−0.009***
	(−5.64)	(−3.34)	(−3.76)	(−3.99)
Constant	3.0***	2.6***	0.4***	0.3***
	(6.39)	(7.99)	(5.80)	(5.25)
Number of observations	47	22	23	38
Adjusted R^2	0.6143	0.3023	0.5143	0.2787

Notes: *** 1% significance, ** 5% significance, * 10% significance. Values in parenthesis are t-values. Gap variables are defined as the difference between the variable and its average over the period. Increase in the yen effective exchange rate means appreciation. *GDP* gross domestic product

Table 5.3 Taylor rule regressions by period, annual data

	Model 7	Model 8	Model 9
	1962–1980	1981–1997	1997–2011
	Call rate	Call rate	Call rate
Inflation gap	33.0**	95.3***	16.5**
	(2.57)	(3.21)	(2.95)
GDP growth gap	2.8	26.3	−1.6
	(0.18)	(1.43)	(−0.99)
Yen/US dollar exchange rate gap	−0.0075	−0.0157**	−0.0014
	(0.80)	(2.06)	(0.52)
Constant	5.5***	7.0***	0.8**
	(4.62)	(13.00)	(2.71)
Number of observations	19	17	14
Adjusted R^2	0.2777	0.7026	0.3726

Notes: *** 1% significance, ** 5% significance, * 10% significance. Values in parenthesis are t-values. Gap variables are defined as the difference between the variable and its average over the period. Increase in the yen/US dollar rate means appreciation. *GDP* gross domestic product

Table 5.3 uses annual data in estimating Taylor regressions for various subperiods. The regressions do not provoke confidence in the Taylor rule. The GDP gap is not statistically significant in any of the regressions. The only variable that is consistently significant and properly signed is the rate of change of prices.

Model 7 looks at the early postwar period. Clearly, the Taylor rule specification does not describe this period. The only variable that is statistically significant is the inflation rate. The overall explanatory power of the model is very weak (adjusted $R^2 = 0.28$). Something else is going on in this period. This is a period of quantitative controls when interest rates were administratively determined and when bank lending was administratively guided. The call rate, by informed accounts, was not the Bank of Japan's (BOJ's) main policy instrument. It was the celebrated period of high growth and economic miracle, but Japanese policy makers were clearly not following either the descriptive or prescriptive forms of the Taylor rule.

Model 8 provides Taylor estimates for the modern period up through 1997. It is a period of financial liberalization and the adoption of modern operating policies by the BOJ. Two variables, the inflation and exchange-rate gaps, are correctly signed and statistically significant. The GDP gap is correctly signed but not statistically significant at conventional levels. This is the one period where there seems to be some support for the Taylor rule specification. This is roughly the period covered by most studies that report evidence favoring the Taylor rule specification for the Japan case. Ironically, it is not a period which most modern observers would associate with effective BOJ policies since it covers both the bubble economy of the 1980s and the "Lost Decade" of the 1990s.[2]

Model 9 covers the period since the Asian Crisis. The overall explanatory power of the regression is very weak (adjusted $R^2 = 0.38$). This was a period of sustained and moderate (roughly 1%) deflation and steady yen appreciation. The only variable that is statistically significant is the rate of changes of prices. The policy rate during this period was effectively at the zero bound making a Taylor-based policy unworkable. It was a period of quantitative easing and other unconventional monetary experiments. It was also a period when BOJ economists increasingly viewed Japan's problems as structural in nature.

5.4 Tentative Conclusions and Future Research

The Taylor rule has become the standard model for representing monetary policy. It is commonly used both as a description of actual monetary policies and as a prescription for efficient policies. It is commonly claimed to be a good description of actual monetary policy in many countries, including Japan. Consequently, a Taylor equation for the policy interest rate has displaced equations for money in new Keynesian models.

We believe there is room to doubt that the Taylor rule is an accurate description of Japan's monetary policies over the postwar period. In our regressions, the GDP gap was usually insignificant and, often, incorrectly signed. The only period where there is modest support for a Taylor rule is in the troubling decades of the bubble economy

[2]Even more ironic is the fact that John Taylor, Milton Friedman, and many other prominent economic observers are on record praising BOJ policies of the 1980s. At the time, few if any economists were warning of an economic bubble, much less a subsequent catastrophe.

and subsequent collapse. Extending the period of investigation to the early postwar period raises substantial doubts about the validity of the Taylor rule specification for this early period of high growth. If there was any long-term consistency in Japanese monetary policy, it was in the response to inflation and the exchange rate. Policy makers generally leaned against the wind in times of inflation and yen variability.

In the various subperiods considered, there was no discernible adjustment in the call rate to changes in the output gap. This is despite fairly substantial fluctuations in output throughout the postwar period. This should not be taken to imply that the output gap is not important to Japanese policy makers. Fiscal policy, interpreted broadly to include government loans, may well have been the preferred instrument for dealing with output fluctuations. Rhodes (1998), for example, found evidence that government lending institutions follow countercyclical lending policies through the Fiscal Investment and Loan Program.

We believe that the Taylor rule is a misleading guide to Japanese monetary policy in the postwar period. The implicit assumption in the literature is that the Japanese monetary authorities faced similar constraints, had similar motivations, and used similar policy instruments as their counterparts in the United States. We believe the constraints, motivations, and instruments were different. This version of our chapter is a tentative first step in raising doubts about the simple Taylor rule formulation. Subsequent work will concentrate on flushing out the historical differences in the Japanese approach to monetary policy and the changes over time. It is particularly important to distinguish between the early postwar periods of quantitative controls (ca. 1955–1971) and the more recent periods of qualitative control mechanisms. In the quantitative control period, the call rate was not the primary policy instrument. Likewise, it is important to recognize the gradual evolution of monetary policy over the long period of financial liberalization (1971–1990) that culminated in the collapse of the "bubble economy." Rhodes and Yoshino (2007) was a preliminary attempt to explain these developments. In a more recent study on the Japanese economy and effectiveness of the monetary policy in this economy, Yoshino and Taghizadeh-Hesary (2015), by development of an aggregate demand–aggregate supply model by incorporating a Taylor rule equation, found that quantitative easing may not be able to stimulate the Japanese economy. Aggregate demand, which includes private investment, did not increase significantly in Japan with lower interest rates. Private investment displays this unconventional behavior because of the uncertainty about the future and because Japan's population is aging. The paper concludes that the remedy for Japan's economic policy is not to be found in its monetary policy.

It is little appreciated that the Japanese monetary authorities used direct controls of commercial bank lending as a policy instrument up until 1990. Rhodes and Yoshino (1999) show that this policy of "window guidance" was effective in regulating bank lending. It remains to be shown that window guidance was an importance instrument of monetary policy in the quantitative control period (roughly 1955–1971). It was only after a long period of liberalization that the BOJ had the tools, motivation, and independence to pursue a modern monetary policy. Ironically, it is in the post-liberalization period that monetary policy has faced its greatest challenges and received its most damning criticism. Our subsequent work will also look at non-Taylor rules in the recent periods of quantitative and qualitative easing brought on by the collapse of the call rate toward the zero bound and negative interest rate policy. With the birth of Abenomics, a new phase in monetary history has been started. We have, it seems, a questioning of central tenants of modern monetary theory and practice. After tracing the evolution of Japan's monetary policy, we will be in a better position to understand the thinking and motivation behind Abenomics. (For more information on Abenomics and its three arrows, see Yoshino and Taghizadeh-Hesary 2014.)

References

Miyazawa K (2011) The Taylor rule in Japan. Jpn Econ 38(2):79–104

Rhodes JR (1998) The cyclical behavior of government lending institutions in Japan. J Econ 23:1–15

Rhodes JR, Yoshino N (1999) Window guidance by the Bank of Japan: was lending controlled? Contemp Econ Policy 17(2):166–176

Rhodes JR, Yoshino N (2007) Japan's monetary policy transition, 1955–2005, GRIPS discussion papers 07-04. National Graduate Institute for Policy Studies (GRIPS), Tokyo

Yoshino N, Taghizadeh-Hesary F (2014) An analysis of challenges faced by Japan's economy and Abenomics. Jpn Polit Econ 40(3–4):37–62

Yoshino N, Taghizadeh-Hesary F (2015) Effectiveness of the easing of monetary policy in the Japanese economy, incorporating energy prices. J Comp Asian Dev 14(2):1–22

Yoshino N, Taghizadeh-Hesary F (2016) Causes and remedies of the Japan's long-lasting recession: lessons for China. Chin World Econ 24(2):23–47

Chapter 6
Impact of the Fukushima Nuclear Disaster: Analysis on Japan's Oil Consuming Sectors

Farhad Taghizadeh-Hesary, Naoyuki Yoshino, and Ehsan Rasoulinezhad

Abstract Since the oil price shocks of the 1970s, several studies have found significant impacts of oil prices on macro variables. However, it is particularly crucial to know how each micro sector in an economy, such as the residential, transport, industrial, and nonenergy sectors, respond to oil price impulses. In this research, we try to shed light on the impact of crude oil price volatility on each sector in Japan, the world's third-largest crude oil consumer. To do so, we apply a vector auto regression model and perform impulse response analysis by using quarterly data from 1990Q1 to 2014Q1. The findings indicate that some economic sectors, such as the residential sector, did not have significant sensitivity to the sharp oil price fluctuations. In contrast, some other sectors, like the commercial, industrial, and transport sectors, were strongly sensitive to the drastic oil price fluctuations. Moreover, our findings show that after the Fukushima disaster in 2011, which led to the shutdown of nuclear power plants in Japan and increased the country's reliance on oil imports, the sensitivity of most sectors to oil price volatility declined.

Keywords Oil price • Fukushima disaster • Nuclear power • Japanese economy

JEL Classification C32, O49, Q43

F. Taghizadeh-Hesary (✉)
Faculty of Economics, Keio University, Tokyo, Japan

Graduate School of Economics, The University of Tokyo, Tokyo, Japan
e-mail: farhadth@gmail.com; farhadth@keio.jp

N. Yoshino
Asian Development Bank Institute (ADBI), Tokyo, Japan

Keio University, Tokyo, Japan
e-mail: nyoshino@adbi.org

E. Rasoulinezhad
Tehran University, Tehran, Iran
e-mail: erasolinejad@gmail.com

N. Yoshino, F. Taghizadeh-Hesary (eds.), *Japan's Lost Decade*, ADB Institute Series on Development Economics, DOI 10.1007/978-981-10-5021-3_6

6.1 Introduction

Global demand for oil has risen drastically since the oil price shocks of the 1970s, while at the same time, new energy-related technologies, new energy resources, and government-mandated energy efficiency targets have made global consumers more resistant to oil shocks.

Several studies have found that oil price shocks have played a significant role in economic downturns. In recent years, both the sharp increase in oil prices that began in 2001 and the sharp decline in 2008 following the subprime mortgage crisis have renewed interest in the effects of oil prices on the macroeconomy. Recently, the price of oil almost halved in a period of less than 5 months from September 2014. After nearly 5 years of stability, the price of a barrel of Brent crude oil in Europe fell from more than $100 per barrel on September 2014 to less than $46 per barrel on January 2015. Several studies have evaluated these impacts (see, inter alia, Taghizadeh-Hesary et al. 2013; Taghizadeh-Hesary and Yoshino 2013, 2014; Yoshino and Taghizadeh-Hesary 2014, 2015a; Taghizadeh-Hesary et al. 2015).

However, economic sectors may not respond to oil price fluctuations in the same way. In this research we will determine which economic sectors are more sensitive to oil price volatility. This chapter will help energy policy makers to protect those sectors with higher sensitivity. Then, if another sharp oil price increase occurs, the identified sectors and the whole economy can be shielded from the negative impacts of the shock.

In this survey, we consider Japan as our case study. Japan is a country that is almost fully dependent on energy imports. In March 2011, a devastating earthquake and tsunami hit eastern Japan and damaged the nuclear power plant in Fukushima. This disaster led to the shutdown of all nuclear power plants due to the lack of government safety approvals. Japan replaced this significant loss of nuclear power with energy generated from imported natural gas, low-sulfur crude oil, fuel oil, and coal. Based on the importance of oil for Japan, we chose to focus on it in this survey. In this chapter, we investigate the effects of oil price fluctuations on the oil consuming economic sectors of Japan using quarterly data from 1990Q1 to 2014Q1 through an autoregression approach. Our research questions are the following: (i) Considering the new energy-related technologies and energy resources, and government-mandated energy efficiency targets, do economic micro sectors still react to oil price movements? (ii) If the answer is yes, are the responses of all economic sectors to oil price impulses of the same scale? Which sectors show higher sensitivities?

This chapter is structured as follows. Section 6.2 provides an overview of energy consumption in Japan. Section 6.3 presents the data analysis. Section 6.4 shows the empirical analysis, and Sect. 6.5 discusses the concluding remarks.

6.2 Overview of Energy Consumption in Japan

Japan is one of the world's largest energy consumers. It is the world's largest liquefied natural gas importer, the second-largest coal importer, and the third-largest net oil importer. Domestic energy sources in Japan meet less than 15% of its own total primary energy use.

Figure 6.1 shows the shares of different energy sources in the Japanese energy basket from January 1994 to June 2014.

In March 2011, a 9.0 magnitude earthquake struck off the coast of Sendai, Japan, triggering a large tsunami. The damage to Japan resulted in an immediate shutdown of about 10 gigawatts of nuclear electric generating capacity. Between the 2011 Fukushima disaster and May 2012, Japan lost all of its nuclear capacity as a result of scheduled maintenance and the lack of government approvals to return to operation. Japan replaced the significant loss of nuclear power with generation from imported natural gas, low-sulfur crude oil, fuel oil, and coal. This caused the price of electricity to rise for the government, utilities, and consumers. Japan spent $250 billion on total fuel imports in 2012, a third of the country's total import charges (Taghizadeh-Hesary and Yoshino 2016). Despite strength in export markets, the yen's depreciation and soaring natural gas and oil import costs due to a greater reliance on fossil fuels continued to deepen Japan's trade deficit throughout 2013. In the wake of the Fukushima nuclear incident, oil is still the main energy carrier in Japan, although the share of oil consumption in total energy consumption has

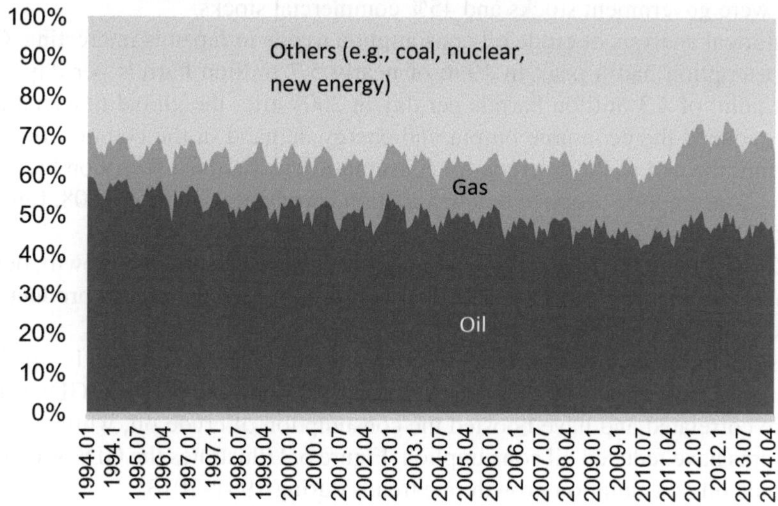

Fig. 6.1 Shares of different energy sources in the Japanese energy basket, January 1994 to June 2014 (*Notes:* Shares are calculated by the calorific value of the energy sources. Oil is imported crude oil plus imported petroleum products. Gas is imported liquefied natural gas. Other energy sources include coal, nuclear power, hydropower, and new energy. *Source:* Yoshino and Taghizadeh-Hesary (2015b))

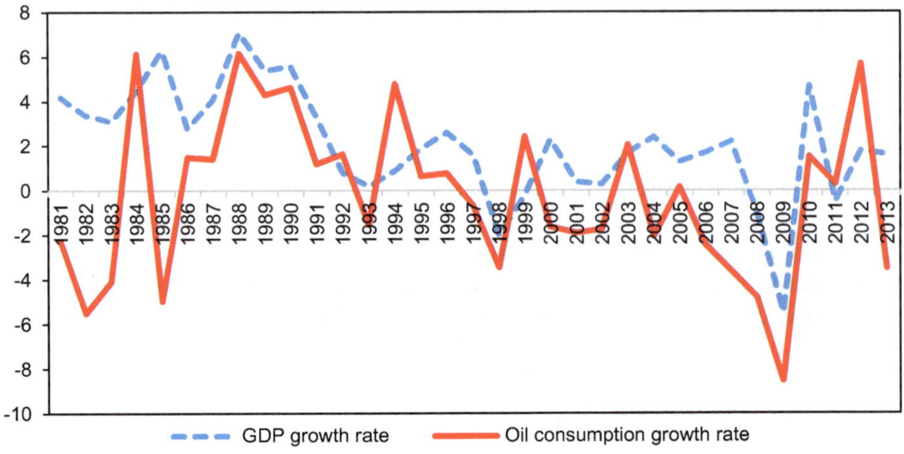

Fig. 6.2 GDP growth rate and crude oil consumption growth of Japan, 1981–2013 (%) (*Note:* GDP is annual change in constant prices. *GDP* gross domestic product. *Source*: International Energy Agency database and World Economic Outlook (WEO) database of the International Monetary Fund (accessed April 2015)).

reduced from about 80% in the 1970s to 43% in 2011. Japan consumed over 4.7 million barrels per day of oil in 2012 (Taghizadeh-Hesary et al. 2015).

According to the U.S. Energy Information Administration, strategic crude oil stocks in Japan totaled 590 million barrels at the end of December 2012, 55% of which were government stocks and 45% commercial stocks.

Historical analysis of crude oil consumption trends in Japan is interesting. Crude oil consumption had a peak in 1996 of nearly 5.7 million barrels per day[1] and a lowest point of 4.3 million barrels per day in 2009 after the global financial crisis, which reduced the economic output and energy demand in the country. From late 1980 until the end of 2006, crude oil consumption was almost 5 million barrels per day, but consumption dropped below 5 million barrels per day from 2008, following the global financial crisis.

In 2015, due to the relative improvement in Japanese economic growth, demand for energy (including oil) rose and total consumption of petroleum products now exceeds 5 million barrels per day.

Besides the aforementioned trends, crude oil consumption in Japan is a procyclical variable. This means that increases in the gross domestic product (GDP) growth rate are correlated and have boosted the consumption of crude oil, while economic downturns have reduced oil consumption. Figure 6.2 illustrates the GDP growth rate and crude oil consumption growth rate trends during 1981–2013.

[1]Average total consumption of petroleum products in February 1996 was 6.8 million barrels per day.

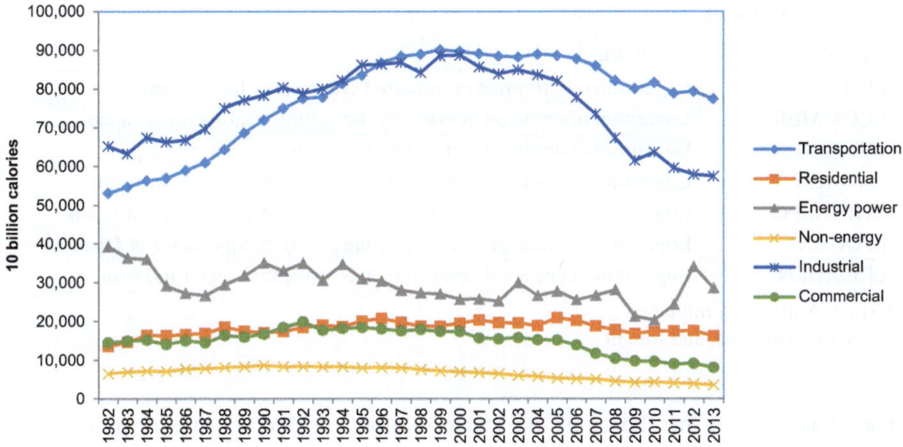

Fig. 6.3 Crude oil consumption by sector in Japan, 1982–2013 (*Source*: Energy Data and Modelling Center database of the Institute of Energy Economics, Japan)

Oil Consumption in Japan by Sector

Generally, there are six oil consuming sectors in an economy: the commercial, energy power generation, industrial, non-energy, residential, and transportation sectors.

Figure 6.3 shows the oil consumption in each of these six sectors in Japan during 1982–2013. Clearly, the transportation and industrial sectors had the highest consumption during this period and importantly, until early 1990, the industrial sector used more crude oil than the transportation sector. However, after the burst of the Japanese asset price bubble in the 1990s, the Japanese economy started suffering from sluggish economic growth and recessions (Japan's so-called "Lost Decade") and the industrial sector's oil demand started to shrink (Yoshino and Taghizadeh-Hesary 2016). Another reason for the reduced demand for oil in the industrial sector was the huge foreign direct investment from Japan in other Asian countries, including Malaysia, Thailand, and the People's Republic of China, which moved a significant part of industrial production to other countries. Since that period, the transportation sector has remained the major consumer of oil in the country, and its consumption has been almost constant. However, in recent years, mainly because of the increased share of hybrid cars and higher energy efficiency in Japanese automobiles, demand for oil in the sector has started to decrease. Industrial sector demand has a negative slope and demand for oil for the Energy Power Generation sector has also been decreasing because of substitution with liquefied natural gas Taghizadeh-Hesary et al. (2016).

In 1982, shares of the transportation, residential, energy power, non-energy, industrial, and commercial sectors in total oil consumption were 28%, 7%, 20%, 3%, 33%, and 9%, respectively. However, it is interesting that by 2013, these ratios

Table 6.1 Variables and definitions

Variable	Definition
LOILP	Logarithm of CIF price of imported crude oil to Japan (yen)
LCOMMER	Logarithm of crude oil demand by the commercial sector in Japan
LINDUS	Logarithm of crude oil demand by the industrial sector in Japan
LNONEN	Logarithm of crude oil demand by the non-energy sector in Japan
LTRANSPO	Logarithm of crude oil demand by the transportation sector in Japan
LPOGEN	Logarithm of crude oil demand by the power energy sector in Japan
LRESIDEN	Logarithm of crude oil demand by the residential sector in Japan

Source: Authors' compilation
CIF cost, insurance, and freight

had changed and the shares of the transportation, residential, energy power, non-energy, industrial, and commercial sectors were measured at 40%, 8%, 15%, 2%, 30%, and 5%, respectively.

6.3 Data Analysis

Variables

The seven variables used in this analysis are comprised of the six energy-consuming sectors and the oil price, all in logarithmic terms. Data on these seven variables are for 1990Q1–2014Q1.The source of the data is the Energy Data and Modelling Center Database of the Institute of Energy Economics, Japan.

Table 6.1 describes the symbols and definitions of these variables.

Unit Root Test

To evaluate the stationarity of all series, we performed two unit root tests on all variables at levels and first differences. The tests used are the augmented Dickey-Fuller test and Phillips-Perron test. The results are summarized in Tables 6.2 and 6.3.

Augmented Dickey-Fuller Test

Our results in Table 6.2 imply that almost all variables are non-stationary in levels. These variables include the crude oil prices and the oil consumption in all six sectors, in logarithmic form. However, the first differences of almost all the variables using the augmented Dickey-Fuller test show stationary results. These

Table 6.2 Unit root test using the augmented Dickey-Fuller test

	Variable	ADF test statistic	1% critical value	5% critical value	10% critical value	H0	Stationary
In levels	Lcommer	0.46	−3.48	−2.88	−2.57	Accept	No
	Lindus	−2.19	−3.48	−2.88	−2.57	Accept	No
	Lnonen	1.31	−3.48	−2.88	−2.57	Accept	No
	Lpogen	−2.93	−3.48	−2.88	−2.57	Accept	No at 1%
	Lresiden	−2.31	−3.48	−2.88	−2.57	Accept	No
	Ltranspo	−2.19	−3.48	−2.88	−2.57	Accept	No
	Loilp	−0.20	−3.48	−2.88	−2.57	Accept	No
First difference form	D(Lcommer)	−5.69	−3.48	−2.88	−2.57	Reject	Yes
	D(Lindus)	−4.97	−3.48	−2.88	−2.57	Reject	Yes
	D(Lnonen)	−5.88	−3.48	−2.88	−2.57	Reject	Yes
	D(Lpogen)	−4.97	−3.48	−2.88	−2.57	Reject	Yes
	D(Lresiden)	−7.94	−3.48	−2.88	−2.57	Reject	Yes
	D(Ltranspo)	−1.46	−3.48	−2.88	−2.57	Accept	No
	D(Loilp)	−9.26	−3.48	−2.88	−2.57	Reject	Yes
Second difference form	DD(Ltranspo)	−9.57	−3.48	−2.88	−2.57	Reject	Yes

Source: Authors' compilation
Note: D refers to first differences, DD refers to second differences. *ADF* augmented Dickey-Fuller test

Table 6.3 Unit root test using the Phillips-Perron test

	Variable	Philips-Perron test statistic	1% critical value	5% critical value	10% critical value	H0	Stationary
First difference form	D(Lcommer)	−23.90	−3.48	−2.88	−2.57	Reject	Yes
	D(Lindus)	−16.49	−3.48	−2.88	−2.57	Reject	Yes
	D(Lnonen)	−19.33	−3.48	−2.88	−2.57	Reject	Yes
	D(Lpogen)	−25.57	−3.48	−2.88	−2.57	Reject	Yes
	D(Lresiden)	−22.26	−3.48	−2.88	−2.57	Reject	Yes
	D(Ltranspo)	−14.48	−3.48	−2.88	−2.57	Reject	Yes
	D(Loilp)	−8.54	−3.48	−2.88	−2.57	Reject	Yes

Source: Authors' compilation
Note: D refers to first differences

results suggest that all variables contain a unit root.[2] Once the unit root test was performed and it was discovered that the variables are non-stationary in levels and stationary in the first differences, they were integrated of order 1, or I(1). Because of the non-stationary series, the next step was to apply a cointegration analysis to examine whether the series are cointegrated and whether long-run relationships exist among these variables.

Phillips-Perron Test

If the time period of analysis includes any structural changes, we should use more than one stationary test in order to confirm the results obtained from the first test. Since the period of our analysis contains several crucial points that affected the energy market—including the 1990–1991 Persian Gulf War, the bursting of the Japanese asset price bubble in 1990–1991, the 1997 Asian financial crisis, the 2008–2009 global financial crisis, and the Fukushima disaster in 2011—we used the Phillips-Perron test for the robustness check.[3] The results of the Phillips-Perron test are shown in Table 6.3. The results confirm the augmented Dickey-Fuller test output for almost all series. The Phillips-Perron test results show that each variable contains a unit root and all series became stationary in first differences.

Cointegration Test

We conducted a cointegration analysis using Johansen's technique by assuming a linear deterministic trend. This approach proposes two likelihood ratio test statistics: the trace and the maximum eigenvalue statistics. Here, we select the maximum eigenvalue statistic and the results are presented in Table 6.4. Based on the results, the series are not cointegrated and there are not any long-run relationships between variables, so we can use the vector autoregressive (VAR) model.

Lag Length Selection

One main issue in VAR models is lag order selection. Normally, six main criteria are available for lag order selection: the Schwarz information criterion, the Hannan-Quinn criterion, the Akaike information criterion, the general-to-specific sequential

[2]With the exception of the transportation sector crude oil demand, which was stationary in the second differences form.

[3]For more information about the causes of energy price elevation following the subprime mortgage crisis and global financial crisis, see Yoshino and Taghizadeh-Hesary (2014).

Table 6.4 Johansen cointegration test

Maximum eigenvalue statistic			
Null hypothesis	Alternative hypothesis	t-statistic	Critical value, 5%
r = 0	r > 0	37.26	46.23
r <= 1	r > 1	31.88	40.07
r <= 2	r > 2	23	33.87
r <= 3	r > 3	15.29	27.58
r <= 4	r > 4	12.20	21.13

Source: Authors' compilation

Table 6.5 Lag length selection

Lag	LogL	AIC	SIC	HQC
0	299.26	−6.56	−6.37	−6.49
1	717.16	−14.8	−13.29	−14.22
2	941.35	−18.7	−15.85[a]	−17.6
3	1027.72	−19.6	−15.32	−17.89
4	1128.24	−20.79	−15.11	−18.50[a]
5	1174.04	−20.72	−13.67	−17.87

Source: Authors' compilation
Note: [a]Shows the optimized lag by the criteria. *AIC* Akaike information criterion, *HQC* Hannan-Quinn criterion, *LogL* log likelihood, *SIC* Schwarz information criterion

likelihood ratio test, a small-sample correction to that test, and the Lagrange multiplier (LM) test. In this present research, we selected optimal lag numbers using the Hannan-Quinn criterion standard, which suggests four lags. Table 6.5 shows the results.

6.4 Empirical Analysis

To answer to the questions raised in the introduction, we developed a vector autoregressive model (VAR).

Vector Autoregressive Model

According to Sims (1980), this approach has the favorable character of endogeneity of the variables. So in this kind of econometric model we cannot divide the variables into two endogenous and exogenous groups. Mathematically, the VAR model can be written as:

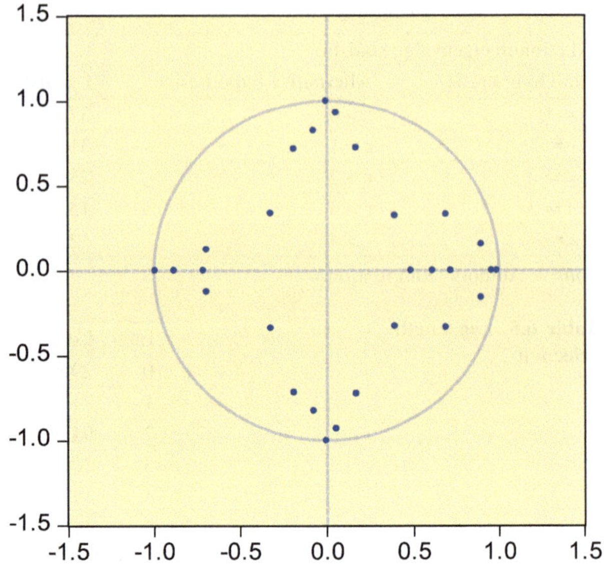

Fig. 6.4 Stability test of the vector autoregressive model (*Source*: Authors' compilation, Note: figure shows the inverse roots of autoregressive characteristic polynomial)

$$y_t = c + \sum_{i=1}^{p} A_i.y_{t-1} + \varepsilon_t \tag{6.1}$$

In Eq. (6.1), y_t is a k*1 vector, c is a vector of intercepts, and y_{t-1} is the lag of the variable y. Furthermore, A_i indicates a time-invariant matrix. To estimate the VAR model, there are further required steps in addition to the stationarity test and lag selection already discussed. We need to consider the stability of the VAR to ensure reliable results, and also need to do an autocorrelation test of the *Lagrange multiplier* (LM), then finally must do the Chow test to capture any structural breaks.

Stability Test of VAR

Agung (2009) shows that for the stability test of the VAR model we can use the inverse roots of the characteristic polynomial. If all model roots are placed inside the circle, our model will be reliable and stable. Figure 6.4 illustrates the result of this test and demonstrates the stability of our model.

Lagrange Multiplier Autocorrelation Test

Before applying the impulse response (IR) analysis, we must perform the autocorrelation test of residuals. This test investigates the problem of autocorrelation between the residuals of the model. The results of the Lagrange multiplier test are shown in Table 6.6.

According to Table 6.6, the null hypothesis, which shows no autocorrelation in the residuals, is not rejected at the 5% critical value, so our model's residuals do not have an autocorrelation problem.

Chow Test for Structural Breaks

To find the presence of structural changes throughout the period of our survey, we tested two significant points. The first was 2008Q3, when oil demand dropped worldwide, including in Japan, due to the recession following the financial crisis. The second point was after the March 2011 Great East Japan Earthquake and tsunami, which shut down all nuclear power generation capacity in Japan, requiring substitution by oil and other fossil fuels. We used the Chow test to check the availability of structural breaks at these points. The results confirm a structural break at 2008Q3, and as a result we can determine two subperiods for our analysis: (i) 1990Q1–2008Q3, and (ii) 2008Q4–2014Q1. we could not find evidence of a structural break in the data following the Fukushima disaster.

As shown in Table 6.7, since the *p*-value is lower than 5%, the null hypothesis can be rejected and hence we can confirm the structural break in 2008Q3.

Table 6.6 Lagrange multiplier autocorrelation test

Lag	LM t-statistic	LM t-statistic
1	59.82	0.138
2	60.58	0.124
3	62.89	0.088
4	82.07	0.210
5	61.76	0.104

Source: Authors' compilation
LM Lagrange multiplier

Table 6.7 Chow test for structural break in 2008Q3

F-statistic	3.16	Prob. F(7,83)	0.005
Log likelihood ratio	22.92	Prob. Chi-square(7)	0.002
Wald statistic	22.13	Prob. Chi-square(7)	0.002

Source: Authors' compilation
Prob. probability

Table 6.8 Granger causality test

Variables	χ^2 Statistic	P-value	Null hypothesis
Lcommer	3.71	0.44	Reject
Lindus	4.13	0.38	Reject
Lnonen	10.18	0.03	Accept
Lresiden	6.54	0.16	Reject
Ltranspo	5.82	0.21	Reject
Lpogen	1.45	0.83	Reject

Source: Authors' compilation

Causality Tests Between Crude Oil Price and Each Sector's Consumption

In this section, we perform the Granger causality test to investigate the short-run relationship between crude oil prices and oil consumption in each economic sector in Japan. Because, according to microeconomic theory, price influences consumption, we can assume that the causality direction is from oil prices to oil consumption. In other words, in this research, the imported oil price in Japan is an active variable whose fluctuations influence oil consumption in the economic sectors. The results of the Granger test represent the causality direction from oil prices to oil consumption for the specified sectors. As can be seen from Table 6.8, the statistic χ^2 is significant in all sectors at the 5% level, with the exception of the non-energy sector. Hence, our null hypothesis is rejected.

Impulse Response Functions

In addition to the causality result obtained in the previous section, we ran an impulse response function. We estimated the responses of each sector to an oil price impulse. According to Lutkepohl and Reimers (1992), impulse response functions (IRFs) are the best way to explore the response of economic variables to the impulse of an indicator. Based on the results of the Chow test for a structural break, we divided our data into two subperiods and then estimated the IRF for each subperiod and the whole period.

Figures 6.5, 6.6, and 6.7 represent the accumulated responses of each oil consuming sector in Japan to oil price impulses.

Figure 6.5 depicts the IRF for the whole period, 1990Q1–2014Q1. As this figure portrays, the power energy sector responds positively to the positive oil price impulse because the majority of Japanese energy is coming from oil, so even if the price of oil rises, demand in the energy sector will still exist and may even increase. Furthermore, a sharp oil price increase leads to an increase in oil consumption by the residential sector until period 4, which can be considered as a short-run period,

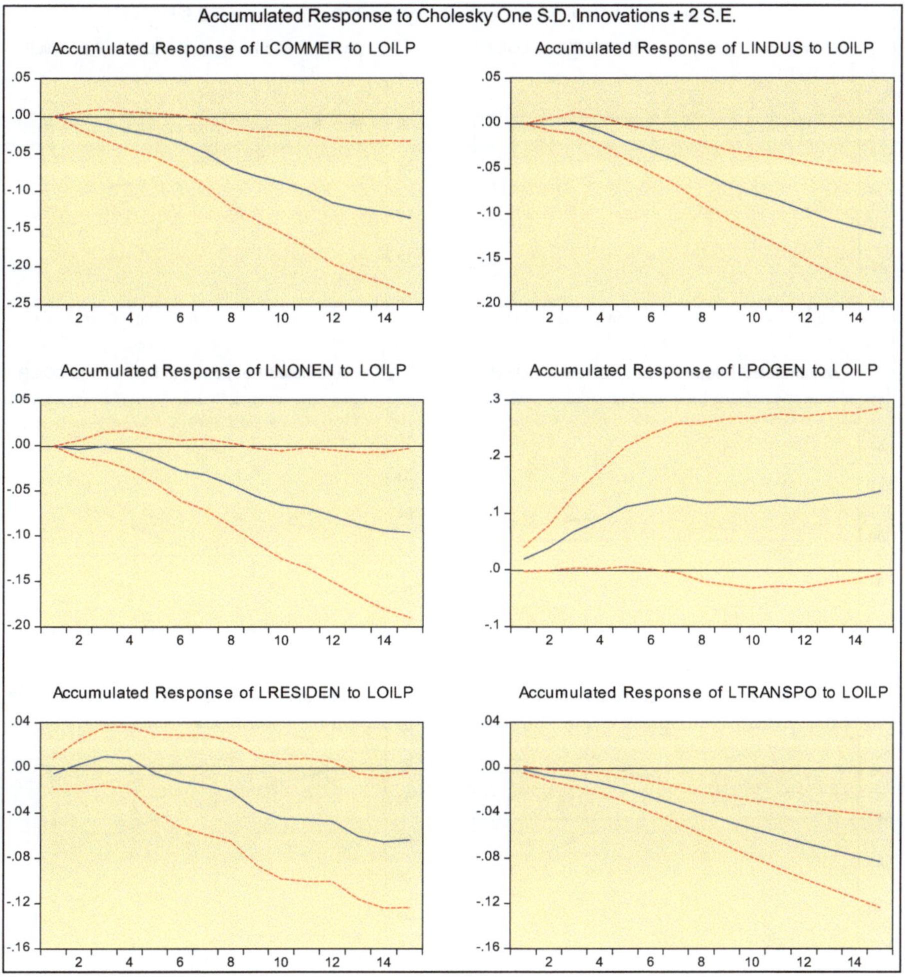

Fig. 6.5 Response of Japan's economic sectors to an oil price fluctuation, 1990Q1–2014Q1 (*Source*: Authors' compilation)

and after that significantly declines. Oil consumption in the other sectors negatively responds to a positive oil price impulse.

Figure 6.6 illustrates the IRF for the period 1990Q1–2008Q3. It is obvious that in this period, the commercial, industrial, and transportation sectors have a high negative sensitivity to oil price positive impulses. The residential sector shows a negative response from period 8, which can be considered as a medium-run period. In this period, the non-energy and power energy sectors showed positive responses for higher oil prices. The reason for the positive response of the non-energy sector is that after several years of recession, during the 2000s, the growth rate of Japanese GDP in real terms was positive. Because of higher economic growth from higher

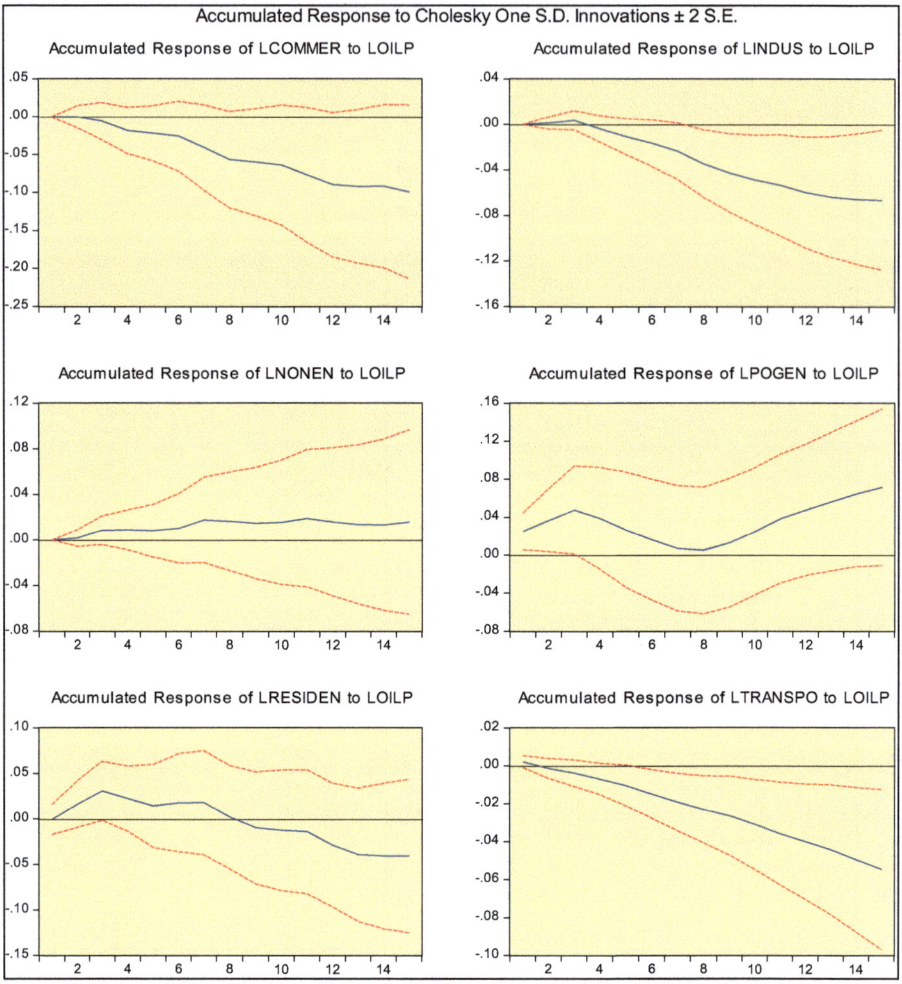

Fig. 6.6 Response of Japan's economic sectors to an oil price fluctuation, 1990Q1–2008Q3 (*Source*: Authors' compilation)

consumption and higher exports, demand for oil as a raw material in petrochemical and industrial production sectors was boosted.

Figure 6.7 depicts the IRF for the years after the global financial crisis of 2008, which includes the Fukushima incident in 2011. It can be seen from the figure that for the period 2008Q4–2014Q1, the sensitivity of oil consumption by the economic sector to oil price fluctuations is low because of the nuclear power shutdown—the economy had higher demand for oil, hence the lower sensitivity to oil price fluctuations. Some sectors, such as the industrial, commercial, and non-energy sectors, respond negatively, while the power energy sector responds positively, to oil price fluctuations. In this period, while the price of oil increased, oil was being

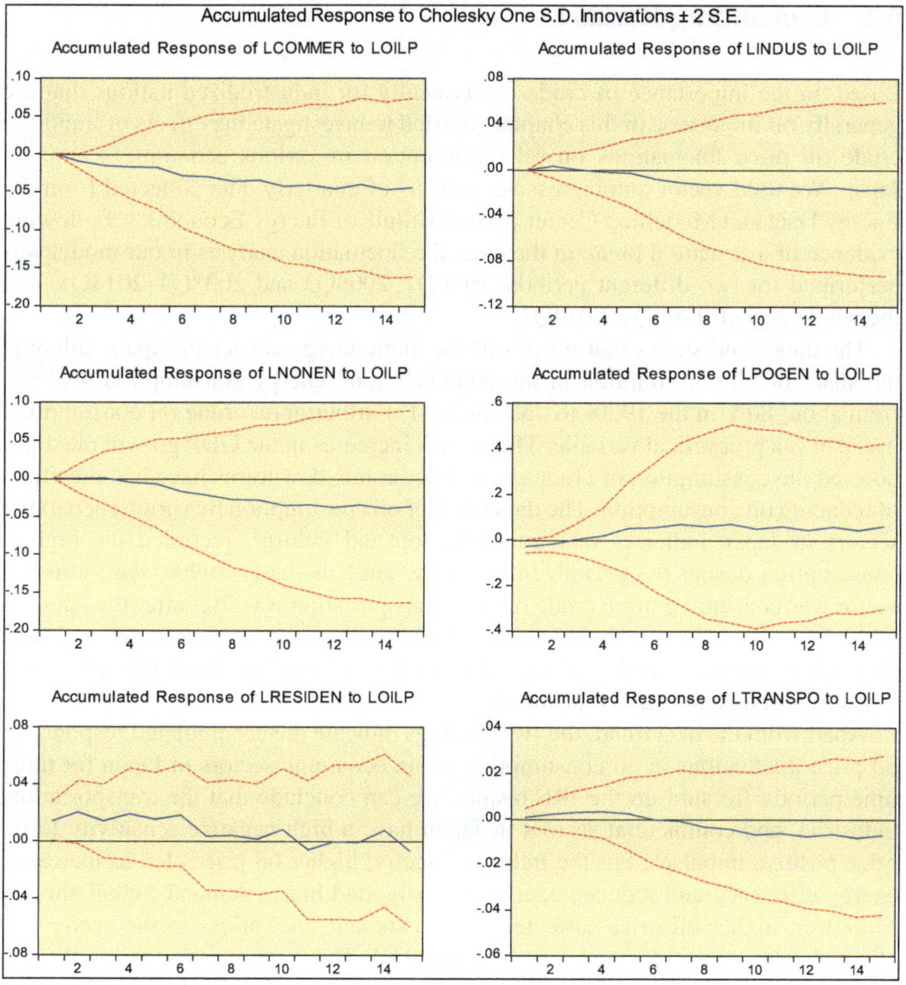

Fig. 6.7 Response of Japan's economic sectors to an oil price fluctuation, 2008Q4–2014Q1 (*Source*: Authors' compilation)

used more in the power generation sector than before because of the lack of nuclear power in Japan. This is the reason for the positive impulses of the oil price, and consumption of oil in the power generation sector also increased. Additionally, the transportation and residential sectors have a positive–negative response. The non-energy sector in the second subperiod shows negative responses to an increase in oil price, which is contrary to the findings for the first subperiod. This is because in the second subperiod, the economy was in recession, so demand for oil as a raw material in petrochemical and other non-energy sectors shrank because of lower aggregate demand. All in all, we can see that the transportation, industrial, and commercial sectors in Japan have a high negative sensitivity to oil price fluctuations.

6.5 Concluding Remarks

Based on the importance of crude oil, typically for industrialized nations that are generally oil importers, in this chapter we tried to investigate the effects of imported crude oil price fluctuations on oil consumption in various economic sectors in Japan. We used vector autoregressive analysis of quarterly data collected from the Energy Data and Modelling Center of the Institute of Energy Economics. Following evidence of a structural break in the data, the fluctuation analysis in our model was performed for two different periods, 1990Q1–2008Q3 and 2008Q4–2014Q1, and the whole period, 1990Q1–2014Q1.

The data trend shows that oil is still the main energy carrier in Japan, although the share of oil consumption in the country's total energy consumption declined from about 80% in the 1970s to 43% in 2011. Furthermore, crude oil consumption in Japan is a procyclical variable. This means increases in the GDP growth rate have boosted the consumption of crude oil, and economic downturns have had the effect of reducing oil consumption. The data trend of oil consumption by various economic sectors in Japan indicates that transportation and industry recorded the highest consumption during the period. Importantly, until the early 1990s, the industrial sector was consuming more crude oil than transportation was. But after the bursting of the Japanese asset price bubble in the 1990s, the Japanese economy suffered from sluggish economic growth and recession—Japan's so-called "Lost Decade"—and industrial oil demand started to shrink.

Apart from the data trend, the IRF findings indicate the accumulated response of oil price fluctuations in oil consumption of six economic sectors in Japan for three time periods. To sum up the IRF results, we can conclude that the transportation, industrial, and commercial sectors in Japan have a high negative sensitivity to oil price positive impulses. For the industrial sector, higher oil prices led to increased energy efficiency and reduced energy intensity, and hence demand for oil shrank. Moreover, higher oil prices affected total costs and final prices in the sector and affected sales, hence demand for oil diminished. The same reasons are applicable to the commercial sector. As for the transportation sector, with higher oil prices, Japanese households used their private automobiles less and demand for public transportation increased. Japanese automotive manufacturers have also increased the energy efficiency of their products in recent years and the share of hybrid cars has risen Taghizadeh-Hesary et al. (2017).

The power generation sector shows a positive response to an oil price increase in both subperiods and for the whole period. The reason for this is the lack of energy resources in Japan and the almost full dependency of the economy on energy imports, especially oil imports. Oil is the main mover of the Japanese economy, hence even at higher prices, the country still needs oil for generating energy.

The responses of the residential and non-energy sectors vary in different subperiods. The second period of our analysis includes the Fukushima nuclear disaster. The results show that in the second subperiod, in the wake of the Fukushima nuclear incident, the country's increased dependence on oil reduced the sensitivity of almost all economic sectors to oil price fluctuations.

References

Agung IGN (2009) Time series data analysis using eviews. Wiley, Hoboken

Lutkepohl H, Reimers H-E (1992) Granger–causality in cointegrated VAR processes, the case of the term structure. Econ Lett 40(3):263–268

Sims CA (1980) Macroeconomics and reality. Econometrica 48:1–48

Taghizadeh-Hesary F, Rasoulinezhad E, Kobayashi Y (2016) Oil price fluctuations and oil consuming sectors: an empirical analysis of Japan. Econ Policy Energy Environ 2(19):33–35. doi:10.3280/EFE2016-002003

Taghizadeh-Hesary F, Yoshino N (2013) Which side of the economy is affected more by oil prices: supply or demand? USAEE research paper 13–139. United States Association for Energy Economics, Cleveland

Taghizadeh-Hesary F, Yoshino N (2014) Monetary policies and oil price determination: an empirical analysis. OPEC Energy Rev 38(1):1–20

Taghizadeh-Hesary F, Yoshino N, Abdoli G, Farzinvash A (2013) An estimation of the impact of oil shocks on crude oil exporting economies and their trade partners. Front Econ China 8(4):571–591

Taghizadeh-Hesary F, Yoshino N, Abadi M, Farboudmanesh R (2015) The response of macro variables of emerging and developed oil importers to oil price movements. J Asia Pac Economy. doi:10.1080/13547860.2015.1057955

Taghizadeh-Hesary F, Yoshino N, Rasoulinezhad E (2017) Impact of fukushima nuclear disaster on oil-consuming sectors of Japan. J Comp Asian Dev 16(2):113–134. doi:10.1080/15339114.2017.1298457

Taghizadeh-Hesary F, Yoshino N (2016) Monetary policy, oil Prices and the real macroeconomic variables: an empirical survey on China, Japan and the U.S. China: Int J 14(4):46–69

US Energy Information Administration. Japan. http://www.eia.gov/beta/international/analysis_includes/countries_long/Japan/japan.pdf. Accessed 3 Feb 2015)

Yoshino N, Taghizadeh-Hesary F (2014) Monetary policies and oil price fluctuations following the subprime mortgage crisis. Int J Monetary Econ Financ 7(3):157–174

Yoshino N, Taghizadeh-Hesary F (2015a) What's behind the recent oil price drop? In: Yoshino N, Taghizadeh-Hesary F (eds) Monetary policy and the oil market. Springer, Tokyo

Yoshino N, Taghizadeh-Hesary F (2015b) Effectiveness of the easing of monetary policy in the Japanese economy, incorporating energy prices. J Comparative Asian Dev 14(2):227–248

Yoshino N, Taghizadeh-Hesary F (2016) Causes and remedies of Japan's long-lasting recession: lessons for China. Chin World Econ 24(2):23–47

Chapter 7
Three Arrows of "Abenomics" and the Further Remedy for the Japanese Economy

Naoyuki Yoshino and Farhad Taghizadeh-Hesary

Abstract "Abenomics" refers to the economic policies advocated by Prime Minister Shinzo Abe, who became Prime Minister of Japan for a second time when his party, the Liberal Democratic Party, won an overwhelming majority at the general election in December 2012. Abenomics is distinguished by sets of policies that comprise "three arrows": (i) an aggressive monetary policy, (ii) fiscal consolidation, and (iii) a growth strategy. The Japanese economy faces an aging population and expanding social welfare expenses. No other country has experienced Japan's rapid growth of retired people. In this chapter we will explain these three aspects of Abenomics and the current state of the Japanese economy and examine what further remedies may be required if Japan is to recover from its long-term deflation. Among remedies we will highlight hometown investment trust (HIT) funds, as a new way of financing start-up businesses and SMEs. The sector that dominates the Japanese economic output and employment.

This chapter is the revised version of a paper presented at the Western Economic Association International (WEAI) 89th Annual Conference, held on 29 June 2014, in Denver, Colorado. We are grateful to all participants of our seminar at the International Monetary Fund (IMF) in Washington, DC on 30 June 2014 for their valuable comments, which helped us to improve this paper. Moreover, we would like to extend our thanks to all commentators at the "Abenomics and Its Impact on the Asian Economy" seminar at the Brookings Institute, 30 June 2014, and to participants of the executive seminar on "Financing for Sustainable Development: Local and Global Perspectives" at the United Nations Economic and Social Commission for Asia and the Pacific (UNESCAP) on 31 October 2014 for their valuable feedback on this paper. Another version of his chapter is published as Yoshino and Taghizadeh-Hesary (2014a).

N. Yoshino
Asian Development Bank Institute (ADBI), Tokyo, Japan

Keio University, Tokyo, Japan
e-mail: nyoshino@adbi.org

F. Taghizadeh-Hesary (✉)
Faculty of Economics, Keio University, Tokyo, Japan

Graduate School of Economics, The University of Tokyo, Tokyo, Japan
e-mail: farhadth@gmail.com; farhadth@keio.jp

N. Yoshino, F. Taghizadeh-Hesary (eds.), *Japan's Lost Decade*, ADB Institute Series on Development Economics, DOI 10.1007/978-981-10-5021-3_7

Keywords Abenomics • Monetary policy • Fiscal consolidation • Home town investment trust funds (HIT)

JEL Classification E52, E62, G21

7.1 Introduction

In the early 1990s, Japan's real estate and stock market bubble burst[1] and the economy went into a tailspin. Since then, Japan has suffered from sluggish economic growth. Two decades later, the collapse of Lehman Brothers in September 2008 and the global financial crisis threatened the entire world economy. In March 2011, a catastrophic earthquake and tsunami struck northeastern Japan. Japan's government budget deficit–gross domestic product (GDP) ratio breached 200% in 2010, mainly because of the high share of pension fund payments in government spending, and the efficiency and effectiveness of public investment was called into question. The Japanese economy required a stimulus to escape from this pattern of long-term sluggish growth. In December 2012, the Liberal Democratic Party won a general election, making Shinzo Abe Prime Minister of Japan, a post that he had held previously in 2007. "Abenomics" refers to the economic policies advocated by the Prime Minister after the election, which were designed to revive the sluggish economy with policy sets that unleash "three arrows": (i) fiscal consolidation, (ii) more aggressive monetary easing by the Bank of Japan (which settled on an inflation target of 2%), and (iii) structural reforms to boost Japan's competitiveness and economic growth. By the end of February 2013, these measures were credited for a 22% rise in the Tokyo Stock Price Index (TOPIX) since Abe's and the Liberal Democratic Party's electoral win. In this chapter we will explain the contributions of the three arrows of Abenomics and the current state of the Japanese economy. We will also propose some further remedies that may be required for Japan to recover from its long-term deflation, such as hometown investment trust (HIT) funds, postponement of the retirement age by introducing a flexible wage rate system, and reduction of subsidies from the central government to local governments (see Yoshino and Taghizadeh-Hesary 2014a, b).

This chapter reviews aspects of the three arrows of Abenomics, identifies a chief financial barrier to realizing progress on the third arrow, and proposes a way forward through the creation of a new funding mechanism. In Sect. 7.2 we review aggressive monetary policies and fiscal consolidation being pursued under Abenomics (the first two arrows). In Sect. 7.3 we review Japan's growth strategy (third arrow of Abenomics). In Sect. 7.4 we present some concluding remarks.

[1] For more information on stock market pricing and stock bubbles, see Yoshino et al. (2014).

7.2 Aggressive Monetary Policy and Fiscal Consolidation in Abenomics

Aggressive Monetary Policy

The government and the Bank of Japan (BOJ) delivered a joint statement on 22 January 2013 on overcoming deflation and achieving sustainable economic growth. The BOJ set a price stability target at 2% (year-on-year rate of change in the consumer price index). The government set an expectation that the BOJ implement aggressive monetary easing to achieve this target as soon as possible. The BOJ pursued this goal by buying long-term government bonds and increasing the monetary base, in contrast to previous attempts at an expansionary monetary policy that mainly focused on buying short-term government bonds.[2] Although prices started to rise after the BOJ implemented monetary easing,[3] a major reason for this was higher energy prices,[4] and at the time of writing the 2% target has not been achieved.

Although prices started to rise after the BOJ implemented monetary easing, it was unable to raise levels of investment and aggregate demand. The achieved inflation in Japan mainly stemmed from other sources, such as the higher energy prices that resulted from the depreciation of the Japanese yen after the easing of monetary policy.

---

[2]On 4 April 2013, the BOJ announced that, based on a decision at the Monetary Policy Meeting, it would purchase Japanese government bonds effective 5 April 2013. This decision was taken at the first Monetary Policy Meeting after Haruhiko Kuroda had taken up his post as the new governor of the BOJ. Approximately Y7.5 trillion per month of Japanese government bonds (2-year bonds, 5-year bonds, 10-year bonds, 20-year bonds, 30-year bonds, 40-year bonds, floating-rate bonds, and inflation-indexed bonds) would be purchased.

[3]Easy monetary policy reduces the interest rate, which increases demand in the commodities market, including the crude oil market, creating inflationary trends in these markets. Since Japan is currently experiencing a high level of demand for oil and liquefied natural gas, inflation in the energy market can disrupt economic growth (see, inter alia, Taghizadeh-Hesary and Yoshino 2013a, 2014; Yoshino and Taghizadeh-Hesary 2014c).

[4]In March 2011, a 9.0 magnitude earthquake struck off the coast of Sendai, Japan, triggering a large tsunami. The damage to Japan resulted in an immediate shutdown of about 10GW of nuclear electric generating capacity. Between the 2011 Fukushima disaster and May 2012, Japan lost all of its nuclear capacity as a result of scheduled maintenance and lack of government approvals to return to operation. Japan replaced the significant loss of nuclear power with generation from imported natural gas, low-sulfur crude oil, fuel oil, and coal. This caused the price of electricity to rise for the government, utilities, and consumers and caused inflation. Increases in the cost of imported fuel have resulted in Japan's top 10 utilities losing over $30 billion in 2012 and 2013. Japan spent $250 billion on total fuel imports in 2012, a third of the country's total import value. Japan consumed over 4.7 million barrels per day of oil in 2012. The increased cost of imported energy had significant negative impact on the Japanese economy. (For more information regarding the impact of higher energy prices on the economy see, inter alia, Taghizadeh-Hesary and Yoshino 2013b, 2016; Taghizadeh-Hesary et al. 2013, 2016.)

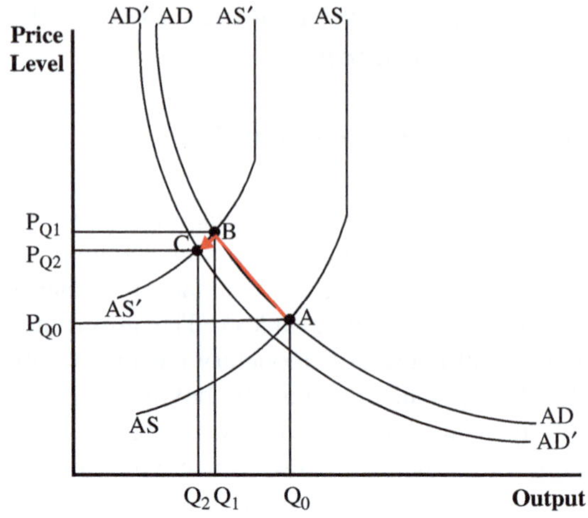

Fig. 7.1 How higher energy prices created inflation in Japan (*Note:* We assume that there is technological progress; that is why the output level in full employment also increased. *AD* aggregate demand, *AS* aggregate supply. *Source*: Taghizadeh-Hesary and Yoshino (2015))

A simple aggregate supply and demand model will clarify the analysis of how higher energy prices created inflation in Japan.

In Fig. 7.1, the economy initially is in equilibrium with price level PQ0 and real output level Q0 at point A. AD is the aggregate demand curve and AS stands for the aggregate supply curve. The aggregate supply curve is constructed with an increasing slope to show that at some real output level, it becomes difficult to increase real output despite increases in the general level of prices. At this output level, the economy achieves full employment.

Let us suppose that the initial equilibrium, point A, is below the full employment level. As the relative price of energy resources (crude oil, natural gas, coal, etc.) increases, the aggregate supply curve shifts to AS'. The employment of existing labor and capital with a given nominal wage rate requires a higher general price for output, if sufficient amounts of the higher-cost energy resources are to be used.

The *productivity* of existing capital and labor resources is reduced so that potential real output declines to Q1. In addition, the same rate of labor employment occurs only if real wages decline sufficiently to match the decline in productivity. This, in turn, happens only if the general level of prices rises sufficiently (PQ1), given the nominal wage rate. This moves the economy to the level of output (Q1) and price level (PQ1). This point is indicated in Fig. 7.1 at point B, which is a disequilibrium point. Given the same supply of labor services and existing plant and equipment, the output associated with full employment declines as producers reduce their use of relatively more expensive energy resources and as plant and equipment become economically obsolete.

On the other hand, on the demand side of the economy, when the price of energy resources rises their consumption declines. Because of this drop in consumption, the aggregate demand curve shifts to AD', which in turn reduces the prices from the previous disequilibrium level at PQ1 and sets them to PQ2 as the final equilibrium

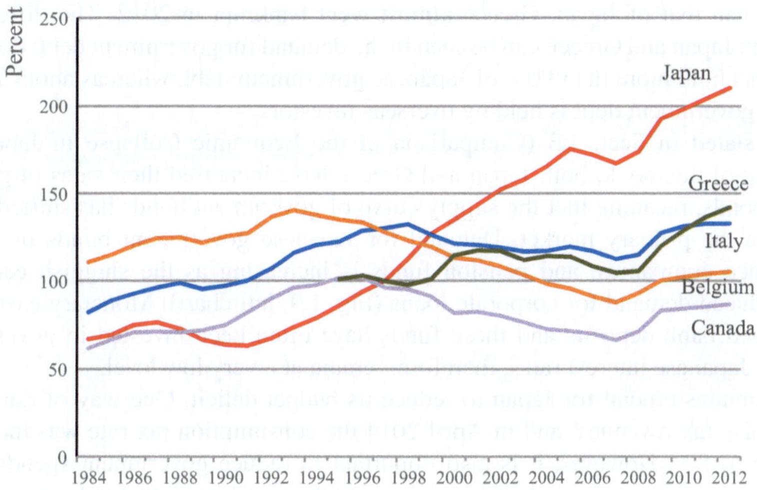

Fig. 7.2 The GDP–debt ratio of selected OECD countries (%). *GDP* gross domestic product, *OECD* Organisation for Economic Co-operation and Development (*Source*: OECD Economic Outlook)

price. Due to less consumption in the economy, this lowers the output levels from the previous point of Q1 to Q2. This point is indicated in Fig. 7.1 at point C, which is the final equilibrium point.

The economy may not adjust instantaneously to point C, even if point C is the new equilibrium. For example, price rigidities due to slow-moving information or other transaction costs can keep nominal prices from adjusting quickly. Consequently, output and prices move along an adjustment path such as that indicated by the arrow in Fig. 7.1.

Fiscal Consolidation

Figure 7.2 compares the gross debt–GDP ratio of selected Organisation for Economic Co-operation and Development (OECD) countries.[5]

Japan's debt–GDP ratio is the highest among OECD countries, yet budget deficits are still sustainable. Although the Greek government debt–GDP ratio is

[5]If we take into account national assets such as highways, government properties, and so on, we can compute net debt to GDP ratio. However even the net debt–GDP ratio of Japan is growing due to an aging population. Social welfare payments such as pensions and health care for the elderly are growing very rapidly (Hoshi et al. 1993).

lower than that of Japan, Greece almost went bankrupt in 2012. The differences between Japan and Greece can be seen in the demand for government debt: domestic investors hold more than 90% of Japanese government debt, whereas about 70% of Greek government debt is held by overseas investors.

As stated in Sect. 1.3 (Comparison of the Economic Collapse in Japan and Greece) of this book, both Japan and Greece have increased their sales of government bonds, meaning that the supply curve of government bonds has shifted to the right in the primary market. Demand for Japanese government bonds by banks, insurance companies, and pension funds is increasing as the sluggish economy has reduced demand for corporate loans (Fig. 1.9, left chart). Monetary easing has increased bank deposits and these funds have often been invested in government bonds. Japanese interest rates, therefore, remain at a very low level.

It remains crucial for Japan to reduce its budget deficit. One way of doing this is to raise tax revenues, and in April 2014 the consumption tax rate was increased from 5 to 8%. However, it is also important to reduce government spending. To reduce government expenditure on social welfare and pension funds, people will have to work longer and not rely wholly on social security and pensions after retirement. This could mean that the retirement age needs to be postponed and wage rates must be based on productivity rather than seniority, as is the case among many Japanese companies. The rationale for this is explained in Sect. 7.3. The Abe government is presently considering these options. (For more information about fiscal consolidation of Japan, see Doi et al. 2011.)

In conclusion, the government will need to manage short-term fiscal policy in a timely and flexible manner, while firmly expressing the political will to restore Japan's fiscal balance over the medium and long term. The government knows that it must credibly reach the current fiscal consolidation target, which aims to achieve a fiscal surplus by FY2020.

7.3 Growth Strategy

The third arrow of Abenomics is putting forth a growth strategy. The Japanese government has pledged that over the medium and long term, it will take measures to strengthen the competitiveness of domestic firms, overcome energy constraints, and enhance the innovation platform based on a well-defined growth strategy, while at the same time accelerating the removal of domestic institutional obstacles, including regulations. In this section, we review the growth strategies of the current government in Japan and propose additional remedies to foster economic growth. We then define one of these remedies—the use of hometown investment trust funds as new way for financing SMEs and start-ups.

Growth Strategies of the Current Japanese Government

In January 2014, during a National Diet meeting, Minister of Finance Taro Aso identified 10 major aspects of Japan's growth strategy:

(i) The government will encourage companies to increase employee wages, which will encourage the expansion of domestic consumption.
(ii) To cover increasing social security spending, the government will increase taxes.[6]
(iii) The government's deficit targets are (a) by 2015, the budget deficit over GDP ratio should be half of the 2010 level; and (b) by 2020, the ratio should be zero. To achieve this goal, the government will make its spending much more efficient.
(iv) Since Japan's population is aging, the government will encourage greater female participation in the labor force, in part by improving child care facilities. The government will also encourage older people to keep working and retirees to rejoin the workforce.
(v) The expenses of medical care for the elderly have been increasing drastically. The government will monitor prices of medicine and health care to ensure they reflect market prices. The government will put in place a regional medical care system.
(vi) The government will ensure there is sufficient funding for disaster preparedness.
(vii) The government will provide more scholarships to students, and increase expenditure on research and development.
(viii) The government will provide sufficient funding for repairing aging infrastructure.
(ix) The government will ensure SMEs have access to easy financing for research and development.
(x) The farming population is aging and the government will provide sufficient funds to ensure an efficient and competitive agriculture sector.

In addition to these remedies, there are others that we believe are necessary to foster the economic growth in Japan, which include the following:

(i) reduction of transfers from central to local governments,
(ii) diversification of households' asset allocation,
(iii) switching asset allocation pension funds and insurance companies from pay-as-you-go to 401(k)-style,
(iv) review of asset management fees,
(v) optimal mix of public and private funds,
(vi) review of monetary policy goals,
(vii) diversification of the energy basket, and
(viii) use of hometown investment trust funds to finance riskier businesses.

[6]The rate of consumption tax in Japan was raised from 5% to 8% on 1 April 2014.

These remedies are completely explained in Chapter 1 of this book. Below we explain the potential role of hometown investment trust funds in fostering the growth of Japan's small business sector.

Hometown Investment Trust Funds

In Japan, like other Asian countries, the economy is dominated by small and medium-sized enterprises (SMEs).

As shown in Fig. 7.3, more than 99% of all businesses in Japan are SMEs; they also employ most of the working population and account for a large proportion of economic output.

On the other hand, the Japanese economy, like other Asian economies, is more bank-oriented than capital-market-oriented compared with western economies (see Fig. 1.12 in Chap. 1).

Due to strict Basel capital requirements, banks have to keep much more capital when lending to risky borrowers such as SMEs and start-up businesses (Yoshino and Hirano 2011). The Japanese economy is dominated by bank loans that have to follow stricter Basel capital requirements (Basel III). Hence banks are reluctant to lend to SMEs and start-up businesses, because they consider these sectors to be risky. Therefore, it is urgent to develop regional funds (or hometown investment trust funds) to provide money to SMEs and start-up businesses in Japan and other parts of Asia. Then, if these regional trust funds are sold through branch offices to regional banks, post offices, credit associations, and large banks, this would increase the opportunities for regional companies to raise funds.

However, such trust funds would not be guaranteed by the Deposit Insurance Corporation and risks would be borne by investors.[7] The terms of a trust fund would

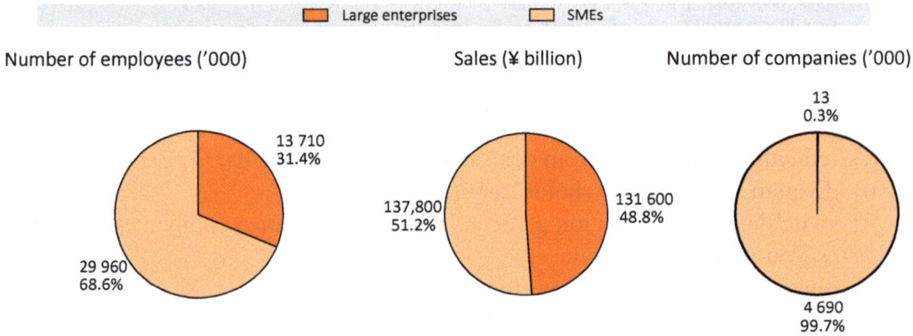

Fig. 7.3 Small and medium-sized enterprises in Japan. *SME* small and medium-sized enterprise (*Source*: Government of Japan, Ministry of Economy, Trade, and Industry (2011) White Paper on SMEs)

[7]For more information about the deposit insurance mechanism, see Yoshino et al. (2015).

have to be fully explained to investors (for example, where their funds would be invested and the risks associated with the investment) in order to strengthen investor confidence and help the trust fund market to grow (Yoshino 2013; Yoshino and Taghizadeh-Hesary 2014d). Examples of such funds in Japan include wind power generators and musicians' funds. In the first example, in order to construct 20 wind power generators, public–private partnerships were launched and local residents invested between $1000 and $5000 in a fund. They receive dividends every year through the sale of electricity from each wind power generator in which they invest. Musicians' funds gather many small investors who buy units for $150–$500. If a musician becomes successful and their music sells well, the sales will generate a high rate of return for the fund.

Examples can be found of both successful and failed funds. Project assessors play a key role in evaluating each project to limit the number of nonperforming investments and losses by investors. Some of Japan's funds are regarded as charities, with some investors seeing them as a way to invest in their region to support new business ventures.

Such new ventures pose a problem for banks, as although some will have high expected rates of return, the high risks involved make it difficult for banks to finance them. However, if the projects are financed by hometown investment trust funds rather than by deposits transformed into bank loans, they will not create nonperforming loans for banks. Banks can still benefit, and compete with each other, by selling hometown investment trust funds through their branch offices. Investors must be advised that their investment is not guaranteed, although they may receive a high rate of return. If a bank sells successful hometown investment trust funds, it will attract more investors; if it sells loss-making funds it will lose investors. Competition will improve the quality of projects and enhance the risk-adjusted returns for investors.

The hometown investment trust fund has three main advantages. First, it contributes to financial market stability by lowering information asymmetry. Individual households and firms have direct access to information about the borrowing firms, mainly SMEs, to which they lend. Second, it is a stable source of risk capital. The fund is project driven. Firms and households decide to invest by getting to know the borrowers and their projects. In this way the fund distributes risk, but not so that it renders risk intractable, which was the problem with the "originate-to-distribute" model.[8] Third, it contributes to economic recovery by connecting firms and households with SMEs that are worthy of their support. It also creates employment opportunities at the SMEs as well as for retirees from financial institutions who can help assess the projects.

Introduction of the hometown investment trust fund has huge global implications. The world is seeking a method of financial intermediation that minimizes information asymmetry, distributes risk without making it opaque, and contributes

[8]In the "originate-to-distribute" model, lenders make loans with the intention of selling them to other institutions and/or investors, as opposed to holding the loans through maturity.

to economic recovery. Funds similar to Japan's hometown investment trust fund can succeed in all three ways—after all, the majority of the world's businesses are SMEs (Yoshino 2013).

7.4 Conclusion

To address the high level of Japan's government budget deficit-GDP ratio and the sluggish economic growth the government of Shinzo Abe, which was elected in December 2012, introduced a reform program called Abenomics, which aimed to revive the sluggish economy with "three arrows": fiscal consolidation, more aggressive monetary easing from the Bank of Japan, and structural reforms to boost Japan's competitiveness and economic growth.

As for the first arrow, fiscal consolidation, the government aims to implement its short-term fiscal policy in a timely and flexible manner, while also firmly expressing the political will to restore the fiscal balance over the medium and long term by cutting the primary deficit of the central and local government in half between FY2010 and FY2015 and achieving a fiscal surplus by FY2020.

As for the second arrow, aggressive monetary policy, the BOJ set a price stability target of 2% (year-on-year rate of change in the consumer price index). The government expects the BOJ to implement aggressive monetary easing to achieve this target as soon as possible. Although prices started to rise after monetary easing, this was largely due to higher oil prices, and the 2% inflation rate target has still not been achieved. The current governor of the BOJ, Haruhiko Kuroda, is pursuing a monetary policy that involves buying long-term government bonds and increasing the monetary base (this is in contrast to the former government, when an expansionary monetary policy was mainly carried out by buying short-term government bonds).

As for the third arrow, the growth strategy, the government has encouraged higher wages to encourage the expansion of domestic consumption, raised taxes to cover increasing social security spending, encouraged female participation in the labor force, postponed the retirement age, prepared for a transition to a regional medical care system for the elderly and taken measures to reduce health care costs, provided a sufficient budget for disaster preparedness, increased the share of R&D and education in government expenditure, improved access to financing for SMEs, and is carrying out agricultural reforms to overcome the inefficiency of this sector.

As part of the growth strategy, we put forth a proposal for a new form of financial intermediation called the hometown investment trust (HIT), with the goal of connecting fund providers and their hometowns. The Japanese government is currently considering this new form of financial intermediation as one remedy for addressing Japan's sluggish growth.

References

Doi T, Hoshi T, Okimoto T (2011) Japanese government debt and sustainability of fiscal policy. J Jpn Int Econ 25(4):414–433

Hoshi T, Kashyap A, Scharfstein D (1993) The choice between public and private debt: an analysis of post-deregulation corporate financing in Japan. NBER working paper series no 4421. National Bureau of Economic Research, Cambridge

Taghizadeh-Hesary F, Yoshino N (2013a) Empirical analysis of oil price determination based on market quality theory. Keio/Kyoto Joint Global COE discussion paper series 2012-044. Keio University, Tokyo

Taghizadeh-Hesary F, Yoshino N (2013b) Which side of the economy is affected more by oil prices: supply or demand? USAEE research paper 13–139. United States Association for Energy Economics, Cleveland

Taghizadeh-Hesary F, Yoshino N (2014) Monetary policies and oil price determination: an empirical analysis. OPEC Energy Rev 38(1):1–20

Taghizadeh-Hesary F, Yoshino N (2015) Macroeconomic effects of oil price fluctuations on emerging and developed economies in a model incorporating monetary variables. Economics and Policy of Energy and the Environment. n. 2/2015:51–75

Taghizadeh-Hesary F, Yoshino N (2016) Monetary policy, oil prices and the real macroeconomic variables: an empirical survey on China, Japan and the U.S. China Int J 14(4):46–69

Taghizadeh-Hesary F, Yoshino N, Abdoli G, Farzinvash A (2013) An estimation of the impact of oil shocks on crude oil exporting economies and their trade partners. Front Econ China 8(4):571–591

Taghizadeh-Hesary F, Yoshino N, Abadi MH, Farboudmanesh R (2016) The response of macro variables of emerging and developed oil importers to oil price movements. J Asia Pac Econ 21(1):91–102

Yoshino N (2013) The background of hometown investment trust funds. In: Yoshino N, Kaji S (eds) Hometown investment trust funds: a stable way to supply risk capital. Springer, Tokyo

Yoshino N, Hirano T (2011) Pro-cyclicality of the Basel capital requirement ratio and its impact on banks. Asian Econ Papers 10(2):22–36

Yoshino N, Taghizadeh-Hesary F (2014a) An analysis of challenges faced by Japan's economy and Abenomics. Jpn Polit Econ 40(3–4):37–62

Yoshino N, Taghizadeh-Hesary F (2014b) Three arrows of "Abenomics" and the structural reform of Japan: inflation targeting policy of the central bank, fiscal consolidation, and growth strategy. ADBI working paper no 492. Asian Development Bank Institute, Tokyo

Yoshino N, Taghizadeh-Hesary F (2014c) Monetary policy and oil price fluctuations following the subprime mortgage crisis. Int J Monetary Econ Finance 7(3):157–174

Yoshino N, Taghizadeh Hesary F (2014d) Hometown investment trust funds: an analysis of credit risk. ADBI working paper 505. Asian Development Bank Institute, Tokyo

Yoshino N, Taghizadeh-Hesary F, Hassanzadeh A, Danu Prasetyo A (2014) Response of stock markets to monetary policy: the Tehran stock market perspective. J Comparative Asian Dev 13(3):517–545

Yoshino N, Taghizadeh Hesary F, Nili F (2015) Estimating dual deposit insurance premium rates and forecasting non-performing loans: two new models. ADBI working paper 510. Asian Development Bank Institute, Tokyo

Chapter 8
The Ineffectiveness of Japan's Negative Interest Rate Policy

Naoyuki Yoshino, Farhad Taghizadeh-Hesary, and Hiroaki Miyamoto

Abstract In April 2013, the Bank of Japan (BOJ) introduced an inflation target of 2% with the aim of overcoming deflation and achieving sustainable economic growth. But due to lower international oil prices it was unable to achieve this target and was forced to take further measures. Hence, in February 2016, the BOJ adopted a negative interest rate policy by massively increasing the money supply through purchasing long-term Japanese government bonds (JGB). Previously the BOJ only purchased short-term government bonds. This policy has flattened the yield curve of JGBs. One the one hand, banks reduced the numbers of government bonds because short-term bond yields had become negative, and even the interest rates of long-term government bonds up to 17 years became negative. On the other hand, bank loans to the corporate sector did not increase, due to the Japanese economy's vertical investment–saving (IS) curve. This chapter firstly explains why, in the view of the authors, the BOJ must reduce its 2% inflation target in the present low oil price era. Secondly, it argues that Japan cannot make a sustainable recovery from its long-lasting recession and tackle its long-standing deflation problem by means of its current monetary policy, and its negative interest rate policy in particular. It is of key importance to make the IS curve downward sloping rather than vertical. That means the rate of return on investment must be positive and companies must be

---

Another version of this chapter is available as Yoshino et al. (2017).

N. Yoshino
Asian Development Bank Institute (ADBI), Tokyo, Japan

Keio University, Tokyo, Japan
e-mail: nyoshino@adbi.org

F. Taghizadeh-Hesary (✉)
Faculty of Economics, Keio University, Tokyo, Japan

Graduate School of Economics, The University of Tokyo, Tokyo, Japan
e-mail: farhadth@gmail.com; farhadth@keio.jp

H. Miyamoto
Graduate School of Public Policy, The University of Tokyo, Tokyo, Japan

College of Business, Rikkyo University, Tokyo, Japan
e-mail: hmiyamoto@imf.org

N. Yoshino, F. Taghizadeh-Hesary (eds.), *Japan's Lost Decade*, ADB Institute Series on Development Economics, DOI 10.1007/978-981-10-5021-3_8

willing to invest if interest rates are lowered. Japan's long-term recession is due to structural problems that cannot be solved by its current monetary policy. The last section reports the results of our simulation of tackling Japan's aging population by introducing a productivity-based wage rate and postponement of the retirement age, which will help the recovery of the Japanese economy.

Keywords Negative interest rate policy • Japanese economy • Oil price • Abenomics

JEL Classification E43, E52, E12

8.1 Introduction

On 22 January 2013, the Government of Japan and the Bank of Japan (BOJ) delivered a joint statement on overcoming deflation and achieving sustainable economic growth. The BOJ set the price stability target at 2% (year-on-year rate of change in the consumer price index). Since then, the BOJ has been implementing aggressive monetary easing through buying long-term government bonds and increasing the monetary base, in contrast to previous expansionary monetary policy attempts, which mainly focused on buying short-term government bonds to achieve this target.

Although for some short periods in 2014 inflation reached the 2% target, this was mainly caused by higher energy prices, especially of oil, and because the consumption tax rate was raised from 5 to 8%. Following the start of the global oil price decline in June 2014, general price levels in Japan also started to decline. Oil prices dropped from over $100 per barrel in June 2014 to less than $30 per barrel in February 2016. Oil and other petroleum products' imports make up a significant portion of total Japanese imports. That is why the price fluctuation of oil has a significant impact on Japanese macroeconomic variables, including on the inflation rate.

Although the price of oil is now less than half of what it was in early 2014, the BOJ has maintained its 2% inflation target. When the price of oil decreases, production becomes cheaper and the aggregate supply curve shifts to the right, which decreases the equilibrium price level. That means the target inflation rate needs to be reviewed and lowered.

On the other hand, the BOJ could not achieve a stable 2% inflation rate and hence further eased the interest rate. At its monetary policy meeting of 29 January 2016, the BOJ policy board decided to introduce "quantitative and qualitative monetary easing (QQE) with a negative interest rate" to achieve the price stability target of 2% at the earliest possible time. The BOJ implemented this policy by increasing the money supply through purchasing long-term Japanese government bonds (JGBs). This policy has flattened the yield curve of JGBs and banks started to reduce their purchases of government bonds because government bond yields up to 17 years became negative.

In this chapter we first shed light on the role of oil prices in the Japanese economy and on prices in Japan. We show why, in the current low oil price era, the BOJ needs to deflate the inflation targets. We also investigate whether the recent negative interest rate policy of the BOJ was effective, and provide some suggestions for overcoming deflation and achieving sustainable economic growth.

The chapter is structured as follows. Section 8.2 provides an overview of recent global oil price movements. Section 8.3 discusses oil prices and the Japanese economy, and Sect. 8.4 lower oil prices and the negative interest rate policy of the BOJ. Section 8.5 presents our simulation results and Sect. 8.6 provides our concluding remarks.

8.2 Recent Global Oil Price Movements

Oil prices dropped from more than $100 per barrel in June 2014 to less than $30 per barrel in February 2016 (Fig. 8.1). They started rising again in early April 2016 because of a fragile improvement in demand, but they are still less than half of the 2014 level. The sharp drop was due to several reasons related to supply and demand conditions and expectations in the oil market (for more information, refer to Yoshino and Taghizadeh-Hesary 2016a). In this section, we shed light on the reasons for the sharp drop.

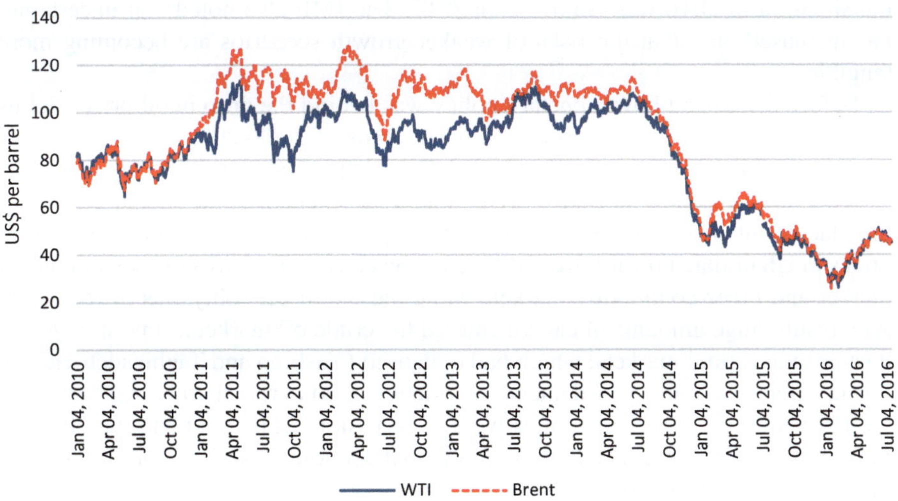

Fig. 8.1 Recent global spot oil price movements (4 Jan 2010–18 July 2016) (*Note:* WTI price is Cushing, OK West Texas Intermediate (WTI) Spot Price free on board (FOB) (US dollars per barrel); Brent price is Europe Brent Spot Price FOB (US dollars per barrel). *Source:* Thomson Reuters. Spot Prices for Crude Oil and Petroleum Products. Release date: 20 September 2016)

Causes of Oil Price Drop

The price of oil is determined partly by actual supply and demand, and partly by expectations. Some of the recent price collapse can be attributed to a new glut in oil supply. Unconventional energy resources, such as shale oil, shale gas, and oil sands, have increased the global oil supply. Massive discoveries of oil in North Dakota and Texas in the United States (US) have driven down prices, and even amid tensions in the Middle East, roughly 3 million barrels a day more are being produced now than in 2011.

Moreover, while oil prices were falling, the Organization of Petroleum Exporting Countries (OPEC), which controls nearly 40% of the world market, failed to reach an agreement on production curbs at its 2014–2015 meetings, thus sending the price down even further.

In 2014 and again in 2015, supply exceeded demand by massive margins—0.9 million barrels per day (mb/d) and 2 mb/d.

In 2014, global economic activity was subdued. The International Monetary Fund (IMF) reported global gross domestic product (GDP) growth of 3.4% in constant prices. Growth in emerging markets and developing economies—while still accounting for over 70% of global growth—declined for the fourth consecutive year, mostly driven by the People's Republic of China, Brazil, and Russia. In 2015, global economic activity declined further, with GDP growth falling to 3.1%. The IMF downgraded its global growth outlook for 2016 by 0.2–3.2%, which is broadly in line with 2015. Although it forecast a strengthening of the recovery in 2017, the situation in 2016 was almost as in 2015. The IMF also noted that uncertainty has increased, and that the risks of weaker growth scenarios are becoming more tangible.

Before discussing how monetary policy was behind the drop in oil prices, let us look further back to the subprime mortgage crisis of 2008–2009 and review what happened to the US money market and global oil prices at that time.

After the subprime mortgage crisis, the weak exchange rate of the US dollar that had resulted from the Federal Reserve's quantitative easing policy pushed oil prices in US dollars upward over 2009–2012 by causing investors to invest in the oil market and other commodity markets while the world economy was in recession. As a result, huge amounts of capital entered the crude oil market as investors found it safer than capital markets, which had collapsed (Yoshino and Taghizadeh-Hesary 2014a). Because of this new demand, oil prices started to rise sharply in 2009, when the US and many other economies were in recession. This trend had the effect of imposing a longer recovery time on the global economy, as oil is one of the most important production inputs.

Let us move to the second half of 2014 to see what has happened more recently. In 2014, financial conditions eased compared with 2013. In particular, long-term interest rates declined in developed economies because of the economic recovery and expectations of a lower neutral policy rate in the US over the medium term.

Equity prices have generally risen and risk premiums declined in developed economies and emerging markets. In the US, both the Dow Jones Industrial Average and Standard and Poor's (S&P) 500 Index powered to record highs, boosted by the strengthening US economy and liquidity provided by the Federal Reserve's unprecedented quantitative easing. The Dow, up 8.5%, surpassed two key psychological levels during 2014—17,000 and 18,000—and the S&P 500, 12.8% higher, surpassed the 2000 milestone.

The liquidity provided mainly by the Federal Reserve, especially during the 2008–2009 financial crisis, transferred to the oil market and created huge speculative demand, causing a surge in oil prices. In 2014, because the US and some other developed and emerging capital markets were recovering, it moved back to the capital markets, resulting in a depressed global oil demand growth rate and a price collapse in the market. This means that this factor may have played a bigger role in reducing oil prices than supply and lower economic growth (Yoshino and Taghizadeh-Hesary 2016a; Taghizadeh-Hesary and Yoshino 2014).

8.3 Oil Prices and the Japanese Economy

In 2015, the total value of Japan's imports amounted to $648 billion, 23% ($150 billion) of which was mineral fuels, $67 billion petroleum, $46 billion liquefied natural gas, $16 billion coal, $15 billion petroleum products, and $5 billion liquefied petroleum gas (LPG) (Fig. 8.2). Although Japan's crude oil imports in 2015 fell to their lowest level since 1988 as demand had been weakening due in part to a declining population, slower economic growth, and more energy-efficient vehicles

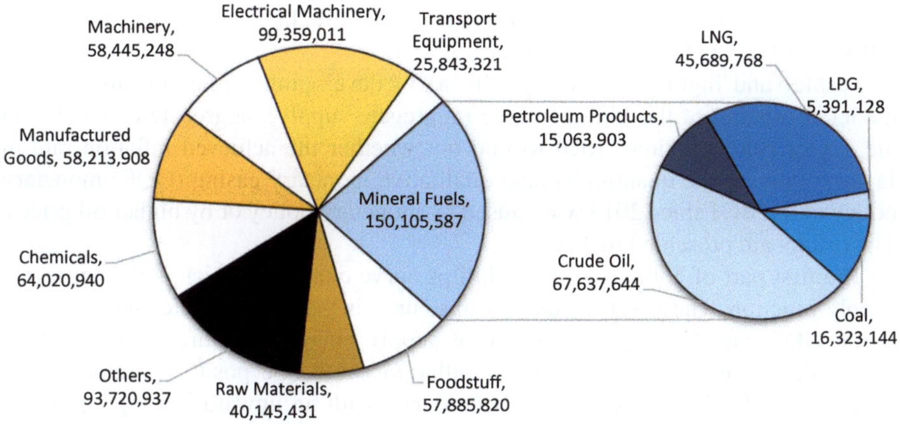

Fig. 8.2 Japan's imports by principal commodity, 2015 (thousands of $). *LNG* liquefied natural gas, *LPG* liquefied petroleum gas (*Source:* Japan External Trade Organization 2016)

and industries, oil is still the main mover of the Japanese economy and Japan remains the third-largest consumer of crude oil behind the US and the People's Republic of China.

Japan is dependent on imports for 91.4% of its energy supply. Since the Fukushima nuclear disaster in 2011, the share of fossil fuels in power generation has been increasing, as a substitute for nuclear power. The level of dependence on petroleum, which had been declining in recent years, increased to 47.2% in fiscal year 2012. In fiscal year 2013, the total primary energy supply in Japan was 21,973 petajoules, up 1.1% from the previous fiscal year, broken down as follows: 45.7% was petroleum, 24.2% coal, 22.5% natural gas, 3.1% hydropower, and 0.4% nuclear power. Other sources were also used, though only in small quantities, including energy from waste, geothermal energy, and natural energy (solar photovoltaic, wind power, and biomass energy, among others) (Ministry of Internal Affairs and Communication 2015).

The result of eliminating nuclear power generation and substituting it with fossil fuels was that the energy self-sufficiency[1] percentage fell from 19.6% in fiscal year 2000 to 8.6% in fiscal year 2013 (Ministry of Internal Affairs and Communication 2015). Before the 2011 Great East Japan Earthquake, Japan had been the third-largest consumer of nuclear power in the world, after the US and France, with nuclear power accounting for about 13% of the country's total energy consumption in 2010 (Taghizadeh-Hesary et al. 2015a). In 2012, the share of nuclear energy fell to 1% of total energy consumption, contributing a similar level to primary energy consumption in 2013, as only two reactors were operating for a little more than half the year. In 2014 Japan did not produce any nuclear power (Taghizadeh-Hesary and Yoshino 2015).

The great importance of oil for the Japanese economy means oil price movements have significant effects on Japanese macroeconomic variables including economic growth and the inflation rate. Several scholars have shown this (Hamilton 1996; Lee et al. 2001; Blanchard and Gali 2007; Kilian 2008; Taghizadeh-Hesary et al. 2013, 2015a; Yoshino and Taghizadeh-Hesary 2015a).

Yoshino and Taghizadeh-Hesary (2015a), by developing a simultaneous equation model consisting of the Phillips curve (aggregate supply), aggregate demand, and the Taylor rule equations, tried to find out whether the achieved inflation rate in Japan following the quantitative and qualitative monetary easing (QQE) monetary policy of the BOJ since 2013 was caused by monetary policy or by higher oil prices. The results are presented in Table 8.1.

The first part of Table 8.1 is the Phillips curve equation, which is the aggregate supply function. The y-axis of the Phillips curve is the inflation rate and the x-axis is the GDP gap. Usually, the aggregate supply curve is upward sloping, which means the GDP gap and the rate of inflation should be positively related. The results for 1994Q2–2001Q4 are in accordance with an upward sloping aggregate

[1]Domestic production of primary energy (including nuclear)/domestic supply of primary energy × 100.

Table 8.1 Oil prices and the inflation rate in Japan

	1994Q2–2001Q4	2002Q1–2014Q2
Phillips curve (Inflation rate)		
Lagged inflation rate	0.89(4.08)**	−0.36(−1.12)
GDP gap	0.69(2.18)*	−0.24(−0.45)
Crude oil price	0.06(3.27)**	0.07(2.59)**
Gas price	0.03(0.45)	0.05(1.17)
Aggregate demand (GDP gap)		
Long-term real interest rate	−0.02(−4.71)**	−0.02(−1.09)
Lagged GDP gap	−0.33(−1.66)	0.42(1.52)
Exchange rate	0.09(2.18)*	0.07(1.17)
Taylor rule (Short-term interest rate)		
Inflation rate	1.21(0.67)	1.94(2.16)*
GDP gap	4.76(2.72)**	3.89(3.01)**

Source: Yoshino and Taghizadeh-Hesary (2015a)
Notes: T-statistics are in parentheses. * indicates significance at 5%. ** indicates significance at 1%. *GDP* gross domestic product

supply, which means a larger GDP gap tended to result in a higher inflation rate in the first period. When the economy is in an inflationary environment, that will accelerate current inflation even more, so in this situation lagged inflation should have a positive impact on the current inflation rate, which is what happened in the first period of this analysis. However, after 2002 Japan was faced with deflation and a decreasing GDP gap, so the results show that the lagged inflation rate and the GDP gap in the Phillips curve are not significant in the second period of this analysis, which is indeed the case. This means (i) the current year's inflation was not affected by lagged inflation rates; and (ii) because the economy was in recession, the GDP gap was negative and had no impact on the inflation rate. However, the rising crude oil price shifted up the aggregate supply curve, because imports of oil created inflationary pressure. Therefore, the positive sign of the crude oil price in both periods is correct. This finding is in accordance with our hypothesis. Although inflation was created after the adoption of QQE, we believe this was due mainly to other factors, especially higher oil prices. Following the easy monetary policy of the BOJ, the yen started to depreciate heavily, which increased prices of crude oil and other energy imports, pushing up production costs and creating inflation. Yoshino and Taghizadeh-Hesary's (2015a) results support this assertion. In the second period, the sign of the output gap in the Phillips curve equation was not significant, which means that the economy was in recession and aggregate demand did not rise enough to have an impact on price levels. However, the higher oil price in yen, which is mainly the result of easy monetary policy, had a significant impact on general price levels, which has been a negative development for Japanese manufacturers.

The second part of Table 8.1 is aggregate demand. It is clear that in the second period, long-term interest rates did not have any significant association with the

GDP gap. This means the QQE policies that cut the short-term and long-term interest rates could neither stimulate the economy nor create inflation. And as mentioned above, the general price inflation in that period was due to other factors, mainly the oil price.

The third part of Table 8.1 is the Taylor Rule, which depends on inflation and the GDP gap. If the inflation rate keeps rising, the central bank will tighten monetary policy, so the inflation rate should have a positive sign (Yoshino et al. 2014). It is positive in both periods, but significant only in the second period. The GDP gap widened from 1994Q2 to 2001Q4. When current GDP is higher than full employment GDP, the economy is accelerating, at which point the central bank usually tries to tighten the money market, so the GDP gap should have a positive sign in line with the Taylor rule. After 2002, Japan was faced with recession, so the GDP gap became negative; the central bank then lowered the short-term interest rate, and again the GDP gap should have a positive sign in line with the Taylor rule.

8.4 Lower Oil Prices and the Negative Interest Rate Policy of the BOJ

In 2013, the BOJ set a price stability target of 2% (year-on-year rate of change in the consumer price index). On 4 April 2013, the BOJ announced that, based on a decision at its monetary policy meeting, it would purchase Japanese government bonds, effective 5 April 2013. This decision was taken at the first monetary policy meeting after Haruhiko Kuroda had taken up his post as the new governor of the BOJ.

Figure 8.3 shows the expansion of the monetary base and JGB holdings by the BOJ. Since 2013 there has been a massive increase in the monetary base through implementation of the QQE policy after Prime Minister Abe came to power for the second time. On the liability side of the BOJ's balance sheet, the monetary base increased drastically. Table 8.2 shows the asset side of the BOJ's balance sheet. In April 2013, assets amounted to ¥175 trillion and by May 2016 had expanded to ¥426 trillion, an increase of almost 2.5 times in 3 years. In the same period, JGBs, which were the major purchase of the BOJ, went up from ¥98 trillion to ¥319 trillion (Table 8.2). So in other words, the major part of the asset is the purchase of long-term government bonds. Figure 8.3 shows that there was a parallel increase in the monetary base and the JGB holdings by the BOJ after 2013.

In Table 8.3, the monetary base–GDP ratios of Japan are compared with those of the US and the eurozone. In July 2016, the ratio was 80% in Japan, 21% in the US, and 20% in the eurozone.

As mentioned above, the BOJ has been maintaining its 2% inflation rate target. But only for short periods, mainly during 2014, did the Japanese inflation rate exceed 1.5%. In 2014 this was due mainly to an increase in consumption tax and higher oil prices. But after oil prices fell, the consumer price index fell and the inflation rate dropped to below 1% (Fig. 8.4).

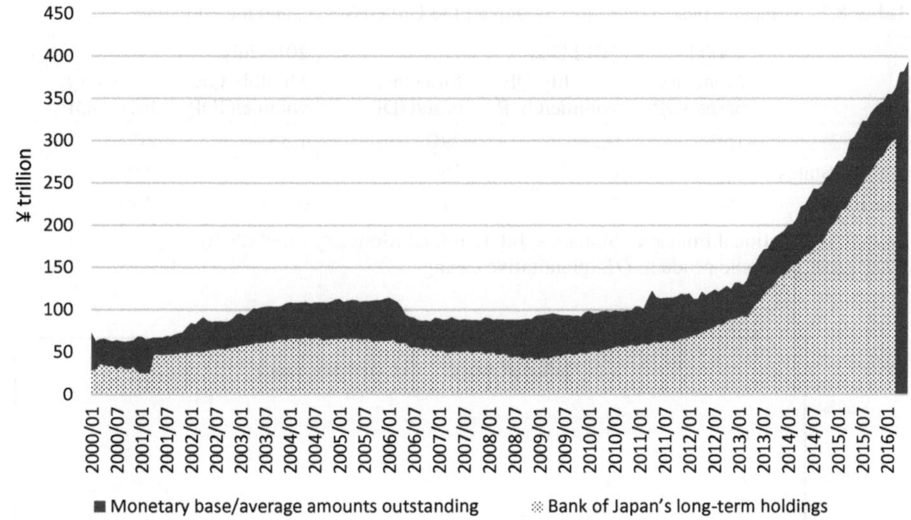

Fig. 8.3 Expansion in the monetary base and Japanese government bond holdings (January 2000–June 2016). ¥ yen (*Notes:* Monetary base is average amounts outstanding in each month. Bank of Japan's long-term JGB holding data was available up to March 2016. *Source:* Bank of Japan time series database (2016). https://www.stat-search.boj.or.jp/index_en.html (accessed 30 July 2016))

Table 8.2 Monetary base and JGB purchase data (Comparison of April 2013 with May 2016) (¥ trillion)

	April 2013 (actual)	May 2016 (actual)	Average annual increase
Monetary base	155	387	About 80 trillion
Japanese government bonds	98	319	About 80 trillion
Commercial paper	1.4	2.3	Outstanding balance maintained
Corporate bonds	2.9	3.2	Outstanding balance maintained
ETFs	1.7	8.0	About 3 trillion
J-REITS	0.13	0.31	About 90 billion
Total assets of the Bank of Japan	175	426	–

Source: Bank of Japan Time series database (2016). https://www.stat-search.boj.or.jp/index_en.html (accessed 30 July 2016)

ETF index-linked exchange-traded fund, *J-REITS* investment equities issued by real estate investment trusts

Due to falling oil prices, on the one hand, the aggregate supply (AS) curve shifts to the right and reduced general price levels because oil as the main energy provider is one of the production inputs. Hence, declining oil prices lead to cheaper input prices for production, which is good news for suppliers and manufacturers of commodities. On the other hand, aggregate demand (AD) also shifts to the right,

Table 8.3 Monetary base–GDP ratio for Japan, the United States, and the eurozone

	2000 Dec	2012 Dec		2016 July	
	Monetary base/GDP	Monthly QE volume/GDP	Monetary base/GDP	Monthly QE volume/GDP	Monetary base/GDP
Japan	15%	0.2%	29%	1.3%	80%
United States	6%	0.5%	16%	–	21%
Eurozone	7%	–	17%	0.8%	20%

Source: International Financial Statistics, International Monetary Fund (2016)
GDP gross domestic product, *QE* quantitative easing

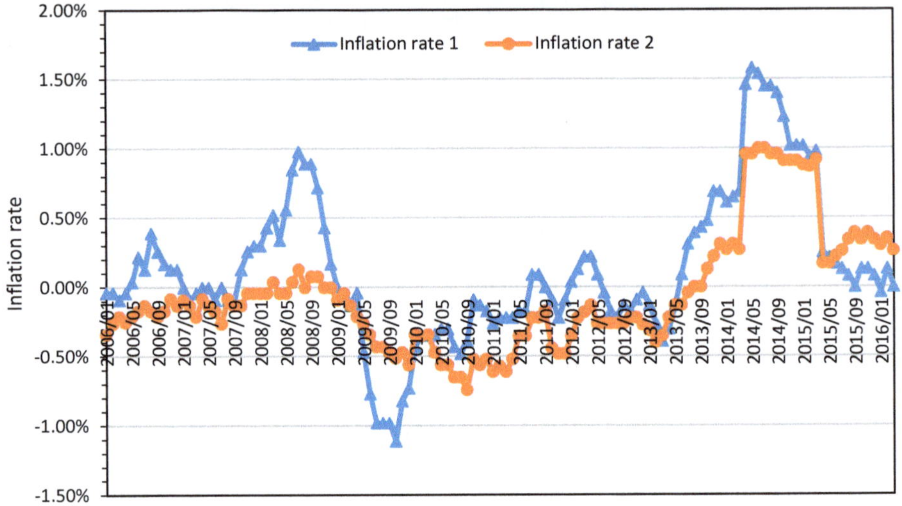

Fig. 8.4 Inflation rate in Japan (January 2006–March 2016) (*Notes:* Inflation rate 1: Consumer price index (CPI) general inflation rate of Japan (year-on-year changes); Inflation rate 2: CPI general inflation excluding food (excluding alcoholic beverage) and energy inflation rate of Japan (year-on-year changes). *Source:* NIKKEI NEEDS database (2016). http://www.nikkeieu.com/needs (accessed 5 August 2016))

because consumption of oil and derivatives become cheaper and this offset part of the earlier price decrease by the shifting of the AS curve. However, the shift in AD in the Japanese case is less for several reasons, two of the most important being the aging population and more efficient automobiles that reduced the consumption and elasticity of oil and petroleum products with respect to prices. Taghizadeh-Hesary et al. (2015b) found that among Japanese oil consuming sectors, the commercial and industrial sectors show a significant response to oil price fluctuations. However, the residential sector does not show a significant response to oil price impulses. They also found that in the wake of the Fukushima nuclear disaster in 2011, because Japan's dependency on oil increased, almost all economic sectors had a lower sensitivity to oil price fluctuations.

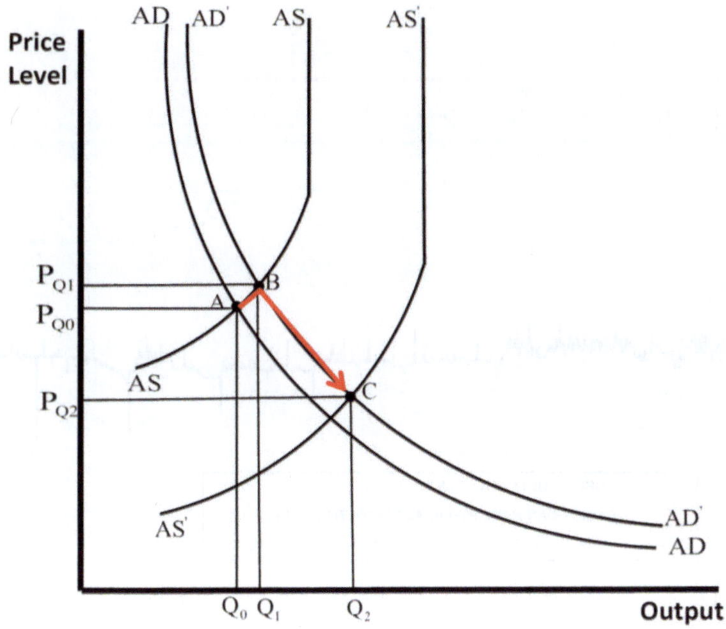

Fig. 8.5 Lower oil prices, lower inflation rate target. *AD* aggregate demand, *AS* aggregate supply (*Source:* Taghizadeh-Hesary and Yoshino 2013)

With a simple AD–AS illustration, Fig. 8.5 shows that following a decline in oil prices, the final equilibrium rate of inflation decreases. This means that the 2% inflation target may not necessarily be appropriate in the current cheap oil era.

At its monetary policy meeting of 29 January 2016, the BOJ policy board introduced quantitative and qualitative monetary easing (QQE) with a negative interest rate to achieve the price stability target of 2% at the earliest possible time. As shown in Fig. 8.6, since February 2016, the short-term interest rate (call rate–overnight uncollateralized interest rate) has been negative.

The BOJ decided to pursue monetary easing by making full use of possible measures in terms of three dimensions: (i) quantity, (ii) quality, and (iii) interest rate, and to do so issued the following guidelines (BOJ 2016):

(i) **Quantity dimension.** "The guideline for money market operations: The BOJ conducts money market operations so that the monetary base increases at an annual pace of about 80 trillion yen."

(ii) **Quality dimension.** "The guidelines for asset purchases: (a) The Bank will purchase Japanese government bonds (JGBs) so that their amount outstanding will increase at an annual pace of about 80 trillion yen. With a view to encouraging a decline in interest rates across the entire yield curve, the Bank will conduct purchases in a flexible manner in accordance with financial market

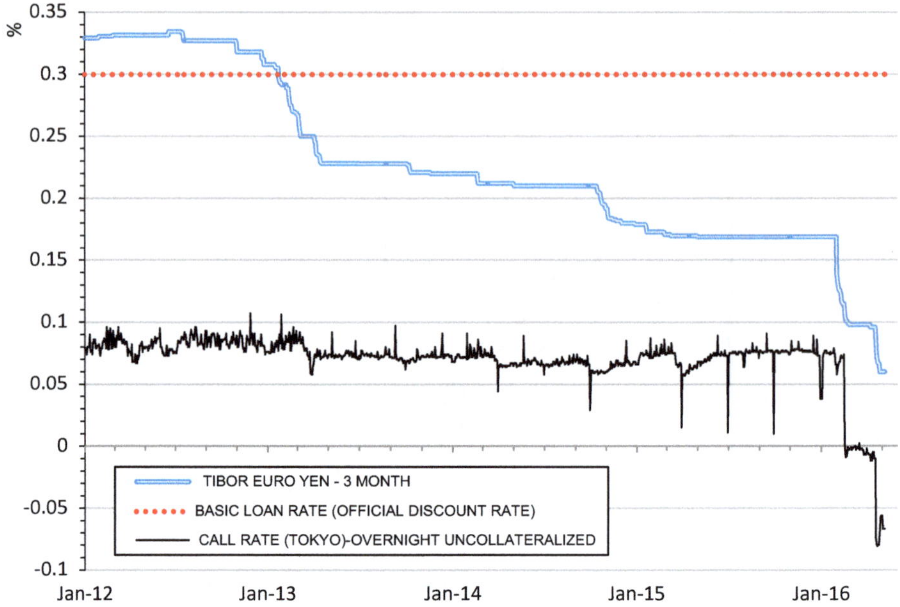

Fig. 8.6 Short-term interest rate in Japan (January 2012–May 2016) (*Source:* Bank of Japan time series database (2016). https://www.stat-search.boj.or.jp/index_en.html (accessed 30 July 2016))

conditions. The average remaining maturity of the Bank's JGB purchases will be about 7–12 years. (b) The Bank will purchase exchange-traded funds (ETFs) and Japan real estate investment trusts (J-REITs) so that their amounts outstanding will increase at annual paces of about 3 trillion yen and about 90 billion yen, respectively. (c) As for CP and corporate bonds, the Bank will maintain their amounts outstanding at about 2.2 trillion yen and about 3.2 trillion yen, respectively."

(iii) **Interest-rate dimension.** "The introduction of a negative interest rate: The Bank will apply a negative interest rate of minus 0.1% to current accounts that financial institutions hold at the Bank. It will cut the interest rate further into negative territory if judged as necessary." Specifically, the BOJ adopted a three-tier system in which the outstanding balance of each financial institution's current account at the bank is divided into three tiers, one of which carries a positive interest rate, one a zero interest rate, and one a negative interest rate.

Although the BOJ published the abovementioned guidelines on 29 January 2016, the short-term negative interest rate also affected the long-term government bond interest rate and the JGB yield curve started to fall and flattened (Fig. 8.7). The BOJ had not expected this to happen. This means it is not rational to hold government bonds until maturity, as the value of 100 at maturity will be less than 100 (i.e., 99, 98, 97, 96, or less). Hence investors, especially overseas investors, are trading the bonds, rather than keeping them until maturity. The nominal interest rate has

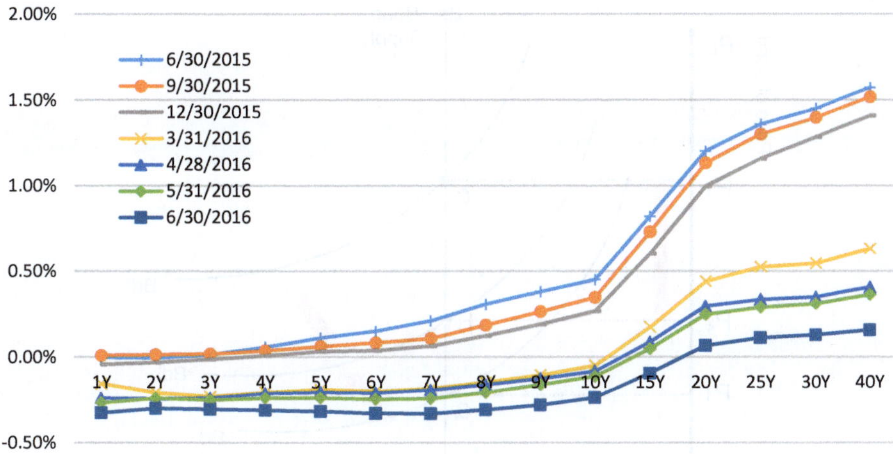

Fig. 8.7 Japanese government bond yield curves. *JGB* Japanese government bond (*Source*: Ministry of Finance of Japan, Financial Bureau 2016)

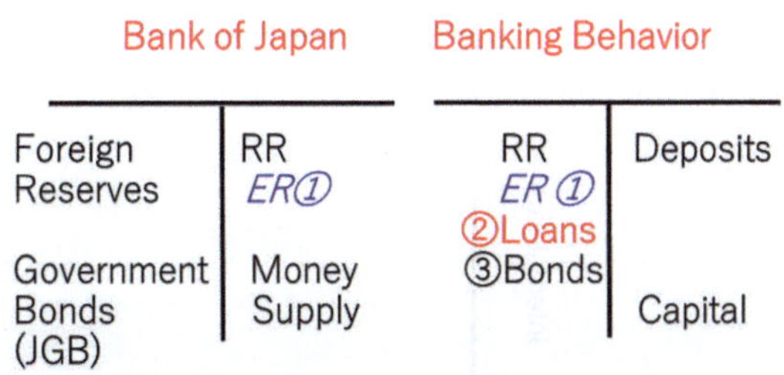

Fig. 8.8 Bank of Japan's and Japanese banks' more recent balance sheets. *ER* excess reserve, *RR* reserve requirement (*Source*: Authors' compilation)

dropped (Fig. 8.9), but the volatility of the bond market has increased because of higher trading of bonds. As for holdings of government bonds, long-term bonds longer than 17 years have a positive yield, but nobody wants to keep bonds that are shorter than 17 years until maturity because the interest rate is negative.

Following its 29 January meeting, the BOJ started charging a negative interest rate on excess reserves kept by commercial banks at the BOJ. Despite a massive increase of the money supply by the BOJ, bank loans have not increased, but have in fact decreased, as shown in Fig. 8.11. (See Fig. 8.8 for the recent behavior of Japanese banks.)

More recently there has been greater demand from overseas investors for short-term bonds (Treasury or T-bills). As shown in Fig. 8.10 (b), 49% of the holders of Treasury bills are foreigners who are buying and selling short-term Japanese government bonds and making a profit. This is the reason for the recent increase in volatility of the Japanese bond market.

As shown in Table 8.2, the BOJ increased its purchases of government bonds from ¥98 trillion in April 2013 to ¥319 trillion in May 2016. The BOJ started to purchase long-term government bonds. As shown in Fig. 8.9, the shift in demand is mainly a result of the BOJ's policy, which increases the price of long-term

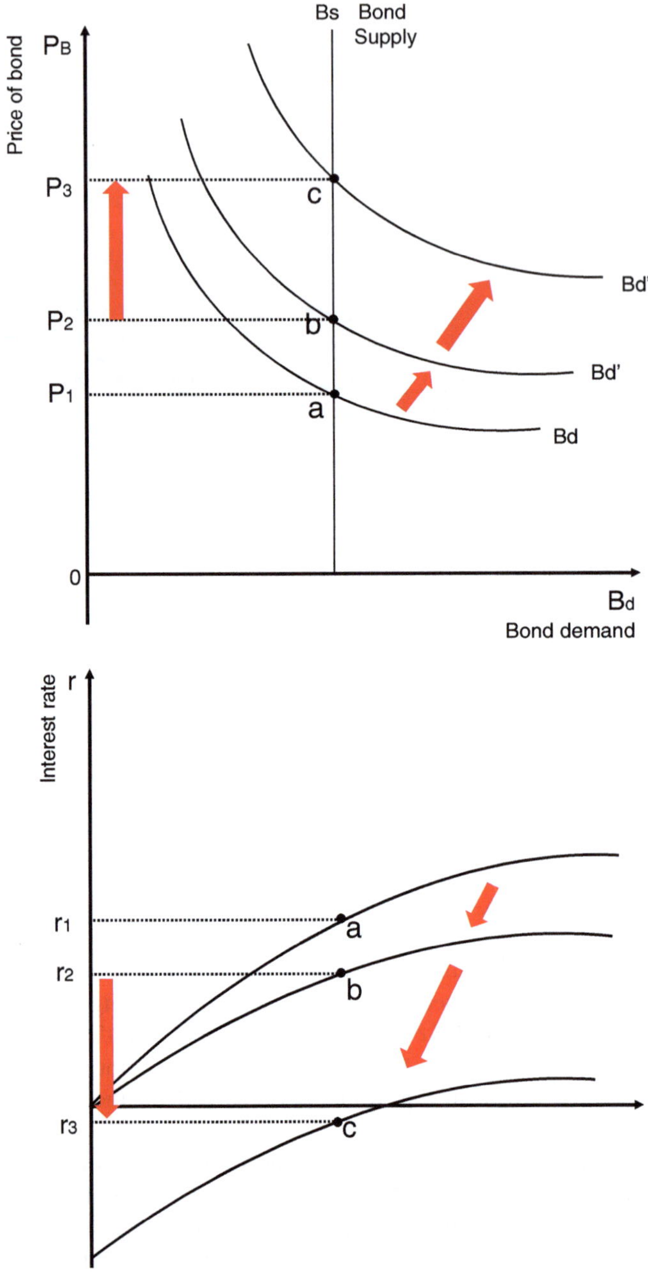

Fig. 8.9 Inverse relationship between price of bonds and interest rate (*Source:* Authors' compilation)

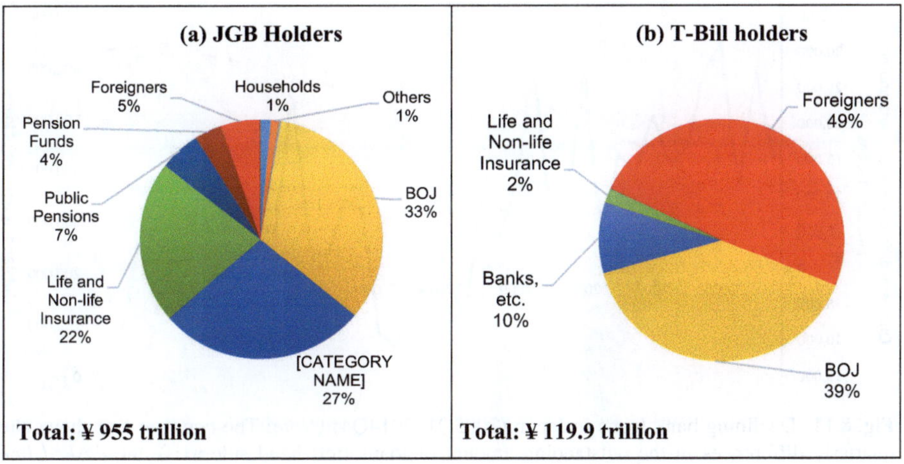

Fig. 8.10 Breakdown by JGB and T-bill holders (March 2016). *BOJ* Bank of Japan, *JGB* Japanese government bond, *T-bill* treasury bill. (**a**) JGB holders. Total: ¥955 trillion. (**b**) T-bill holders. Total: ¥119.9 trillion (*Source*: Ministry of Finance of Japan, Financial Bureau 2016)

government bonds and decreases the interest rate of long-term government bonds. That is why the JGB yield curve shifted downward (Fig. 8.7).

The BOJ wants the yield curve to become positive in the long term and to become steeper compared with the current yield curve. To do so, the BOJ will start to purchase short-term government bonds rather than long-term bonds.

On the other hand, as can be seen in Fig. 8.10, the share of households holding JGBs is very small (1%) as they are no longer interested in holding these bonds because of negative interest rates.

Among households, the Japanese saving rate is falling because of the aging population and lower economic growth rate, while the corporate sector saves more than households. Corporate savings are going to banks or insurance companies. In conventional cases, banks should lend money; however, because of the decreased demand for loans, bank lending is decreasing (Fig. 8.11). Due to the Japanese economy's vertical investment–saving (IS) curve, the rate of return on investment and companies' willingness to invest has become very low. Hence, loans are diminishing and banks are holding government bonds instead. So on the asset side of Japanese banks, we can see predominantly JGBs.

During the Japanese government's present term, attention is focused on monetary policy rather than structural issues, but the problem of the Japanese economy is its vertical IS curve (Fig. 8.12). Private investment did not grow despite very low interest rates. Expected rates of return are low, and as a consequence, not many new technologies are developed in Japan. Even though the central bank's short-term interest rate is now negative, depressed investment in Japan means that the economy is not able to recover (Yoshino and Taghizadeh-Hesary 2016b). This is in

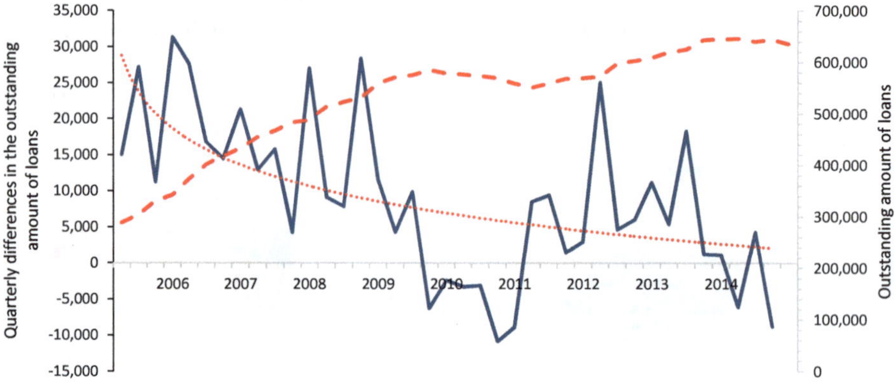

Fig. 8.11 Declining bank loans in Japan (2005Q1–2014Q4) (*Note:* The *constant line* shows the quarterly differences in the outstanding amount of loans (left hand side axis), the *dashed line* shows the outstanding amount of loans (right hand side axis), and the *dotted line* is the logarithmic trend of the quarterly differences in the outstanding amount of loans. *Source:* Japanese Bankers Association database (2016))

accordance with Table 8.1. The aggregate demand row, where during the second period real interest rate movements had no significant impact on the GDP gap, reflects the vertical IS curve.

Corporate restructuring to reduce idle capacity and start new investments was not pursued, with too much energy expended on expansion of monetary policy and not enough on accelerating corporate restructuring (Yoshino and Taghizadeh-Hesary 2014b).

However, there has been a recent change in banking behavior. After 2012, demand for JGBs fell in both large city banks and regional banks. Instead, because of higher interest rates on deposits at BOJ, banks increased their excess reserves at the BOJ. But this new negative interest rate policy forced banks to withdraw their excess reserves from the central bank and spend it in other ways. More recently, especially among regional banks, the demand for investment overseas has been increasing. Because they are collecting deposits in yen and investing in Europe and the US in euros and dollars, there is an exchange-rate risk. Banks are advised to keep some portion of deposits in foreign currencies (euros and dollars, among others) to minimize the exchange-rate risk.

8.5 Simulation Results

Yoshino and Miyamoto (2017) examined how an aging population affects economic performance and effectiveness of macroeconomic policies by using a New Keynesian dynamic stochastic general equilibrium (DSGE) model. They demonstrate that the effects of monetary and fiscal policies are weakened when the working

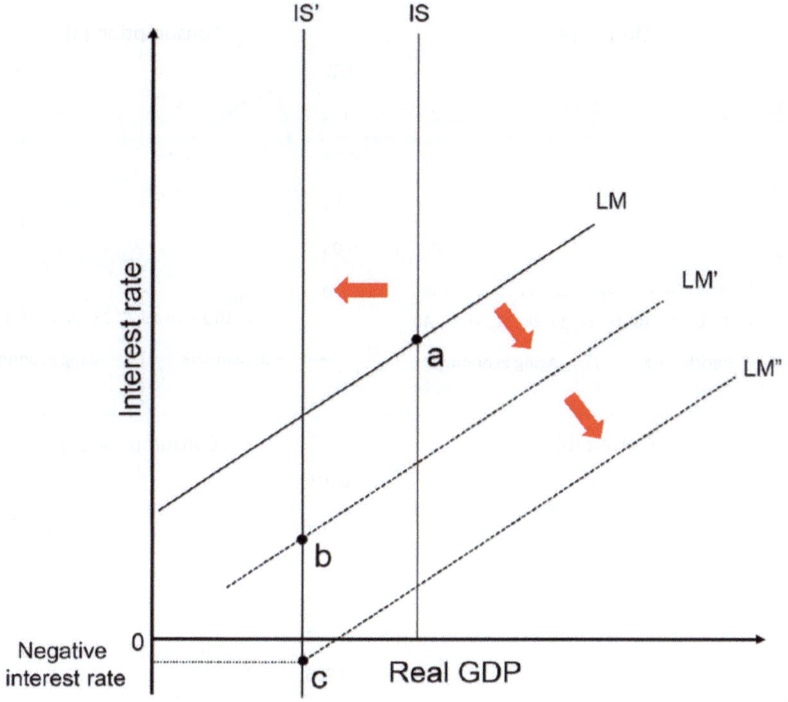

Fig. 8.12 The ineffectiveness of monetary policy in Japan. *GDP* gross domestic product, *LM* liquidity preference/money supply equilibrium (*Source*: Adapted from Yoshino and Sakakibara 2002)

population becomes smaller. They also found that an increased proportion of workers boosts output, consumption, and investment. Thus, their analysis shows that the best policy for Japan would be to keep elderly people working by paying them the marginal product of labor. To do so, it is necessary to abolish the seniority wage rate and flatten the wage curve.

Figure 8.13 shows that the effect of monetary policy on the economy is weakened when the proportion of retirees is larger (i.e., the proportion of working population is smaller). Although the effect of an expansionary monetary policy (interest rate policy) on output may be similar between two economies, the effect of the policy on consumption in an economy with higher labor participation is much larger than that in an economy with fewer workers.

Figure 8.13 also shows that the effect of a positive government investment shock on output and consumption is larger than in an economy with a higher proportion of workers in the total population.

These results mean that both monetary and fiscal policies become less effective in an aging economy.

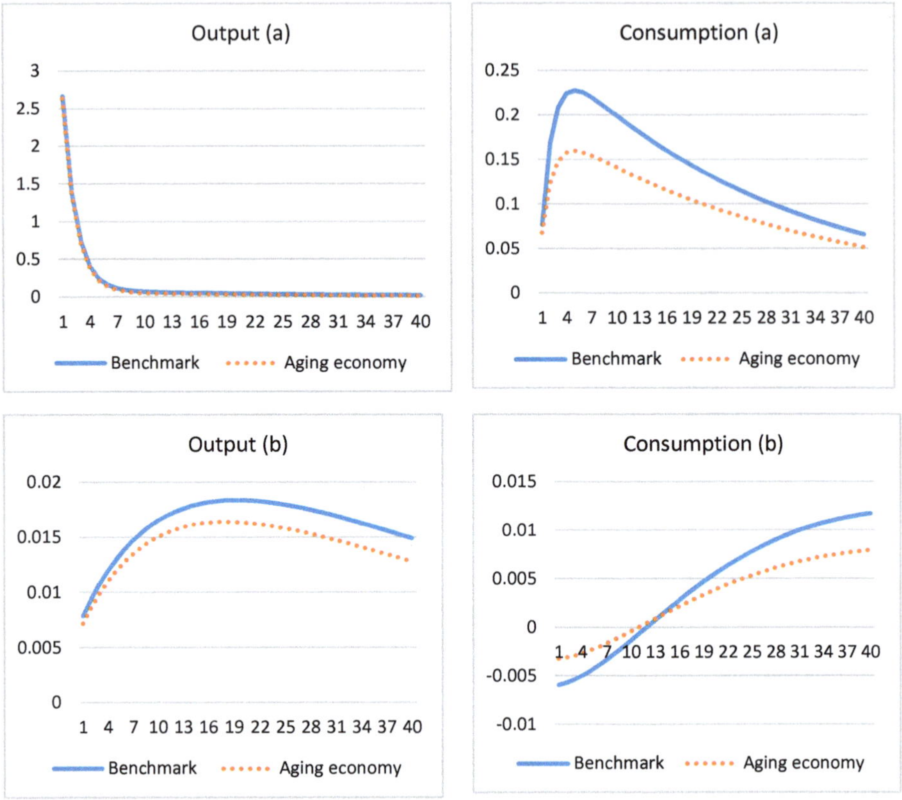

Fig. 8.13 Effects of monetary and fiscal policy shock on the economy (**a**) Effects of an expansionary monetary policy. (**b**) Effects of a positive government investment shock (*Note:* For an expansionary monetary policy, responses to a decrease in the nominal interest rate are reported. For a positive fiscal policy shock, responses to an increase in government investment are reported. The *solid lines* labeled "Benchmark" plot the impulse responses in the economy with large working population. The *dotted* labeled "Aging economy" plot the impulse responses in the economy with lower working population. The horizontal axis represents quarters after the shock. The vertical axis represents percentage deviations from the steady-state value. *Source:* Yoshino and Miyamoto (2017))

We examine how an increase in the proportion of workers affects the economy. Figure 8.14 shows that an increase in labor participation increases output and aggregate consumption.

This effect can be understood by looking at the responses of taxes paid by workers. In the economy, retirees receive pension benefits that are financed by imposing taxes on workers. Thus, pension benefits are transfers from tax payment by workers. Given the amount of pension benefits per retiree, an increase in the proportion of working population reduces the tax paid by each worker. This leads to an increase in consumption of workers and thus aggregate consumption. An increase in working population increases labor supply, which increases output.

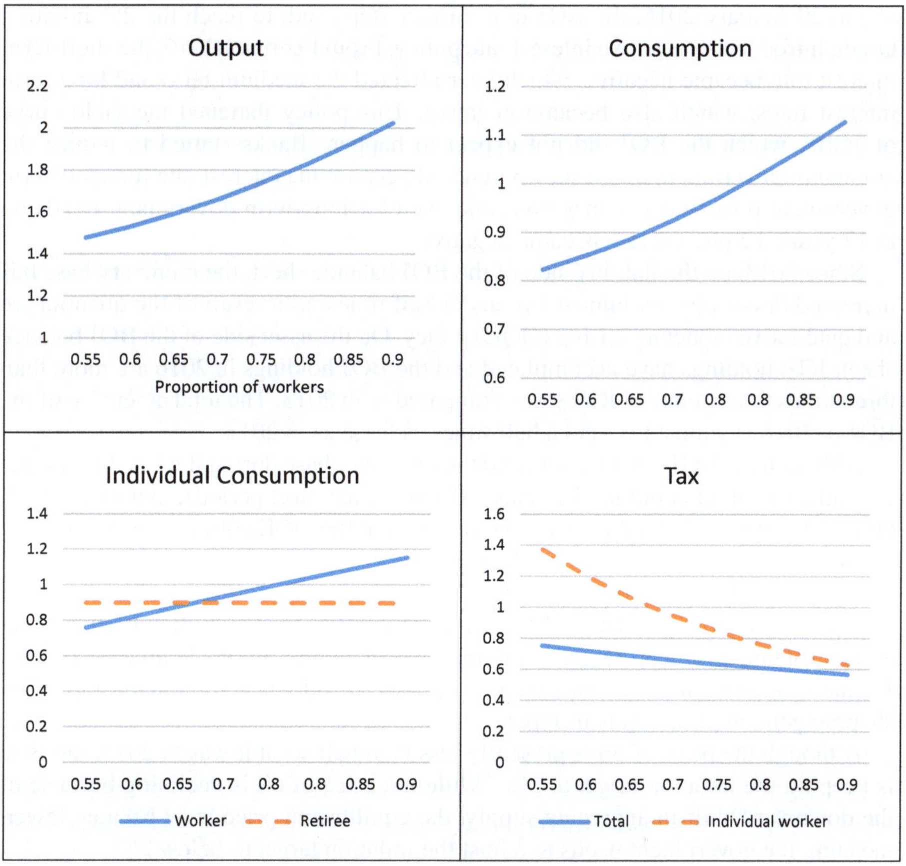

Fig. 8.14 Effect of a change in the ratio of workers to population (*Source:* Yoshino and Miyamoto 2017)

Figure 8.14 implies that necessary policy to cope with an aging population is to keep older people working. (Figs. 8.13 and 8.14 imply that in an aging society, macroeconomic policies become less effective and it is better to increase the working population to boost the economy.)

8.6 Concluding Remarks

Japan has reached the limits of conventional macroeconomic policies. To overcome deflation and achieve sustainable economic growth, the BOJ since 2013 has had an inflation target of 2% and implemented an aggressive monetary policy with a view to achieving this target as soon as possible.

On 29 January 2016, the BOJ took further steps and, to reach the 2% inflation target, introduced a negative interest rate policy. From February 2016, the short-term interest rate became negative, which later affected the medium-term and long-term interest rates, which also became negative. This policy flattened the yield curve of JGBs, which the BOJ did not expect to happen. Banks started to reduce the amount of government bonds they purchased because the interest rate for short-term government bonds became negative, and even for long-term government bonds up to 17 years the interest rate became negative.

Since 2013, on the liability side of the BOJ balance sheet, the monetary base has increased drastically, by almost two and a half times, as a result of the quantitative and qualitative monetary easing (QQE) policy. On the asset side of the BOJ balance sheet, JGB holdings have accumulated and the BOJ holdings in 2016 are more than three times the amount of JGB stock compared with 2013. The total asset size of the BOJ in 2016 is almost two and a half times as large as in 2013.

Although the BOJ drastically raised the monetary base during the last 3 years, the 2% inflation target could not be achieved, except for short periods, mainly in 2014. One of the reasons behind the unsuccessfulness of the QQE policy for achieving the 2% inflation target is the drop in oil prices.

Oil prices dropped from above $100 per barrel in June 2014 to less than $30 per barrel in February 2016. In 2015, Japan imported over $80 billion of petroleum and petroleum products. Mineral fuel imports, including oil, made up 23% of total Japanese imports in 2015. This means the price of oil has a significant impact on shaping general price levels in Japan.

Although the price of oil is presently less than half what it was in 2014, the BOJ is keeping the inflation target at 2%. While the price of oil is declining because of the downward shift in aggregate supply, the equilibrium price level became lower, meaning the government needs to adjust the inflation target to below 2%.

The BOJ introduced a negative interest rate policy so that banks would withdraw excess reserves from the central bank and increase lending to the corporate sector and households, stimulating aggregate demand, raising prices, and accelerating economic growth. Following the BOJ's negative interest rate policy, banks did indeed withdraw excess reserves from the BOJ, but lending to the corporate sector did not increase. This is due to the vertical IS curve. Because of the aging population, a shrinking labor force, low participation of females in the workforce, a conservative banking system, less productive local governments, low levels of technological development, and slow growth in small and medium-sized enterprises and startup businesses (Yoshino and Taghizadeh-Hesary 2014c, 2015b), the marginal productivity of capital is very low and the corporate sector's interest in investment has decreased, causing the IS curve to become vertical. This means that, although the BOJ is now strictly following the QQE policy, it could neither boost the economy nor raise the prices. This means the problems of the Japanese economy are structural and remedies cannot be found in monetary policy. The Japanese government needs to focus more on the growth strategies of "Abenomics" (see Yoshino and Taghizadeh-Hesary 2015b) than on monetary policy.

References

Bank of Japan (BOJ) (2016) Introduction of quantitative and qualitative monetary easing with a negative interest rate. 29 January. Tokyo. https://www.boj.or.jp/en/announcements/release_2016/k160129a.pdf. Accessed 10 Apr 2016

Blanchard OJ, Gali J (2007) The macroeconomic effects of oil shocks: why are the 2000s so different from the 1970s? NBER working paper 13368. National Bureau of Economic Research, Cambridge, MA. doi:10.3386/w13368

Government of Japan, Ministry of Internal Affairs and Communication (2015) Statistical handbook of Japan 2015. Statistics Bureau/Ministry of Internal Affairs and Communication, Tokyo

Hamilton JD (1996) This is what happened to the oil price–macroeconomy relationship. J Monet Econ 38(2):215–220

Japan External Trade Organization (2016) Japanese trade and investment statistics 2016. Tokyo

Kilian L (2008) A comparison of the effects of exogenous oil supply shocks on output and inflation in the G7 countries. J Eur Econ Assoc 6(1):78–121. doi:10.1162/jeea.2008.6.1.78

Lee BR, Lee K, Ratti RA (2001) Monetary policy, oil price shocks, and the Japanese economy. Jpn World Econ 13(3):321–349

Taghizadeh-Hesary F, Yoshino N (2013) Which side of the economy is affected more by oil prices: supply or demand? USAEE research paper 13-139. United States Association for Energy Economics, Cleveland

Taghizadeh-Hesary F, Yoshino N (2014) Monetary policies and oil price determination: an empirical analysis. OPEC Energy Rev 38(1):1–20

Taghizadeh-Hesary F, Yoshino N (2015) Macroeconomic effects of oil price fluctuations on emerging and developed economies in a model incorporating monetary variables. Econ Policy Energy Environ 2:51–75. doi:10.3280/EFE2015-002005

Taghizadeh-Hesary F, Yoshino N, Abdoli G, Farzinvash A (2013) An estimation of the impact of oil shocks on crude oil exporting economies and their trade partners. Front Econ China 8(4):571–591

Taghizadeh-Hesary F, Yoshino N, MMH A, Farboudmanesh R (2015a) The response of macro variables of emerging and developed oil importers to oil price movements. J Asia Pac Economy 21(1):91–102. doi:10.1080/13547860.2015.1057955

Taghizadeh-Hesary F, Rasolinezhad E, Kobayashi Y (2015b) Oil price fluctuations and oil consuming sectors: an empirical analysis of Japan. ADBI working paper 539. Asian Development Bank Institute, Tokyo

Yoshino N, Miyamoto H (2017) Declined effectiveness of fiscal and monetary policies faced with aging population in Japan. ADBI working paper. Asian Development Bank Institute, Tokyo

Yoshino N, Sakakibara E (2002) The current state of the Japanese economy and remedies. Asian Econo Pap 1:110–126

Yoshino N, Taghizadeh-Hesary F (2014a) Monetary policies and oil price fluctuations following the subprime mortgage crisis. Int J Monetary Econ Finance 7(3):157–174

Yoshino N, Taghizadeh-Hesary F (2014b) An analysis of challenges faced by Japan's economy and Abenomics. Jpn Political Economy 40(3–4):37–62

Yoshino N, Taghizadeh-Hesary F (2014c) Analytical framework on credit risks for financing SMEs in Asia. Asia–Pac Dev J 21(2):1–21

Yoshino N, Taghizadeh-Hesary F (2015a) Effectiveness of the easing of monetary policy in the Japanese economy, incorporating energy prices. J Comparative Asian Dev 14(2):227–248

Yoshino N, Taghizadeh-Hesary F (2015b) Analysis of credit risk for small and medium-sized enterprises: evidence from Asia. Asian Dev Rev 32(2):18–37

Yoshino N, Taghizadeh-Hesary F (2016a) Introductory remarks: what's behind the recent oil price drop? In: Yoshino N, Taghizadeh-Hesary F (eds) Monetary policy and the oil market. Springer, Tokyo

Yoshino N, Taghizadeh-Hesary F (2016b) Causes and remedies of Japan's long-lasting recession: lessons for China. Chin World Econ 24(2):23–47

Yoshino N, Taghizadeh-Hesary F, Hassanzadeh A, Prasetyo AD (2014) Response of stock markets to monetary policy: the Tehran stock market perspective. J Comp Asian Dev 13(3):517–545

Yoshino N, Taghizadeh-Hesary F, Miyamoto H (2017) The effectiveness of the negative interest rate policy in Japan. Credit Cap Mark – Kredit und Kapital 50(2):189–212

Index

N. Yoshino, F. Taghizadeh-Hesary (eds.), *Japan's Lost Decade*, ADB Institute Series on Development Economics, DOI 10.1007/978-981-10-5021-3

MIX
Papier aus verantwortungsvollen Quellen
Paper from responsible sources
FSC® C105338

If you have any concerns about our products,
you can contact us on
ProductSafety@springernature.com

In case Publisher is established outside the EU,
the EU authorized representative is:
Springer Nature Customer Service Center GmbH
Europaplatz 3, 69115 Heidelberg, Germany

Printed by Libri Plureos GmbH
in Hamburg, Germany